Building Character through Literature

A Guide for Middle School Readers

Rosann Jweid
Margaret Rizzo

The Scarecrow Press, Inc.
Lanham, Maryland, and London
2001

SCARECROW PRESS, INC.

Published in the United States of America
by Scarecrow Press, Inc.
4720 Boston Way, Lanham, Maryland 20706
www.scarecrowpress.com

4 Pleydell Gardens, Folkestone
Kent CT20 2DN, England

British Library Cataloguing in Publication Information Available

Library of Congress Cataloging-in-Publication Data

Jweid, Rosann, 1933–
  Building character through literature : a guide for middle school readers / Rosann
Jweid, Margaret Rizzo.
    p. cm.
Includes bibliographical references and index.
ISBN 0-8108-3951-2 (alk. paper)
  1. Best books—Children's literature. 2. Children's literature—Bibliography. 3. Middle
school students—Books and reading. 4. Characters and characteristics in literature. 5. Middle
school libraries—Book lists. I. Rizzo, Margaret. II. Title.
Z1037 .J93 2001
809'.89283—dc21   00-046401

♾™ The paper used in this publication meets the minimum requirements of
American National Standard for Information Sciences—Permanence of
Paper for Printed Library Materials, ANSI/NISO Z39.48-1992.
Manufactured in the United States of America.

Contents

Preface

With the recurring incidences of violence in our schools, society is asking several questions. Why is this happening? What can we do to eliminate the violence? Who is responsible for teaching the values that will eliminate violence?

In other words, character education has become an important issue for parents, educators, and community leaders. It is being argued that character education is the responsibility of every part of society rather than the sole priority of the family unit. Many institutions of higher education are designing programs to assist teachers and administrators in incorporating character education into the elementary and secondary curriculums. Though character or values education has been a controversial issue for at least the last twenty years, this book is not a philosophical treatise on this question. Instead it is an endorsement of the need to educate children about the positive values essential to a society. It is intended to assist the educators, parents, and other adults working with children who have embraced the concept of character education.

As school librarians whose previous publications involve cooperative library and curriculum units, we have often discussed authoring a book dealing with our first loves—reading and literature. In the process of considering several approaches, we decided to write a book about novels with strong plots and themes in which the characters make good and bad decisions, face and surmount life's problems, and learn life's lessons. This is the focus of *Building Character through Literature: A Guide for Middle School Readers.*

Our primary purpose is to introduce novels that show strength of character with guidance for discussions that can raise character issues. Our intention is that the reader will be able to identify with the character issues that appear in the book and develop the ability to evaluate them, determining those worthy of emulation. Our secondary purpose is to encourage a love of reading and of quality literature through a greater understanding of the relevance of literature to our everyday lives. Writers of literature for children and young adults have often concerned themselves with these same purposes: catching the interest of the reader, expanding awareness and knowledge of the world, and helping the reader to grow and develop into a thoughtful, caring adult.

Because of the wealth of excellent novels for our age group, children nine through fourteen, the selection of fifty novels has been difficult. First and foremost, we selected books that exemplified strong character traits. Next, we gave preference to novels written by authors with a body of critically acclaimed work and novels that had been awarded literary prizes. Our hope is that the work done with each of these will be useful for librarians working with individuals and groups, for teachers leading class discussions, and for librarians and teachers working together. Parents who educate their children at home and parents who read with their children will also find the information useful and stimulating.

Reading will never go out of style. In the age of video games, cable television, and the Internet, young readers need to be exposed to quality literature and encouraged to see the beauty and the power of the written word.

Introduction

Building Character through Literature: A Guide for Middle School Readers is designed to assist the library teacher, classroom teacher, and parent in selecting novels, guiding students, and discussing books that demonstrate character building.

In the first section, the fifty novels chosen for inclusion are appropriate for students in grades four through eight, and are arranged alphabetically by title. The same format has been used to discuss each novel:

Awards
Characters
Setting
Plot
Questions for Discussion
Projects
Vocabulary
About the Author
From the Author

Specifically, the Awards section includes major literary honors given to the book. The sections entitled Characters, Setting, and Plot, taken together, provide an overview of what happens in the book to assist in evaluating the appropriateness of the novel for the reader. Questions for Discussion stimulate children to think about the characters, evaluate their actions and their motives, and question their own reactions to the characters. They test the reader's comprehension of the novel's meaning and encourage a critical appreciation of literature and a love of reading. These questions may be used by class groups or individual students. Ideas given in the section Projects appeal to a broad range of interest and ability levels and can be used for library research, curriculum correlation, and parental involvement. Vocabulary is given in direct quotations. The section About the Author provides brief information about the author and his or her motivations to guide the user in promoting the novel. Whenever possible, authors were contacted about their motivations for writing the books and their feelings about the finished works. These comments are included in the section From the Author.

The rest of the book includes the following:

Titles Arranged by Genre and Theme
Character Traits in the Novels
Interesting and Useful Websites
Bibliography of Novels
Bibliography of Sources

Novels

After the Rain
Author: Norma Fox Mazer
Publication date: 1987

Awards
> Newbery Honor Book
> *School Library Journal* Best Book of the Year
> American Library Association Notable Books for Young Adults
> American Library Association Best Books for Young Adults
> *Horn Book* Fanfare Book

Characters
> Rachel Cooper
> Izzy Shapiro, Rachel's grandfather
> Mr. and Mrs. Cooper, Rachel's parents
> Helena
> Lewis

Setting
> Present day

Plot

Fifteen-year-old Rachel lives with her parents, and her maternal grandfather, Izzy, lives nearby, so there is close and consistent contact with him. Each Sunday, Rachel and her parents spend the day with Izzy, who is not an easy man to be close to. Rachel also phones him weekly but finds it almost impossible to carry on a conversation with him.

Eighty-three-year-old Izzy is independent and seems indestructible. He lives alone and walks four miles a day, but complaints about a stomachache lead to tests and a diagnosis that Izzy has mesothelioma, a lung cancer affecting people who worked with asbestos. He has two or three months to live. At this point the doctor recommends that Izzy not be told of his prognosis because Izzy might lose all hope and become depressed.

When Izzy falls during one of his walks, Rachel is the one who takes the call. After this, Rachel offers to walk with him. Although he initially feels bullied, before long Izzy waits for Rachel to come. Rachel begins by thinking of these walks as a job. She and Izzy hardly communicate, and she has given up her own activities, but when she realizes her grandfather expects her, she cannot refuse.

Her friend Helena suggests that Rachel use the time with Izzy to find out things about him, in other words, to do an oral history. Rachel begins to ask questions. Izzy is sometimes not very talkative and is sometimes in a bad mood. He staunchly tries to keep up as he always has and is fiercely independent. At one point, when he has insisted on carrying his own groceries all the way home from the store and does not want her to come up on the elevator with him, Rachel overhears him congratulating himself on doing what he wanted to do. One rainy day, Izzy and Rachel play Scrabble, and Izzy beats her soundly.

Through all of this, Izzy still does not know his true condition. Finally, Izzy asks Rachel what she knows about his condition, and she tells him. He does not ask if he is going to die, and Rachel does not volunteer this information. They continue their walks, although he is getting progressively weaker. One day he takes her across town to look at bridges he has built when he worked as a stonemason. He wants to find his handprint and initials that he carved in one of them. Izzy and Rachel are not successful in finding these.

Rachel and Izzy experience the same feelings of jealousy. When Rachel's boyfriend, Lewis, comes to meet him, Izzy is unfriendly and tells Lewis he has weak hands and couldn't be a mason. Conversely, when Helena, her boyfriend, and Lewis bring Helena's birthday party to Izzy's apartment, Rachel is jealous of the attention that Izzy gives to Helena.

When Izzy goes into the hospital in his final days, Rachel spends as much time as she can with him. She even gets her school assignments so that she can be there during the day. The night she insists on staying with him through the night, Izzy dies. Rachel is grateful that she finally got to know him but angry that it happened at the end of his life. She misses him and dreams of him, but after months she adjusts to his absence. She thinks occasionally of the handprint he left on the bridge, and eventually she and Lewis find the print with Izzy's initials. Rachel is comforted by the fact that the print has been there for years and will be there for many more.

Questions for Discussion

1. How would you characterize the relationship between Rachel and her parents? How does she feel about the fact that they are much older than the parents of her friends? Do you think that Rachel and her parents have a good relationship?

2. What kind of man is Izzy? Do you know anyone like him? What is likable and admirable about Izzy? Is there anything about him you do not admire?

3. What qualities does Rachel have that you admire? Is there anything about her that you do not like? Would you like to have Rachel for a friend? Why?

4. Why does Rachel suggest walking with Izzy? How does their attitude about these walks change as time goes on?

5. In what ways do Rachel and Izzy grow closer as they spend more time together? Can you understand the jealousy that Izzy feels toward Lewis and Rachel feels toward Helena? Have you ever experienced these feelings?

6. Describe the friendship of Rachel and Helena. Would you like to have Helena for a friend? Why? How does she affect Rachel's relationship with Izzy?

7. Why does the doctor suggest that Izzy not be told of his prognosis? Why do Rachel's parents go along with this suggestion? Do you think they are making the right decision?

8. Why does Izzy ask Rachel to tell him what she knows about his medical condition? What does this tell you about the bond between Izzy and Rachel? Do you think Rachel is right to tell him what she knows? Do you think she did the right thing by not volunteering that he was going to die in a short time?

9. Uncle Frederick and Rachel's brother, Jeremy, both wish they had settled things with Izzy before he died. What could have been done to settle their problems? Who is responsible for the fact that they were not worked out before Izzy died? Have you ever shared the feelings of Jeremy and Frederick in wishing you could change something that could no longer be changed? Did you learn anything from this?

10. What does Rachel sacrifice to spend time with Izzy? What does this tell you about the value that Rachel places on family?

Projects

1. Helena suggests that Rachel take an oral history from Izzy. Select a family member such as a parent, grandparent, aunt, uncle, friend, or a neighbor to interview. Write your questions first, concentrating on what the person's school was like, how the person spent his or her leisure time, and what special memories the person has. Ask your interviewee if you can take notes or record the interview. When the interview has been completed, compile your notes into an oral history of the person. Be sure to share your essay with your subject when it has been completed.

2. Izzy lives alone but is lucky to have family members living close by. Not all elderly people have this fortunate situation. Phone your local social service agency to find out what services are available for the elderly who live alone in their own homes. How do they get to appointments? Is there help for them to shop, prepare, or receive meals? What opportunities are there for them to socialize with other people? Compile this information into a booklet including brief descriptions of the available services and phone numbers. When it has been completed, share your booklet with your local social service agency.

3. When Izzy was fifteen, he was an apprentice to a bricklayer. Look at your home and your school. What building and construction jobs were needed to construct these buildings? Find out how a person could learn this trade. Make a chart listing the trade, job description, and training.

4. Rachel is afraid of dogs and walks to her grandfather's by a route that takes her past only fenced-in dogs. Make a poster showing what Rachel should do to deal with the animals that frighten her.

Vocabulary

Each of the following quotations chosen from *After the Rain* includes one or more vocabulary words in **bold print**.

1. "A baby whale in a yellow sport shirt, **voluminous** checked pants . . ."
2. "She has heard the story **innumerable** times."
3. "That's no excuse for my **vile** temper."

4. "Rachel still **mourns** the loss of Thomas Leander."
5. "Helena's honesty hurt, but Rachel preferred it to **hypocrisy**."
6. "Rachel's room is her cave, her **sanctuary**."
7. ". . . he has tight blond curls and large, **prominent** ears."
8. "When Rachel makes a particularly **inept** move, swinging the racket and missing the ball by a mile . . ."
9. ". . . how she's always **hovering** over him and trying to please him."
10. "There's a **vast throng** of kids **milling** around the front steps and sitting on the stone wall."
11. " 'And he was a pretty heavy smoker back then. That makes people much more **susceptible**.' "
12. "As if going with her to Dr. N.'s was some kind of **incredible feat** of moral strength . . . "
13. "She **rummages** through her parents' desk in the living room for a city map."
14. "Lewis's nose **twitches**."
15. "Lewis pretends to **cower** in a corner."
16. "She plays harder this time, **mulls** over her **options**, goes for points instead of the showy stuff."
17. "**Torrents** of rain pour down the windows."
18. ". . . in a voice barely **audible** . . ."
19. ". . . to hear Izzy spoken to as if he's a **deficient** child."
20. "Rachel sits by the bed, makes a **pretense** of studying."

About the Author

Norma Fox Mazer was raised in Glens Falls, New York, and attended Antioch College and Syracuse University. Although she thought of careers in social work or teaching, she always dreamed of becoming a writer. After her third child was born, she became a freelance writer. She has received many honors and awards for her writing, including the Edgar Allan Poe Award for best juvenile mystery for *Taking Terri Mueller*. She reads and writes daily.

From the Author

"This was a difficult book for me to write, because Izzy's death was based on my father's illness and death, and each time I revised, I went through this all over again. I want to say, though, that Izzy was not my father, as no character ever is a real person.

"I thought of writing this book after my father died. My idea was to write a forthright book about dying that would take some of the terror out of death and invest it with dignity. Years passed, and I wrote other books, but the idea never left me."

Amber Brown Goes Fourth
Author: Paula Danziger
Publication date: 1995

Awards
   Emphasis on Reading, third place

Characters
   Amber Brown
   Amber's mother
   Amber's father
   Hannah Burton
   Ms. Holt
   Brandi Colwin
   Max

Setting
   Present-day suburbia

Plot
   This Amber Brown novel is one of a series that deals humorously, yet realis-
tically, with some of life's changes and problems that challenge today's children.
   Amber Brown is entering fourth grade with several major worries. She misses
her father, who since his divorce from Amber's mother, lives in Paris, France.
This year she must face the first day of school without her best friend, Justin,
who has moved away. Another major worry is that her mother is dating a new
man, Max, seriously shattering Amber's plans for her parents' reunion. Her first
worry is addressed by a phone call from her dad wishing her well for the new
school year, but she still worries that nobody wants to be her best friend.
   Entering the classroom, Amber sees that everyone is sitting in the same seat
as last year, so Justin's seat next to her is empty. Brandi Colwin, returning from
California, takes the seat. Amber's hope that maybe she will have a new best
friend is soon dashed when Brandi informs her that she is not Justin.
   Looking at her first week of school, Amber wishes that she had not compared
Brandi to Justin, wishes that she did not care about having a best friend, wishes
that she had not shown up for Elementary Extension, and wishes that she did not
think about all the things bothering her: her parents' divorce, Justin's distance,
and Max's proximity.

Then, Brandi starts coming to Elementary Extension, an after school day-care for children with working parents, and the ice is broken between her and Amber when they have a giggling fit that earns each of them detention. The friendship grows as Amber assures Brandi that she is not a stand-in for Justin. Amber realizes that she enjoys doing different things like braiding hair and talking about feelings.

Talking to Brandi makes Amber understand how hard it is for new kids to make friends and how everyone needs the support of a friend, even her mother. She knows that her mother has lost the friendship of Justin's mother and of her husband and that maybe Max is filling the void. She begins to see that things change in life and that she has to move on.

Questions for Discussion

1. What does Amber do to keep images of her father around her? Why are there no pictures of him in her house? What does she do with her *Dad Book*? Do you think this helps with her problems? Why?

2. Amber's mother is going on a date with Max. How does Amber react to this? How does she treat her mother? What does her mother do in response? How would you feel in this situation?

3. The first day of school brings changes from the previous year. What are they? Why have these changes occurred?

4. Does your school have a program like Elementary Extension? Why do you think it is necessary?

5. Amber Brown has first-day jitters. What are her concerns? Are these common fears, and have you experienced them? How do you overcome or handle these fears?

6. How does Amber react to her dad's phone call? Is it common to have conflicting feelings? What are some things that make you feel sad and glad?

7. Looking around the playground, Amber realizes that the only person without a best friend is Hannah Burton. How does she feel about this? Why does she feel this way? Do you agree with her? What are some characteristics you want in a best friend?

8. When Brandi arrives, Amber hopes that they can be best friends. Why does Brandi reject her overture of friendship? Do you agree with her? How do you think Amber should have tried to make friends?

9. A giggling fit breaks the ice between the two girls. Why? How do they build on that start? What does Amber learn about Brandi's friendship with Hannah Burton? Have you ever been the new child in class? Did someone help you? How? How do you think new students should be welcomed?

10. What does Amber write to Justin about Max and her father? Why does she feel this way? Is this a normal reaction to the situation?

11. What are Amber's feelings about change? What does she decide to do about it? Do you agree with her? Why?

Projects
1. Write a letter to either a real or imaginary friend who has moved away.
2. Get ready for the first day of school. Prepare a chart of all the things you need to do.

Vocabulary

Each of the following quotations chosen from *Amber Brown Goes Fourth* includes one or more vocabulary words in **bold print**.
1. "Before we would go off to **slay** the dragons, one of us would yell, 'THE BRAVE KNIGHTS GO FORTH!' "
2. " 'What if I get a desk that **wobbles**.' "
3. " 'She'd like to see the sneakers with **rhinestones** on them.' "
4. "I remember how Justin and I **organized** our kindergarten to compete in the Jungle Gymboree Olympics."
5. "My mom is no **pushover**."
6. "I grin a **humongous** grin."
7. "I think of him as Min ..... like in **minimum**."
8. "She holds up lots of different colors of **embroidery** threads."
9. "This alarm is a real person who **rumples** my hair and says different things depending on the day."
10. " 'I'll pick you up right after Elementary **Extension**.' "

About the Author

Formerly an English teacher, Paula Danziger has been a full-time writer since 1978. Though she normally writes for young adults, this Amber Brown series speaks with the voice of younger readers and deals with some of their concerns. Ms. Danziger's books, while dealing with real-life situations, are always peppered with laughter.

Animal Farm
Author: George Orwell
Publication date: 1945

Characters
Major
Mr. Jones
Frederick
Snowball
Napoleon
Boxer
Benjamin
Squeaker

Setting
Modern-day England

Plot

Old Major, the prize boar of Manor Farm, has a dream of the earth without man. With the belief that anything that walks on two legs is the enemy and anything that walks on four legs or flies with wings is a friend, he calls for a rebellion of the animals to overthrow man. Two young boars, Snowball and Napoleon, and a porker, Squealer, put Major's thoughts into a system called Animalism. Although initially the other animals do not greet their plans to rebel with enthusiasm, the Rebellion is successful. The principles of Animalism in the form of Seven Commandments are displayed on the barn wall. The last of these is "All animals are equal."

At the beginning, the animals flourish, and their harvest is a great success. Every problem they have can be solved by the clever pigs that do not work but supervise the others. At the weekly meetings, pigs put forth proposals on which the animals vote; in the debates preceding the votes, Napoleon and Snowball never agree. Snowball's project to tame wild animals and increase egg production does not succeed, but calls to teach the animals to read and write are successful. When pigs take privileges, the other animals are always told that it is necessary to keep the pigs healthy in order to keep man away. As life becomes harder, it is determined that policy decisions will be voted on by everyone but decided by the pigs. Snowball suggests a windmill, which Napoleon opposes, but after Snowball is driven away by Napoleon's dogs, Napoleon says that the windmill is his idea. He also rules that there will be no more debates in the interest of keeping the animals from making the wrong decisions. The pigs take more and more privileges and blame Snowball for everything bad that happens.

The first group of animals to rebel against the tyranny are the hens, who protest when their eggs are taken and sold. Napoleon stops feeding them, and after five days, the rebellions ends. Soon after the ringleaders of this rebellion and other animals are slaughtered as traitors in league with Snowball. The animals are distraught that they are killing each other. Napoleon, now addressed as "our Leader, Comrade Napoleon," sells wood to Frederick, who pays for it with forged notes. Although Frederick attacks and blows up the windmill, Squealer claims victory.

During a hard winter, rations are reduced for all animals except the pigs and dogs. While Napoleon still gets lamp oil, candles, and sugar, the other animals forget their hunger with the weekly songs and speeches that celebrate the successes of Animal Farm. As the only candidate for election, Napoleon is elected unanimously.

Boxer, who has exhibited tremendous physical strength and determination to make the Farm succeed, collapses. He is taken away to be slaughtered, although Squealer says he died happy praising Napoleon. Finally the pigs begin to walk on two legs, carry whips, dress in man's clothing, and drink beer while they play cards with men. The name of the farm is changed back to Manor Farm. It is difficult to tell the pigs from the men. The Seven Commandments for living on Animal Farm have been reduced and altered to one—"All animals are equal but some animals are more equal than others."

Questions for Discussion

1. Describe the feelings of pride and ownership the animals have in the farm. How do they remain loyal even in hard times?
2. Whose idea is the windmill? Is the disagreement over the windmill the reason for Snowball's being driven away? How are lies about Snowball used to manipulate the animals throughout the book?
3. What is Boxer's slogan for his life? Do his actions support his words? Do you admire Boxer? Why or why not? Do you have a motto or a slogan that describes how you act?
4. Napoleon and Snowball disagree on the treatment of adults and children. Napoleon wants to concentrate on the young. Do you agree with Napoleon? How do you think our culture treats the young and the elderly? What is the importance to society of people of all ages?
5. After their battles, the animals devise medals and holidays of commemoration. What holidays have we created to remember significant times of our history? Why are these important?
6. How does Napoleon take over as the authority of Animal Farm? How is protest contained? How does he preserve his authority? What does he increasingly resemble?
7. In what ways is Squealer a dangerous character? Does he have any admirable qualities? Do you know anyone who shares some of his traits?
8. What is the significance of the name change from Animal Farm to Manor Farm?

9. Major says that the animals must not come to resemble man or adopt his ways. How does the behavior of the pigs contradict this as the novel progresses? Explain the significance of the end when the pigs walk on two legs, wear clothes, and carry whips.
10. Major says that all animals are equal. When and why does this begin to change? In what important ways are all men created equal?
11. What is the significance of the destruction of knives, reins, nosebags, and whips after the Rebellion? What does Mollie's worry about her ribbons tell you about her? Have you ever seen this quality among people?
12. How do the Seven Commandments change as the book progresses? Do the new commandments support the philosophy of Animalism as Major envisioned?
13. *Animal Farm* is a satirical novel. What was Orwell criticizing when he wrote the book? In what ways is his satire relevant today?

Projects

1. The animals decide to build a windmill to supply the farm with power. Consulting reference materials or Internet sources, find out how a windmill works. Make a poster of the outside of a windmill or a cross section showing the interior. Identify the parts of the windmill and how they function.
2. Throughout the book, the pigs are described as the most clever of the animals. Locate information on pigs, including their physical characteristics and mental capabilities. Put your information into a written report or a multimedia presentation.
3. Napoleon, the leader of Animal Farm, shares a name with Napoleon I, military leader and emperor of France. Research the life of Napoleon I, and write a brief report about his life and personality. Compare and contrast him with the character who bears his name in the novel.
4. Soon after the Rebellion, Snowball creates a flag for Animal Farm. Its green background represents the fields of England, and its white hoof and horn represent the future when man will be overthrown. Real flags also are made with significant colors and symbols. Select five flags from United States history or the flags used today by five countries of the world. Draw each flag, and explain the meaning of its colors and symbols. Organize this information on a poster.

Vocabulary

Each of the following quotations chosen from *Animal Farm* includes one or more vocabulary words in **bold print**.

1. "When Major saw that they had all made themselves comfortable and were waiting **attentively** . . ."
2. " 'And remember, comrades, your **resolution** must never **falter**. No argument must lead you **astray**.' "
3. "At the beginning they met with much stupidity and **apathy**."
4. ". . . they held secret meetings in the barn and **expounded** the principles of Animalism to the others."

5. "The others **reproached** her sharply. . . ."
6. ". . . the **implements** had been designed for human beings and not for animals. . . ."
7. "He did his work in the same slow **obstinate** way as he had done it in Jones's time, never **shirking** and never volunteering for extra work either."
8. "First came the **hoisting** of the flag."
9. ". . . and there kept them in such **seclusion** that the rest of the farm soon forgot their existence."
10. "Bulls which had always been **tractable** suddenly turned savage, sheep broke down hedges and **devoured** the clover. . . ."
11. ". . . all the animals **dispersed**."
12. "The corn **ration** was **drastically** reduced. . . ."
13. "The potatoes had become soft and discoloured, and only a few were **edible**."
14. "Napoleon **inhabited** separate apartments from the others."
15. "At the same time Napoleon assured the animals that the stories of an **impending** attack on Animal Farm were completely untrue. . . ."
16. ". . . the **flimsy** white things stirred and rustled in his breath."
17. "It was impossible now to **venture** out of the shelter of the buildings."
18. ". . . since Boxer's death, more **morose** and **taciturn** than ever."

About the Author

George Orwell was born in India in 1903 and returned to England with his family when he was four years old. When he was eight, he attended a preparatory school that, he claimed later, colored his views on the class system in England. From the time he was an adolescent, he wanted to be a writer. He taught and wrote articles on the downtrodden until he could support himself with his writing. He began writing *Animal Farm* in 1943 and finished it the next year, but several publishers refused to print it because of its political message. Critics say that George Orwell's honesty marks his life as a man and a writer.

Around the World in Eighty Days
Author: Jules Verne
Publication date: 1873

Characters
Phileas Fogg
Jean Passepartout
Detective Fix
Princess Aouda

Setting
1872—The World

Plot
It is the year 1872 and the *Daily Telegraph* estimates that the world can be circumnavigated in eighty days. Phileas Fogg wagers twenty thousand pounds with members of his club that he can accomplish this feat. Returning to his home, he announces to his valet, Passepartout, that they are leaving immediately to travel around the world. A former gymnast and fireman, Passepartout, who has taken the job with Fogg in search of a more peaceful life, is astounded.

Armed only with a carpetbag containing a couple of shirts and stockings as well as twenty thousand pounds in Bank of England notes, Fogg and Passepartout begin their journey by crossing the English Channel. On reaching the Suez Canal, they encounter Fix, who has identified Fogg as a wanted bank robber. For the rest of the trip, Fix dogs the footsteps of the pair, in hopes of arresting Fogg. When on British soil, Fix does all to impede the progress of the journey but on reaching the United States does all to facilitate the trip.

The first serious impediment of the trip is the fact that the railway from Bombay to Calcutta is missing fifty miles of track. Undaunted, Fogg arranges for transport on an elephant. Traveling through the forest, the group, most particularly Passepartout, rescues Princess Aouda from being cremated with her dead husband. Fogg brings Aouda with them until a safe haven can be found for her.

In crossing the United States, the foursome is delayed by a herd of buffalo and an attack on the train by the Sioux Indians. Though the savior of the day, Passepartout is captured and causes Fogg to miss the train in order to save him. Fix arranges for a sledge with sails to take them to Omaha.

When they finally again reach British soil in Ireland, Fix wrongly arrests Fogg for the bank robbery, causing an insurmountable delay. Released, Fogg travels to London prepared to pay his debt. While waiting for Passepartout to collect his bank funds, Fogg, realizing that he is deeply in love with Aouda, ac-

cepts her marriage proposal. Passepartout discovers that due to the fact that they
had always traveled east, they have gained a day and have gone around the
world in the specified time. Fogg is triumphant and collects his wager.

Questions for Discussion
1. What is Passepartout's background before being employed by Phileas
   Fogg? What type of life is he searching for? Why does he think Fogg is his
   perfect employer?
2. Why did the majority of people think Fogg's task was impossible? What
   were some of the obstacles they foresaw to ruin his chances? Why do you
   think Fogg did not agree with them?
3. Detective Fix has no doubt that he will arrest Mr. Fogg for the bank robbery. What is there about Fix that makes him so positive? Is this a good or
   bad attribute?
4. What does Passepartout say to Fix that further convinces him of Fogg's
   guilt? Why do you think Passepartout is so forthcoming with information?
   Fix convinces the consul that appearances are against Fogg. Should appearances be the best reason in judging a person?
5. Fogg is indifferent to the beauty and the hazards of his journey. Is this a
   helpful characteristic in the completion of his task? Why?
6. What is Sir Francis Cromarty's opinion of Phileas Fogg? What does Fogg
   do while in India to prove this opinion false? What qualities do you think
   Fogg must have possessed to do these kindnesses? Why did Passepartout
   begin to love Fogg? Are these characteristics that you admire in a person?
7. How does Fogg repay the Parsee for his special efforts in saving Princess
   Aouda? Why was this a better reward than money might have been?
8. What qualities does Passepartout show is his rescue of Princess Aouda?
9. How does Fogg react to the serious delay caused by the storm while they
   are steaming toward Hong Kong? How does Passepartout react? Which
   man's actions resemble what you would do?
10. Why does Passepartout refuse to help Fix keep Fogg in Hong Kong? What
    course of action does Fix take when he cannot get Passepartout's coopera-
    tion? Is their anything to be admired in Fix's actions?
11. How does Fix become obliged to Fogg? Do you think this will change his
    intentions? Why?
12. When Passepartout reaches Yokohama, he is without funds or a way to get
    to the United States. How does he resolve his problem? Is this the first time
    he has used his skills from his former life? Is it well to know our abilities
    and recognize places where they can be used to good advantage? Think of a
    time in your life when you have done so.
13. Why does Fix decide to help Fogg once they get to the United States? How
    does Passepartout react to this change? What has Passepartout learned from
    his dealings with Fix?
14. The demonstration for the election of a justice of the peace in San Francisco
    is an example of "irony." What is irony and how does Verne use it here?

15. Why does Fogg feel that he must retaliate against Colonel Stamp Proctor? Do you think most people today would feel the same, or has national pride become less important?
16. How does Passepartout think the people should cross the shaky railroad trestle? Do you think his idea has merit over the way it was done? Why is he ignored?
17. What action does Fogg take when the Indians capture Passepartout? Is this at a cost to his goal? How is Fix affected by Fogg's decision?
18. What does Fix do when the party lands on English soil? Are you surprised by his actions? How does Fogg react when he is freed? Is this in keeping with his usual behavior? How would you have acted?
19. When all is seemingly lost, Aouda proposes to Fogg. Why does she do this? How does Fogg respond?
20. List the character qualities of Phileas Fogg, Jean Passepartout, and Princess Aouda that make you like them. Would you like to possess these qualities? Why?

Projects

1. On a map of the world, identify the British Empire in 1872 when Phileas Fogg traveled around the world. For each area, write a brief history of how it became a part of the empire and the present status.
2. Many religions are practiced in India; research one of these religions and write a report on your findings.
3. Investigate the burial practices of the Hindu religion. Write a brief report about them.
4. On a map of the world, draw the time zones of the world. Starting at the Greenwich meridian with noon on Sunday, identify the day and time of day in each zone.
5. Imagine you are a worker on either the Union Pacific or Central Pacific Railroad, and keep a diary of your days for two weeks before the completion of your trip in Utah.
6. Create a diorama or large poster depicting the Sioux Indian attack on the railroad or the screw steamer in which the group traveled from Calcutta to Hong Kong.
7. Following the same route and stopping in the same locations but using any type of modern transportation you desire, estimate the amount of time and the amount of money needed to complete Phileas Fogg's trip around the world today. Convert the time from days into hours and then minutes, as Mr. Fogg did. Convert the money needed into English pounds.

Vocabulary

Each of the following quotations chosen from *Around the World in Eighty Days* includes one or more vocabulary words in **bold print**.

1. "But he could not take root in any of these; with **chagrin**, he found his masters invariably whimsical and irregular, constantly running about the country on the lookout for adventure."

2. "Having **scrutinized** the house from top to bottom. . . ."
3. "Stuart, whose turn it was to deal, gathered them up, and went on: 'You are right **theoretically**, Mr. Fogg, but practically—' "
4. "A memorandum of the wager was at once drawn up and signed by the six parties, during which Phileas Fogg preserved a **stoical** composure."
5. "As for his antagonists, they seemed much agitated; not so much for the value of their take, as because they had some **scruples** about betting under conditions so difficult to their friend."
6. "But surely a gentleman so **chary** of his steps would stop there . . . ."
7. "Phileas Fogg, snugly **ensconced** in his corner, did not open his lips."
8. ". . . and blamed his Reform Club friends for having accepted a wager which betrayed the mental **aberration** of its proposer."
9. " 'Consul' remarked the detective, **dogmatically**, 'great robbers always resemble honest folks.' "
10. "Fix, left alone was more impatient than ever, having a **presentiment** that the robber was on board the *Magnolia*."
11. "And they walked off together, Passepartout chatting **volubly** as they went along."
12. "In which the Red Sea and the Indian Ocean prove **propitious** to the designs of Phileas Fogg."
13. "But the Red Sea is full of **caprice**, and often boisterous, like most long and narrow gulfs."
14. ". . . which Passepartout never failed to accept with graceful **alacrity** . . . "
15. ". . . who sang a **lugubrious** psalm . . ."
16. ". . . they decided to make a **reconnaissance** around the **pagoda**."
17. "The cries of the **fakirs** were just ceasing. . . ."
18. ". . . whether the priests were watching by the side of their victim as **assiduously** as were the soldiers at the door."
19. ". . . an **extradition** warrant would be necessary."
20. ". . . he conducted her to a **palanquin**. . . ."

About the Author

Jules Verne, born in 1828, has been called by many the "father of science fiction." Through his novels, he predicted many twentieth-century inventions, the nuclear submarine and the helicopter to name just two. The heroes in his novels traveled to the bottom of the sea, the center of the earth, and the moon. Though man has not journeyed to the center of the earth, he has accomplished the other two feats. Jules Verne died in 1905, but his novels are still read and enjoyed by readers the world over.

Bambi: A Life in the Woods
Author: Felix Salten
Publication date: 1928

Characters
    Bambi
    His mother
    The old stag
    Aunt Ena
    Faline
    Gobo
    He

Setting
    Present day—The Forest

Plot

Children and adults the world over are familiar with the deer, Bambi, through the Disney production of the same name, but few are as familiar with the novel by Felix Salten, first published in 1928. John Galsworthy in the foreword to the book states, "For delicacy of perception and essential truth I hardly know any story of animals that can stand beside this life study of a forest deer."

Beginning with his birth in the hidden forest thicket, Bambi lives the idyllic life of the very young. Guided by his loving mother, he ventures from his birth place to the deer trails that wind through the forest, meeting along the way the other forest denizens: the chattering magpie, the scurrying squirrel, the quarrelsome blue jays, and the suave and cautious hare. Always curious, he constantly questions his mother and sometimes is satisfied with her answers and other times is puzzled and mystified by her responses.

As he grows and strengthens, he and his mother venture farther from the glade and eventually come to the meadow. Bambi is truly excited by the openness and wishes to leap into the clearing to romp and play. His mother cautions him that walking in the meadow is dangerous and he may enter only if his mother has deemed it safe. On a visit to the meadow, he meets his Aunt Ena and her two children, Gobo and Faline. Once when his mother has left Bambi alone, he spies a creature on the edge of the clearing. The sight fills him with an overwhelming dread and fear. From his mother he learns that the terrifying creature is "He." Another time when Bambi is left alone, he meets his father, who berates him for crying because he is alone.

The winter changes life for Bambi and all the other animals in the forest, for they must face the bitter, bone-chilling cold and the pangs of hunger. But worst of all is "He" and the terrible weapon he carries that kills with a thundering boom. When Bambi's mother is killed, he is left to reach adulthood on his own. Soon, as described by the squirrel, he is " 'so tall, so stately and with such long bright prongs to your antlers.' " With strange longings, he clashes with the other stags for mastery and mates with Faline. Following the ways of male deer, he leaves his family for the solitude of the forest. Assisted by the old stag, Bambi eludes "He," recovers from a bullet wound, and grows to be the leader of the herd. The old stag schools Bambi to wisdom and eventually shows him the truth about "He."

Questions for Discussion
 1. Why did Bambi find it perfectly normal to ask his mother many questions? Why do you think his mother did not always tell him all she knew? Does this ever happen in your family?
 2. When Bambi, Faline, and Gobo first meet, the just stare at each other. Why does it take them time to play together? How do you react when you meet someone new? What helps you get past the strangeness?
 3. When Bambi and his cousins discuss the hedgehog, Faline thinks the hedgehog doesn't like people, but Gobo says he may just be afraid. Who do you think is right? Why?
 4. How does Bambi feel when his mother leaves him alone? How did you feel the first time you were all alone? Why does the old stag admonish Bambi?
 5. " 'Relatives are never as good as friends' " is the advice given by the screech owl. Do you agree with him? Do you rely more on relatives or more on friends for help and advice? Is there someone special whom you count on? Why did you choose this person?
 6. What is the advice the old stag gives Bambi when he inquires about "He"? Could you apply it to your own life?
 7. Winter brings great hardship. How do the forest creatures react? Are humans sometimes affected in the same way by trouble? Is Marena's thought worth applying when you are suffering?
 8. Why are all the woodland creatures frightened when "He" comes into the forest? What happened to Bambi's mother?
 9. What is the second piece of advice that the old stag gives to Bambi? Why does Bambi take his advice?
 10. Why do Bambi and the old stag misinterpret the feelings of each other when they encounter each other in the forest? Do you ever feel people are misinterpreting your feelings because of outward appearances or that you misunderstand others? How could these mistakes be avoided?
 11. Why does the old stag pity Gobo when he talks of his time with man? How has Gobo's time in captivity affected his ability to survive in the forest?
 12. What is the final lesson the old stag teaches Bambi?

Projects
 1. The ferret capturing the mouse is an example of part of the forest food chain. Draw a food chain that might be found in a temperate forest.

2. Research one of the animals mentioned in *Bambi*. Write a report that includes its scientific name, physical description, habitat, feeding habits, and importance to man.
3. Investigate the rules covering the hunting of deer in your community. Report your findings to the class in an oral presentation.
4. View the Disney movie version of *Bambi,* and create a chart or a multimedia presentation showing the similarities and differences. State which version you prefer.
5. Felix Salten gives a beautiful description of the coming of winter. Pick a season and write your own lyrical description.
6. Draw a picture of the meadow as it is when first viewed by Bambi.

Vocabulary

Each of the following quotations chosen from *Bambi* includes one or more vocabulary words in **bold print**.

1. ". . . and to be **eternally** on guard lest something happen to them."
2. "She continued **zealously** washing her newly-born."
3. "The whole forest resounded with **myriad** voices, was **penetrated** by them in a joyous **agitation**."
4. "The wood thrush rejoiced **incessantly**. . . ."
5. ". . . he hunted eagerly around and found **nourishment** for his life."
6. ". . . so that the soil of the twilit forest floor shone with a silent, **ardent**, colorful gladness."
7. ". . . such **anticipation**, that he would become anxious and happy at the same time, and grow silent."
8. "A threadlike little cry shrilled out **piteously**. . . ."
9. ". . . but Bambi stopped **inquisitively**."
10. ". . . or the tender, **dappled** light that played through the branches."
11. "It tossed and waved **luxuriantly**."
12. "He was very friendly and civil, but a little **condescending**.
13. ". . . and let himself be **mollified**."
14. ". . . and pleasantly **ruminating**, went farther and farther into the woods."
15. "Bambi kept a **discreet** distance."
16. "The stag looked at Bambi **appraisingly** and smiled a very slight, hardly noticeable smile."
17. ". . . for it was always exciting, **unfathomable**, mysterious and terrible."
18. ". . . answered Ronno **evasively**, and walked quickly away."
19. ". . . he whispered **solicitously**, while his voice quavered. . . ."
20. ". . . and felt an **inexplicable** desire driving him to find him."

About the Author

Felix Salten is the pen name for Sigmund Salzman, born in Budapest, Hungary, in 1869. He became a journalist but later began writing and publishing many historical and romantic novels. He is best known for his works depicting the lives of animals. In 1829, he published his most widely read, *Bambi*. At the invitation of the Carnegie Foundation, he traveled to the United States and recounted his impressions of the country in a book called *Five Minutes America*. With the Nazi invasion of his homeland, he fled to Zurich, Switzerland, where he lived throughout the war, dying in 1945.

Belle Prater's Boy
Author: Ruth White
Publication date: 1996

Awards
Newbery Honor Book

Characters
Gypsy Arbutus Leemaster
Woodrow Prater
Belle Prater
Lady Ball Dotson
Porter Dotson
Granny and Grandpa Ball
Everett Prater
Blind Benny

Setting
1950s—Coal Station, Virginia

Plot
This is the story of Gypsy and Woodrow, cousins whose lives have been affected by the loss of two loved ones. Gypsy's adored father is dead, and
Woodrow's mother has disappeared. Almost a year after Belle Prater has disappeared, Woodrow, her son, moves to Coal Station to live with Granny and
Grandpa Ball. Gypsy lives next door with her mother and stepfather and is determined to discover the mystery of her aunt's disappearance; Woodrow is not
ready to tell what he knows.

As the children of two sisters, Love and Belle, Gypsy's and Woodrow's lives
and their present situation have been seriously affected by what happened to
their mothers in the past. Though named Belle in hopes that she will be the
"belle of the ball," it is Love who has all the looks and all the boyfriends. While
Love is away to college, Belle blossoms and falls in love with handsome Amos
Leemaster, a newcomer in town. However, when Love comes home, it is she
whom Amos asks to marry, and Belle, hurt and brokenhearted, runs away with
Everett Prater, a coal miner.

Like her mother, Gypsy is beautiful and has always lived a sheltered and
privileged life. Like his mother, Woodrow is not very attractive; he is cross-
eyed, wears thick glasses, and usually dresses in very large hand-me-down
clothes. Despite their differences, Gypsy and Woodrow become good friends
and share their secret desires. Woodrow wants his mother to come home and his

eyes to be straightened; Gypsy wants her long hair to be cut because she feels invisible. " 'Like maybe under all this hair nobody can see me.' "

During the summer, Gypsy comes to appreciate Woodrow more and more, for his gift for storytelling, his gift for finding adventure, his innate goodness, and his great compassion. Woodrow, though he misses his mother, enjoys his new life in Coal Station and becomes an integral part of this extended family.

On the first day of school, Gypsy is forced to face the truth of her father's death. She learns to accept his suicide and to live with it through the kindness and understanding of her stepfather, her mother, and Woodrow. On the anniversary of Belle's disappearance, Woodrow reveals that he knows his mother left willingly, wearing his hand-me-down clothes and taking the thirty dollars saved for his eye operation.

Questions for Discussion

1. When Gypsy questions Granny about giving her aunt the name Belle, Granny answers that they wanted her to be the "belle of the ball." Is this a good reason for naming someone? Does Belle fit her name? How does she feel about it? How could she have been helped?

2. How does Granny describe Amos? Is she more impressed by his good looks or his good deeds? Do you judge people by their appearance or their actions? What happened to Belle that spring? What happens when Love comes home? How would you feel if you were Belle?

3. How does Gypsy treat her stepfather? Why do you think she does this? Does Porter deserve this treatment?

4. What does Love say when Gypsy confronts her about Belle being Amos's sweetheart first? Does Love regret her treatment of Belle? How would she change things if she could?

5. Describe Gypsy's room. What does this tell you about Gypsy's life? Do you envy her? Do you think these material things are important?

6. When Belle eloped with Everett Prater, what did Love think of her behavior? What does she think now? Why do you think she changed her mind?

7. What occurs in Gypsy's dream? The dream is an example of the literary device, foreshadowing. What is the purpose of foreshadowing in a novel? Why do you think the author used it here?

8. Woodrow tells Gypsy about his mama feeling like the man in the straight jacket. Why did she feel this way? Where does Woodrow think she has gone? Do you believe this is possible?

9. When Everett comes to visit Woodrow, he has a woman in his car. How does Woodrow show that it bothers him? Why do you think that it does?

10. When Gypsy is recovering from the measles, how does Porter show his kindness? Does Gypsy appreciate it? Why or why not? What does she say to her mother?

11. Why has Gypsy's hair never been cut? What does Grandpa say about appearances? Do you agree with him? What does he say about Belle and Woodrow? When Gypsy says she would like people to admire her for her

talent or her brain, she realizes it is easy for her to say. Why? For what traits do you want to be admired?

12. Why does Gypsy doubt that Woodrow really believes that his mother has gone to the place where two things come together or another world? Do you agree with her?

13. Why was Mrs. Cooper so mean to Woodrow? What do you think of her behavior? How does he retaliate? What is the "power of suggestion"? Why is he not punished? Why is Gypsy jealous of this?

14. How do Woodrow and Gypsy disagree about the song *Pretty Is as Pretty Does*? With whom do you agree?

15. Why do you think that Woodrow will not talk about the thirty dollars saved toward his eye operation? For what reason does Woodrow challenge Gypsy with the fact that Porter did not leave her as her father did?

16. Think about Woodrow's story of Olive Ann. Why do you think that he told it?

17. On the first day of school, Woodrow tells the story of his mother disappearing into thin air. Why do you think he told it? Do you know what a defense mechanism is? Have you ever used one?

18. Gypsy tells the story of her family but is challenged by Buzz Osborne, who tells the real story of Amos Leemaster's death. Who tries to stop him? How does Gypsy react when she is faced with the truth? Why does she do it? Who comes to help her? What does he say that strikes a chord? What does it mean?

19. Why did Gypsy's father commit suicide? Can you empathize with his feelings? Are other people in this story affected by outward appearances? How do you feel about this?

20. When Woodrow brings Blind Benny to Gypsy, what does he tell her about her father and mother? Does this information give you a fuller picture of Amos?

21. Woodrow ends his essay about Blind Benny by writing, " 'Because Benny is able to see beyond appearances.' " Is this the message of this novel? How often do you form an opinion based upon appearances? Will this novel help you to see beyond appearances?

22. What is the truth of Belle's disappearance? What do Gypsy and Woodrow realize about their parents leaving them? Why were they able to forgive them? Would you?

Projects

1. Coal mining has been an important industry in Virginia. Trace its history, and prepare a written report on your findings.

2. Woodrow and Gypsy watched *I Led Three Lives for the FBI,* a television show airing in the 1950s. Find ten other shows appearing in that period. Create a poster or a multimedia presentation depicting the shows, the stars, and the networks on which they appeared.

3. One of the motion pictures Woodrow and Gypsy saw was *Rear Window*. Actor James Stewart starred in the movie *Rear Window*, and actor Christopher Reeve remade the movie as a television drama. Document the life of either man through a pictorial essay.

4. This novel mentions Mammoth Cave in Kentucky. Research ten major caves in the United States. Locate them on a map, and identify their size, depth, and outstanding features.

5. Spelunking is the sport of cave exploring. Locate spelunking organizations either through the Internet or local sources. Contact them for information about local caves and the equipment and training needed for the sport. Present the data in an informational booklet for future spelunkers.

6. Columbia Presbyterian Hospital is the hospital in New York City famous for its success in operating on cross-eyed children. Research when this procedure was first developed and implemented and how this procedure is performed today. Report your findings in the style of a newspaper article or a medical segment on a television newscast.

7. Solve the mathematical riddle about the hotel charges posed by Woodrow. Present two other mathematical riddles for the class to solve. (Answer—The riddle cannot be solved by addition; subtraction must be used. From the thirty dollars, subtract the three returned to the guests and the two kept by the bellhop; you are left with the owner's twenty-five.)

8. Research why measles is no longer a disease contracted by children in the United States. Present your answer in an oral report to the class. You might want to interview a doctor or search the Web for the answer.

Vocabulary

Each of the following quotations chosen from *Belle Prater's Boy* includes one or more vocabulary word in **bold print**.

1. "And no indication that she went **traipsing** off to somewheres else."

2. "And the **speculation** went on."

3. " 'There were **insinuations** in it,' she said."

4. "Then I couldn't help feeling more **plagued** than **privileged**."

5. " 'Now don't you go over and **aggravate** him about Aunt Belle, you hear me.' "

6. "It was a **mystic** twilight I found myself in that first of many times to follow when I raced across the yards to go visit Woodrow."

7. "That sent us into **hysterics** again and Granny had to take her glasses off and wipe them on her apron."

8. " 'Folks always come to my place to **socialize**,' Clint went on, like he was bragging."

9. " 'We were **mesmerized**, brainwashed, hypnotized, whatever you want to call it.' "

10. "I folded my arms in stubborn **resolution**. He said if folks heard me carrying on about a place in the air, they'd think I was **addled** in the head."

11. "And what happened to him when he went **spelunking** alone one day was a sorrowful thing."
12. "Every pore of my body ached right down to my hair **follicles**."
13. "All that night I had strange dreams and **hallucinations**."
14. "Each time I woke up in a **frenzy**, my mama was there, my mama was there, calm, cool and beautiful."
15. "I was **flabbergasted**."
16. " 'It's being **filtered** through two worlds.' "
17. "I was **disgruntled** because it put him way up higher than the rest of us."
18. ". . . I said, **exasperated**."
19. ". . . so now it was bitter acid she was spraying on Woodrow in **retaliation**."
20. "It sat on my chest like some dark **parasite**, feeding on my grief."

About the Author

Born in 1942 in Whitewood, Virginia, White received her bachelor of arts from Pfeiffer College and her master of library sciences from Queens College. Like Woodrow, her father was a coal miner and her childhood years were poverty stricken. For her education she received in public schools she is deeply grateful and feels she has given something back by working as an English teacher and a school librarian in the public school system. Ms. White now lives in Virginia Beach where she works as a technical services librarian.

From the Author

"It is important to me that children of today read these books [about the Appalachian region] and feel they can escape for just a little while into another place and time which once was very real. I want them not only to enjoy my stories and my particular style but also to feel what I used to feel when I was in the habit of reading every book I could find—'This feels right. I love this. Someday I will write books like this.' "

Bud, Not Buddy
Author: Christopher Paul Curtis
Publication date: 1999

Awards
  Newbery Medal
  Coretta Scott King Award

Characters
  Bud Caldwell
  Herman E. Calloway
  Amos family with son, Todd
  Bugs
  Deza Malone
  Lefty Lewis
  Mrs. Sleet, Kim, and Scott Sleet
  Grace Thomas
  Members of the band: Jimmy Wesley, Doug Tennant, Steady Eddie Patrick,
    Chug Cross, Roy Breed

Setting
  1936—Michigan

Plot
    Ten-year-old Bud Caldwell narrates his own story. He has been an orphan for
four years since his mother died. He remembers his mother telling him that Bud,
like the flower waiting to bloom, is his name instead of Buddy, which could be a
dog's name. He is sent to live with the Amos family in his third foster home.
Todd Amos is a bully, and worse yet, a bully whose parents support all his lies
and punish Bud. With his battered suitcase tied with twine, Bud runs away. He
sleeps outside, gets his food from the mission soup line, and stays in the library
during the day. He meets up with Bugs, another orphan on the run, and decides
to catch the train for the West. While waiting for the train, the boys stay in a
Hooverville, where Bud meets ten-year-old Deza. Bud misses the train and decides that he really should stay in Michigan. At the library, he finds out how far
he has to walk to get to Grand Rapids, where he thinks his father lives. With his
suitcase containing his blanket, a picture of his mother with a horse when she
was about ten years old, five stones with writing on them that he found after the
ambulance took his mother away, and five flyers of Herman Calloway and his
band, Bud starts walking. Bud believes that his mother kept these flyers because
Calloway is Bud's father, the father he never knew.

On the road, he is picked up by Mr. Lefty Lewis, who is transporting blood and union flyers. He spends the night with Lefty's family, the Sleets. When Bud gets to Calloway's club, he is surprised that the man is so old and crabby and denies being Bud's father. The other people in his band, and his singer, Grace Thomas, however, make Bud feel at home. They convince Calloway that Bud should stay in Grand Rapids and live with them at Grand Calloway Station, and he is given a room with pictures of horses tacked to a wall. Miss Thomas warns Bud that he will have to be patient with Calloway. When Bud rides back from a playing engagement with him, Calloway asks him to pick up some rocks from the ground. Bud notices that they resemble the rocks he has carried in his suitcase. He shows these to Calloway, who accuses him of taking the rocks from the room in which he has been sleeping.

The rocks are the first step in unraveling the connection between Calloway and Bud. Wherever he performed, Calloway picked up a rock and brought it back to his little girl; he continued to collect them for her after she left home to escape the pressure her father was placing on her to go to college. Calloway is actually his grandfather, the father of Bud's mother, the girl who pinned the horse pictures to her bedroom wall, the woman who treasured the flyers of Calloway's concerts.

Questions for Discussion

1. What admirable qualities does Bud have? Does he have any qualities that you do not admire? Would you like to have Bud for a friend? Why?

2. Why did Bud devise "Bud Caldwell's Rules and Things for Having a Funner Life and Making a Better Liar Out of Yourself"? Are these good or bad rules? In what kind of situations does Bud use his rules? What does this tell you about him? Do you have any rules for yourself similar to Bud's? Do any of his appeal to you?

3. What kind of relationship did Bud have with his mother? What is the significance of the items he carries around in his suitcase? Why doesn't he feel the need to carry everything around with him at the end of the story?

4. Todd, the son in Bud's foster home, is a bully. How does Bud handle him? Do you think that Bud handled Todd's bullying in the correct way? Does Todd learn anything about how he should treat others? How do you deal with bullies?

5. Bud's mother used to tell him that when one door closes, another opens. What did she mean? How does Bud experience this? Have you ever experienced this?

6. Contrast the cruel treatment Bud received from the Amos family with the kindness of the librarians and the family in the mission line. What motivates these people to treat Bud as they do? Whom do you admire?

7. Bud says, "It seemed like the only good thing that came out of going to Hooverville was that I finally kissed a girl." Do you think that Bud really learns more about people, the Depression, and himself? Why does he want to find Deza and her mother after the police burn down the shantytown?

8. What admirable qualities does Herman Calloway have? Does he have any qualities you do not admire? What kind of relationship did he have with his daughter? What kind of relationship does he have with his band? How does he react to Bud's claims that he is Bud's father? How does he react when he discovers Bud is his grandson?

9. In what ways do African Americans experience prejudice in this novel? How does the band handle the prejudice they encounter? Is Mrs. Amos prejudiced toward her own race? Why? What other kinds of prejudice exist besides racial prejudice? Have you been the victim of prejudice or observed incidents of prejudice? How did these make you feel?

10. By means of the literary device of foreshadowing, an author can present clues to the reader about what will happen in the story. Is there any fore-shadowing in *Bud, Not Buddy*? When did you begin to realize that Calloway is Bud's grandfather?

Projects

1. Bud carries his treasures around with him in a suitcase. Use a box that re-sembles a suitcase in shape, and attach the top to the bottom along one long side so that the box can open like a suitcase. Place in it those items that are as important to you as Bud's are to him. On the inside cover of the box, ex-plain the significance of each item you have selected. If an item cannot be placed in the box, describe it and its significance on a card placed inside the box.

2. This novel gives the reader a glimpse into life during the Depression. Re-search this time in American history. What started the Depression? How did people survive? Besides Hoovervilles and bread lines, what characterized this time? Make a multimedia presentation or a poster that will give an overview of this time.

3. The members of the band first give Bud a recorder and then give him an alto sax. Make drawings of each of these instruments and label the parts.

4. Several historical figures were mentioned in this novel, for example Paul Robeson, J. Edgar Hoover, Pretty Boy Floyd, Pinkerton, Baby Face Nelson, George Washington Carver, and Al Capone. Select one of these or another person who lived in America during the Depression. Research the life of this person, and compile your research into a brief biographical sketch.

5. Lefty Lewis is transporting flyers for labor organizers. Write a news story about the struggle to organize labor unions for automobile factory workers or Pullman porters.

Vocabulary

Each of the following quotations chosen from *Bud, Not Buddy* includes one or more vocabulary words in **bold print**.

1. ". . . when perfectly good parts of your body **commence** to loosening up and falling off of you."

2. " 'Not only have you struck him, you have **provoked** his asthma!' "
3. " 'I will not **tolerate** even one night with you under my roof.' "
4. "I **simmered** down and started thinking about getting even."
5. "I walked over to the sink and turned on one of the **spigots**."
6. "I had to be real careful, even if it was the middle of the night, even if I was **crouching** down. . . ."
7. "I got a **whiff** of the leather on all the old books. . . ."
8. ". . . making it look like a **gigantic** black genie . . ."
9. "The one who was doing all the talking saw them **fidgeting** and said, 'Hold steady, men.' "
10. "I'd get a **crick** in my neck. . . ."
11. " '. . . it looks like he provided a pretty **paltry** meal for every mosquito on the way. ' "
12. ". . .even though she was kind of young and **scrawny** . . ."
13. "I slapped him instead and it left a big **welt** on his cheek. . . ."
14. ". . . **twitch** the same way a horse's does when a fly lands on it."

About the Author

Christopher Paul Curtis, like Bud, grew up in Flint, Michigan. He attended the University of Michigan and worked on an auto body assembly line while he was a student there. His first novel for young adults, *The Watsons Go to Birmingham—1963*, was a Newbery Honor Book and a Coretta Scott King Honor Book. He is now a full-time writer and lives in Windsor, Ontario, Canada.

Crazy Lady!
Author: Jane Leslie Conly
Publication date: 1993

Awards
Newbery Honor Book
ALA Notable Books for Children

Characters
Vernon Dibbs
Maxine Flooter
Ronald
Miss Annie
Milt
Miss Marlowe

Setting
1981—Baltimore, Maryland

Plot
Vern looks back two years to 1981, his first year in junior high school, to tell the story of Maxine Flooter and her son, Ronald. Maxine is known as Crazy Lady in the neighborhood because of her garish dress and erratic behavior that is often caused by her drinking. In spite of her unpredictable behavior, Maxine does her best to be a good mother to her retarded son, Ronald.

Vern is the middle of five children; three years before his encounter with Maxine, his mother died suddenly. Vern is still learning to cope with her death. Because he has trouble in school, he feels inadequate in the family, especially next to his older brother, Tony, who is very smart and studious.

Maxine is the laughingstock of the neighborhood, and Vern is not prepared for the circumstances that will draw them together. They meet in Milt's store, both victims of Milt's attempt to cheat them. Maxine remembers that Vern's mother had sewn a coat for Ronald, and Vern tells her he is having trouble in school. A few days later, Maxine leaves a note in Vern's mailbox offering to introduce him to Miss Annie, a former schoolteacher, who can help him with his schoolwork.

Miss Annie does help Vern in return for help she wants him to give to Maxine. Initially, Vern is afraid of what his friends will say. Before long, he recognizes that Ronald doesn't look that different and really knows more than anyone realizes. He learns from Maxine that she insisted on taking Ronald home from the hospital when the doctors had recommended that the baby be institutionalized. She supported him until she was laid off from her job. Soon, Vern objects to his brother's reference to Maxine as the Crazy Lady. However, she is still drinking, and Vern finds out that she has been locked up for being drunk and disorderly. When Ronald's teacher comes to their house to evaluate the care Ronald is receiving, Vern offers to be Ronald's assistant at the Special Olympics. He even organizes a neighborhood carnival to raise money to buy Ronald a pair of sneakers. Unfortunately, Maxine arrives at the carnival drunk.

Maxine becomes more and more difficult as Social Services starts to investigate her care of Ronald. At times, she is reluctant to let Vern see Ronald. She tells Vern that she is lost when she doesn't drink. Finally, she decides to send Ronald to North Carolina to live with his aunt and uncle.

Questions for Discussion
1. Vern says that most of his friends take candy from the store; they also try to take school supplies. What would you say to a friend who shoplifted from a store?
2. How are Maxine and her son treated by the children in the neighborhood? Why do they treat them the way they do? Do you know of anyone like Maxine? How is this person treated?
3. Why does Miss Annie ask Vern to help Maxine? Does she think Vern can benefit from the friendship as well as Maxine and Ronald?
4. Do you understand why Vern is afraid of his friends' reaction to his friendship with Maxine? Why does he lie to them about the carnival?
5. How does Vern's attitude to Maxine and Ronald change? Do you admire the way he treats them? How does he see himself as similar to Ronald?
6. What kind of stress exists in Vern's family? Why does Vern argue with his brother Tony after the carnival? How does his father try to relieve the family's problems? How does his father want them to settle their problems? Do you think Vern's father is correct in his approach?
7. What does the carnival do to help Vern to feel better about himself? Does his work on the carnival help others to see him in a new light?
8. Why does Maxine appear at the carnival and insist that she and her son do not want charity? How do you think Vern feels about this? How would it make you feel if you were Vern?
9. Miss Annie says that she and Vern are "connected" while Maxine is not. What does she mean by this?
10. Maxine says that she and Ronald know that Vern is not dumb. She says that people who put her son down are the "the dumb ones." What does she mean? In what ways is Ronald smart? Have you ever known anyone like Ronald who was smart in some ways and not in others?
11. Miss Annie tells Vern that Maxine is responsible for her own actions. Do you agree? Do you think her alcoholism lessens the responsibility she has for her own behavior? Why does she drink?
12. Miss Annie tells Vern that it is hard to establish friendships with people who are different. Do you agree? Have you ever had a friendship with someone different from yourself?

13. Why does Maxine send Ronald away? Do you think she makes the right decision? Is she a good mother to Ronald? Why does Vern react the way he does?
14. Vern says that the Special Olympics changed things for himself and Ronald. How?

Projects

1. Vern volunteers to help Ronald in the Special Olympics. Find out about the Special Olympics in your area. What kinds of activities does it sponsor? How can someone become involved as a participant or a volunteer? Compile your information into a brief report.
2. Vern organizes a neighborhood carnival to raise money for Ronald's sneakers. Plan a carnival for your own neighborhood that could benefit Special Olympics or another favorite charity. Make a series of posters for the various activities and events that will be part of the carnival. If circumstances permit, actually stage your event, and give the money to the charity.
3. Vern's father cannot read, and he asks Vern to help him learn. Literacy Volunteers is an organization dedicated to teaching adults to read. Find out if this organization exists in your area. How could someone become involved as a client or as a volunteer? Write two radio advertisements, one to attract an adult who wants to learn to read, and another to attract people to volunteer to teach in the program.
4. Vern and his friends are baseball fans. Find out about baseball in 1981. Who was on the Baltimore Orioles team, and how did they finish that year? What other players held the records that year for hitting and pitching? Who won the World Series? Compile your information into a written report or multimedia presentation.
5. Maxine is an alcoholic. Research the effects of alcohol on the body, and present your information in the form of a poster.
6. Contact your local chapter of Alcoholics Anonymous for information on their program for stopping alcoholics from drinking. Write a letter to Maxine explaining to her how the program works and how it will help her to get control of her drinking.

Vocabulary

Each of the following quotations chosen from *Crazy Lady!* includes one or more vocabulary words in **bold print**.

1. "I'd **hunker** down in the last seat and hope the teachers wouldn't call on me. . . ."
2. " 'We could go up to Woolworth's and **snitch** some candy bars. . . .' "
3. ". . . a big red hat with a **tassel** on it."
4. " 'I'm getting so **shriveled** up, I'm more like a tough old vine than a human being.' "
5. "Her lipstick was **fluorescent** orange."
6. "I pointed out the window to **distract** him while I hid it. . . ."
7. ". . . his eyes **bulged**. . . ."

8. ". . . being scared made him **gawky** and pop-eyed. . . ."
9. "I **mimicked** his reedy voice till Steph gave me a look that said be quiet."
10. "I could feel she was getting **agitated**."
11. "Ronald was **cringing** behind her."
12. "I was **sprawled** on the bedspread with my clothes still on."
13. "I gave it to him quick, before Maxine could **intercept** it."
14. "He hated it when we **bickered**."
15. "Her mood was **contagious**."
16. "He **smirked** as he brought them to the register."
17. ". . . either Ben or Sandra would come **slithering** over and grab the page."
18. "She was dressed **shabbily**, in a worn coat and built-up shoes, the kind old ladies wear."

About the Author

Jane Leslie Conly grew up on a farm in Leesburg, Virginia. Both her parents were writers. Her father, in fact, was the recipient of the Newbery Medal for *Mrs. Frisby and the Rats of NIMH*, which she continued in her first book, *Racso and the Rats of NIMH*. Conly attended Smith College and participated in the Writing Seminars Program at Johns Hopkins University. She lives in Maryland.

Dancing on the Edge
Author: Han Nolan
Publication date: 1997

Awards
National Book Award for Young People's Literature
ALA Best Book for Young Adults
School Library Journal Best Book of the Year
Booklist Editors' Choice
New York Public Library Book for the Teenage

Characters
Miracle McCloy
Gigi, Miracle's grandmother
Dane, her father
Aunt Casey
Uncle Toole
Grandaddy Opal
Dr. DeAngelis

Setting
Present day—Southeastern states

Plot
Miracle has her name because of her extraordinary birth, being taken from her mother after her death in an automobile accident. For the ten years since her birth, she has lived with her grandmother, Gigi, and her brilliant father, Dane, who had written and published his first novel when he was fifteen. At seventeen he published his second and married Miracle's mother. Gigi is a psychic, and Miracle has grown up believing in spells, omens, auras, and mystical spirits. It is commonplace for her grandmother, Dane, and her aunt and uncle to use a Ouija board to contact her deceased mother. On one such night, Miracle is allowed to join in place of her father, and the planchette spells out "Dane gone." When the four check his room, his clothes are in a heap on the floor, and Gigi announces that he has melted. When Miracle asks where Dane has melted to, Gigi answers vaguely, leaving Miracle's question unanswered. The town does not accept the story of Dane's melting, and Miracle and Gigi move to live with Grandaddy Opal. There, unknown to Gigi, her grandfather enrolls Miracle in a dance school. Fearing that she will tell Gigi of the lessons, Miracle imagines a giant eraser following her home wiping out all she has learned. In the modern dance portions of the lessons she throws herself about so hard that she bruises herself banging into walls and hitting the floor. A closeness develops between Miracle

and Grandaddy Opal, protecting her in a small way from Gigi's strange beliefs. Miracle, however, continues to feel she was never born, searches for Dane and her mother, and builds a shrine to Dane in the basement.

During Miracle's thirteenth birthday party, a tornado forces everyone into the cellar, where they discover the shrine and Miracle dances for the group. Gigi is angry at Opal, but the force of the tornado hitting the house stops her wrath. Following the tornado, Grandaddy Opal has a heart attack, Gigi leaves for Europe to marry her friend, Mr. Wadell, and Miracle goes to live with her mother's sister, Aunt Casey. The new home does not make many changes in Miracle's private life for she is still an outcast at school and still searching for her father and her own identity, something she is not sure she possesses. Miracle, in an attempt to melt just like Dane, sets herself on fire. When she is ready to be released from the hospital, her Aunt Casey has her charged to the mental section. It is in the hospital that Miracle realizes that the miracle of her birth and her grandmother's treatment of it are the sources of some of her serious problems. With the help of her doctor and Aunt Casey, she begins the road to recovery.

Questions for Discussion

1. What makes Gigi think that Dane had melted? Why does Miracle agree with her? Do Aunt Casey and Uncle Toole? With whom do you agree? Why?
2. What reason does Gigi give Miracle for her decision to move on? Why does she tell Miracle that she is special? How does Miracle feel about this?
3. What does Miracle tell Aunt Casey about her trouble at school? What do they say that disturbs her the most? Why does this frighten her?
4. Miracle misses her father, wears his bathrobe, listens to his tapes, and cuts her hair like his. What is she trying to do? What would you have done?
5. In Dane's last argument with Gigi, he says that Miracle should be with his father since Gigi is not fit to raise a child and never was. Why do you think he feels this way? What does his attitude tell you of his childhood?
6. What is Grandaddy Opal's reaction when he hears the children jeering Miracle from the bus? How does he try to improve her life? What is the problem with the solution?
7. What does Grandaddy Opal tell Miracle about black holes? What does this lead Miracle to plan?
8. During Miracle's birthday party everyone goes to the cellar to avoid a tornado; what do they find there? Why do you think Miracle built this shrine to Dane? What did she expect to happen? How did all the birthday guests react? Why did Miss Emmaline begin to sing? How does Gigi react when Miracle begins to dance?
9. Why does Miracle think Grandaddy's heart attack is her fault?
10. When Miracle goes to school, she keeps erasing her name from the blackboard. Why does she do this? Why does she write the fantasy about the ballerina? Does this tell you what she fears about herself?

11. Miracle interests the girls at school by casting love spells for them. Does this get the friendship she desires? What is the final result?
12. What does Miracle finally do that gets her Aunt Casey's attention? What does her Aunt Casey do? Why does Gigi oppose this move?
13. How does Dr. DeAngelis help Miracle? Why does revealing the secrets of her parents' marriage and her mother's death set Miracle on the road to recovery? Do you agree that secrets can be dangerous? Would you rather know the truth even if it were unpleasant?
14. What does Miracle finally realize about Gigi? What does she realize is the truth about Dane's disappearance? Why does Miracle leave Gigi to return to the hospital? Do you agree that everyone has to feel that they are somebody?
15. Miracle is a disturbed child, but some of her ideas and feelings are common to all of us. What did she learn that could help each of us to see the real truth?

Projects

1. Find resources in your community that treat and assist mentally disturbed children. Record or videotape an interview with a person who works in this field. Present your interview to your class, family, or other interested group.
2. Read ten of the poems written by Emily Dickinson. Record your responses to them in a reading journal.
3. Research the latest findings concerning mentally ill children, and write a report of your findings.

Vocabulary

Each of the following quotations chosen from *Dancing on the Edge* includes one or more vocabulary words in **bold print**.

1. ". . . a **portent** of great things to come. . . ."
2. ". . . worried, then frightened, her pink **jowly** face suddenly pale. . . . "
3. "The night of the **séance**, I grabbed my Barbie doll off the card table and flopped down on the floor with it."
4. "I looked to Gigi and she **squinched** her nose up at me."
5. ". . . they suspected both murder and suicide and had the pond in back of our house **dredged**."
6. "And she emphasized the word making it sound like she meant to say **derangement**."
7. "It was more **conducive** to Dane's work, Gigi had said."
8. "He walked like a **mutant** duck around the trunk of the maple. . . ."
9. "I imagined myself a famous dancer, a **prodigy** at thirteen like Dane."
10. ". . . nothing existed but the swirling sheer **ecstasy** of the dance and the music."
11. "She said Grandaddy Opal and I had **nebulous astral** bodies and she had an **ovoid** one."
12. ". . . when every muscle and bone ached beyond **endurance**."
13. "And that wasn't the only **coincidence**."

14. "The stale odor of cigarettes still **permeated** the house. . . ."
15. " 'Don't try reverse **psychology** on me.' "
16. " 'I come from a long line of mediums and healers and **clairvoyants**.' "
17. " 'Of course, it could just be **psychosomatic**.' "
18. "She'd talk to me, her voice tight, **constricted**."
19. "I saw Gigi's **stricken** face the day of the tornado when I had danced for her."
20. ". . . one of Gigi's **subliminal** tapes for losing weight."

About the Author

Like her protagonist, Miracle, Han Nolan is a dancer, receiving her bachelor's from the University of North Carolina and her master's from Ohio State in dance. Upon graduation, she became a dance instructor until she and her husband adopted children. This prompted a change in careers, and she has been a professional writer ever since. Her audience of choice has always been young adults who she hopes are provoked to thought by her novels. She now lives with her family in Alabama, the state in which she was born in 1956.

From the Author

"I am often asked where I get ideas for my stories. *Dancing on the Edge* was inspired by my children and by other stories about children who, like my own, are adopted. For this book I asked myself two questions: How do you form an identity when those people who should be telling you who you are aren't there for you? And how does it affect a child to grow up 'protected' from family secrets?"

Dear Mr. Henshaw
Author: Beverly Cleary
Publication date: 1983

Awards
  Newbery Medal

Characters
  Leigh Botts
  Bonnie Botts, Leigh's mother
  Bill Botts, Leigh's father
  Bandit, Leigh's dog
  Boyd Henshaw
  Mr. Fridley

Setting
  Present day—Pacific Grove, California

Plot
Boyd Henshaw became Leigh Botts's favorite author when Leigh's second-grade teacher read a Henshaw book to his class. Leigh began writing to Henshaw at that time. He tells his story in the form of letters to Boyd Henshaw and a diary, which Henshaw had suggested he keep because Leigh wants to be a writer himself.

By the time Leigh is in sixth grade, his parents are divorced, he and his mother move to Pacific Grove, and Leigh is in a new school. He misses his father, a long-distance trucker, and is bothered that his father rarely calls him and never says that he misses Leigh. Moreover, his father took Bandit after the divorce so he could have company on long trips. When his father doesn't fulfill his promise to call, Leigh calls him and discovers that his father has left Bandit out in a snowstorm. Furthermore, over the phone, Leigh hears the voice of a boy asking when he, his mother, and Leigh's father are going for pizza.

Leigh doesn't have a lot of friends in school, but he is befriended by Mr. Fridley, the school custodian, who asks him to come to school early in the morning to help him raise the state and national flags. Leigh is upset that the tasty treats his mother brings from her catering job for his lunch are frequently stolen, so he devises a burglar alarm for his lunch box. When he has to get into his lunch box for his food, the alarm goes off, and Leigh becomes the center of attention. A lot of kids want alarms on their boxes, and he is even invited to another boy's house to set up an alarm in his bedroom.

His teacher encourages Leigh to enter a writing contest. The best pieces of writing would be printed in a book, and the writers would have lunch with a famous author. Leigh's story, *A Day on Dad's Rig*, receives honorable mention but he still has lunch with an author since a winning piece of writing had been plagiarized. The author commends Leigh for writing an honest story that made her feel like she was riding in a rig.

His father comes home to see them and brings Bandit. He had asked other truckers for help in finding the dog, and one had picked Bandit up in the storm. Leigh's father also wants to know if there is a chance that he and Leigh's mother can reunite. Leigh's mother is not encouraging. Leigh gives Bandit back to his father to be company on the long rides.

Questions for Discussion

1. Why does Leigh have a hard time making friends? What advice does Mr. Fridley give him? What finally helps Leigh to make friends? What advice would you give any student new to a school? How could you help to make the new person's adjustment easier?
2. Leigh feels better when he writes in his diary. Why? Does writing your thoughts on paper make you feel better?
3. What kind of character is Mr. Fridley? How does he help Leigh?
4. How does Leigh feel about his parents' divorce? Why does he blame himself for their breakup? Are his feelings understandable?
5. What kind of man is Leigh's father? How does Leigh feel about him? Should Leigh's father have done anything differently when Bandit was not in his cab? How does Leigh feel about what his father did? Why is Leigh mad when his father sends him money?
6. How does Leigh feel when he hears another boy talking to his father? Are Leigh's feelings understandable?
7. Leigh is glad he never catches the lunch-box thief. Why? What does this tell you about him?
8. Leigh reread Boyd Henshaw's book many times. Have you ever read the same book several times? What pleasure do you get from reading the same book again?
9. What makes Leigh's father come home? How does Leigh feel about his father when he comes home? Why does Leigh give Bandit back to his father? What does this tell you about Leigh?
10. Do you think Leigh should hold out hope that his parents will reunite? Why?

Projects

1. Mr. Fridley asks Leigh to help him with the flags outside the school. Look up the rules for hoisting, displaying, and lowering your state flag and the American flag. Put this information into a poster or a multimedia presentation.
2. Leigh's mom won't fix their broken television because she wants to keep Leigh's brain intact. Locate a magazine article about television viewing by children. According to the article, what effect does television have on them? How much television viewing is recommended? Write your information in

a letter to Leigh's mother either agreeing with her position or arguing for a change.

3. Watching waves makes Leigh's mother feel better; watching the monarch butterflies makes Leigh feel better. Draw a picture of either of these scenes from the book, conveying the comforting effect it has on the character.

4. Leigh sees a multitude of monarch butterflies in a grove of trees. Locate information on the habits of monarch butterflies. Where do they live? What do they eat? What attracts them to a particular place? Compile your information into a report.

5. Leigh wants to be an author. In writing for the contest, he thinks about but does not enter a story about a wax truck driver who melts when he crosses the desert and a poem about butterflies. Complete one of these writings for Leigh.

Vocabulary

Each of the following quotations chosen from *Dear Mr. Henshaw* includes one or more vocabulary words in **bold print**.

1. "First Mr. Fridley fastened the U.S. flag on the **halyard**. . . ."
2. "I don't want to be a **nuisance** to you. . . ."
3. "When they **hibernated** and then woke up in the middle of winter because they had eaten all the wrong things and hadn't stored up enough fat, I almost cried."
4. "Mr. Fridley noticed me **scowling** again. . . ."
5. "I am filled with **wrath**. . . ."
6. " 'I couldn't get **stranded** up there in the mountains. . . .' "
7. "I let her in and gave her a **demonstration** of my burglar alarm."
8. "Would my sandwich **muffle** the bell?"
9. "I could dash back behind the **partition** and tackle the thief."
10. "The principal, who always **prowls** around keeping an eye on things at lunchtime . . ."
11. "The **fad** didn't last very long. . . "
12. "Mom is not a **snoop**."
13. " '*A Day on Dad's Rig* was **splendid** work for a boy your age.' "

About the Author

Beverly Cleary was born in McMinnville, Oregon. Until she was six, she lived on a farm, and then her family moved to Portland. She graduated from the University of California at Berkeley and received her degree as a librarian from the University of Washington at Seattle. After college, she became a children's librarian. However, by the time she was in sixth grade, she had decided to be a writer, especially of the kind of books she liked to read, about the real problems of children who are able to solve many of these problems on their own. Beverly Cleary lives in Carmel, California.

Deathwatch
Author: Robb White
Publication date: 1972

Characters
Ben
Madec
Eugene Strick, Deputy
Dr. Saunders
Mr. Hondurak, justice of the peace
Ben's uncle
Mr. Barowitz, Madec's lawyer

Setting
Present day—Bighorn sheep region of California

Plot
The bighorn sheep region of California is a rugged barren area, made up of desert, buttes, and the Rocky Mountains. The temperature is sizzling, the sun blazing, and the water scarce. Ben, a college student earning tuition money, guides Madec in his hunt for bighorn sheep. Madec is not a pleasant companion, smiling only when telling stories of his business deals in which he outwits and hurts his adversary.

After several days, they spot a herd of sheep that scatters when spooked. Madec takes aim with his .358 and shoots even though Ben says he did not see horns. The shot hits not a bighorn sheep but an old prospector. When Ben insists they return to report the accident, Madec turns his gun on Ben, making him remove all of his clothes except his underpants. He then forces him to go naked into the desert with no food, water, or the ability to gather either. Each time Ben thinks Madec has made a mistake, he finds himself thwarted and outwitted. Madec even removes the clothes from the dead prospector so that Ben cannot use them. At the prospector's camp, Madec destroys everything useful with the exception of a hunting slingshot and the buckshot ammunition for it. Without water, Ben only has forty-eight hours to live from his last drink. With almost twenty-four hours gone, Ben remembers a butte where there is a water catch basin. Using woodpecker nests and sotol leaves as boots, Ben reaches the butte, but the climb seems impossible. Desperation is a strong incentive, and Ben makes it up the north face of the butte even though Madec has shot him in the arm. While on the butte, Ben uses the slingshot to kill some birds, eats them raw, watches Madec preparing to climb the butte, and realizes that the jeep is the key to survival.

During the night, Ben slides down the funnel of the butte and buries himself alive in the loose sand. When Madec returns to the butte, Ben uncovers himself

45

and tries to start the jeep, but Madec has outsmarted him again; he has taken the keys and the distributor cap with him. Ben knows that he must capture Madec in order to return to safety. Using his slingshot, he wounds and captures Madec. Returning to town, Madec's prediction that no one will believe Ben comes true; even his uncle doubts Ben's tale. Ben, not Madec, is held in jail. Madec has hired a lawyer who twists everything that Ben says. It is not until the doctor who treated Ben and Madec corroborates Ben's story that the town officials, shame-facedly, believe him and release him from jail.

Questions for Discussion

1. Why is Ben sorry that he had agreed to guide Madec to the bighorn sheep? Do you feel that Madec is ruthless in his business dealings?
2. Does Madec actually see horns when he shoots? What does he tell Ben about hunting for a specimen? Why does Ben feel that the biggest ram in the mountains would not satisfy Madec?
3. How does Ben feel when he discovers the old man? What does he say they must do? What does Madec do when Ben goes to get the jeep? Does Madec try to talk Ben out of his decision? What is his justification for his point of view? What does he do when he cannot dissuade Ben? What kind of a man would do such a thing?
4. What is Ben's reaction when Madec strips him of all his clothes and supplies? Is he right to be afraid? What do you think are his chances of surviving in the desert?
5. Why does Madec say Ben is a loser? Why does Madec feel that he is important? Who would you rather be like?
6. Why does Ben think Madec has made two mistakes? What has Madec done to outwit Ben? How does this make it harder for him to survive?
7. When Ben thinks about returning and promising Madec that he will not tell about the prospector, he knows it will not work. Why? What does this tell you about Madec?
8. Why does Ben feel he is chained to Madec?
9. When Ben reaches the butte, how does he reach the top? What emotion helps him in the quest? Do you feel that rage can give you strength? Do you think you could have achieved the top if you were Ben? What qualities do you have that would help you?
10. After Ben has satisfied his thirst, he feels like he has awakened from a nightmare and been comforted. Why do you think he feels this way? How has the water helped him physically? Does it give him strength to look to the next step in his survival?
11. What thoughts bring Ben to his decision to try again to defeat Madec? How does he succeed? Would you have the fortitude to bury yourself alive? What would your thoughts be, as you lay covered by the sand?
12. Driving back to town, Madec says that he is a survivor and that he can get Ben into very serious trouble. Do you believe him? Why do you think Ben does not believe him?

13. When his persuasion does not work, what does Madec offer Ben as they drive back to town? Would you be tempted to accept his offer? Why do you think Ben turns him down? What does he say to Madec?
14. What happens when Ben and Madec return to town? How would you feel if you were charged with felony-aggravated assault after suffering as Ben has? How would you feel if nobody believed you even though they were your friends and relatives? What reason does Hondurak, the justice of the peace, give for why he could not believe Ben?
15. When Ben is absolved of any crime, he does not press charges. What would you do in his position? Why do you think Ben did as he did? Is Ben someone you can admire? What are some of his qualities that you would like to emulate?

Projects

1. Create a time line for the evolution of the California area discussed in the book.
2. Investigate the saguaro cactus or the bighorn sheep, and write a report on your findings.
3. Ben sheltered on a butte. Draw a picture of it and the surrounding area, including Madec's camp.
4. Design a poster that illustrates the gear necessary for this type of hunting trip.

Vocabulary

Each of the following quotations chosen from *Deathwatch* includes one or more vocabulary words in **bold print**.

1. ". . . and cracked the blue **vault** of the sky and rolled the mountains back."
2. ". . . he knew most of the old **prospectors** who still roamed these lonely hills. . . ."
3. " 'Good flat **trajectory**. What's the **muzzle velocity**?' "
4. "Madec's voice had a **chiding** teacherlike quality."
5. " 'For example, using your rifle is what you could call a contingency. . . .' "
6. " 'Your **testimony** about what happened would be completely honest, I know that.' "
7. " 'I resent your thinking I'd ask you to **perjure** yourself in a court of law.' "
8. "Beyond the boulders was a narrow **arroyo**. . . ."
9. "He could not afford to let Madec rest, and **contemplate**. . . ."
10. ". . . and probably add new cuts to his already **lacerated** feet."
11. ". . . but as he started toward it he had a strange feeling of **inevitability**."
12. ". . . the **extrusion** of mountains from the almost liquid surface of the earth had quieted. . . ."
13. "It looked **ominous** and black, threatening, forbidding."
14. ". . . toward the end after the **lassitude** and sleepiness, and odd hunger, a man dying of thirst begins to get dizzy."
15. ". . . as though **maneuvering** separately, found the ledge and snapped over it. . . ."

16. ". . . he was now about fifty feet above the **breccia**."
17. "Where the rock had **abraded** him, the blood stood out like watery red dew."
18. ". . . any speck of dust in their eyes causes **excruciating** pain."
19. "He noted every wrinkle in it, every rough patch, every **stratum**."

About the Author

Born in 1909 in the Philippines, Robb White has lived a life as adventure-some as the novels that he has written for young adults. After receiving his degree from the United States Naval Academy, he resigned his commission to write full time. During World War II, he was recalled to the Navy, where he flew as a pilot and served in submarines, carriers, and battleships. Later he roamed the world, taking many jobs to finance his writing career. Finally he settled in Arizona, where he devoted his time to writing books. His books are fast-paced, and his heroes are always good, decent, courageous people.

Dicey's Song
Author: Cynthia Voigt
Publishing date: 1982

Awards

Newbery Medal

Characters

Dicey Tillerman
James Tillerman
Maybeth Tillerman
Sammy Tillerman
Gram
Mina Smiths
Jeff
Mr. Lingerle
Millie Tydings

Setting

Present day—Crisfield, Maryland, on the Chesapeake Bay

Plot

Because her mother is hospitalized with mental illness and is unable to care for her children, Dicey led her two brothers and sister from Provincetown to her maternal grandmother's house on the Chesapeake Bay in Maryland. This new living arrangement has brought vast changes to the lives of the children and their grandmother. Gram, who has lived alone for years, now has four children to care for, has to have a phone, and even feels compelled to apply for welfare, which she abhors. Since none of the reports on her daughter's recovery is encouraging, she makes plans to adopt the children.

Dicey, who at thirteen has been responsible for her younger siblings, now recognizes that she has less responsibility for them. She also feels it necessary to get a job in a local grocery store owned by Millie Tydings, who had known Gram for many years and tells Dicey about her grandmother as a young woman. Maybeth, who has always had a difficult time with schoolwork, reveals a talent for music and begins to take piano lessons from her teacher, Mr. Lingerle. James has trouble fitting in, and Sammy begins to fight again, but no one knows why.

Dicey keeps to herself at school and feels like an outsider. She wants to take mechanical drawing but has to take home ec instead, and considering the class boring and useless, she makes an apron that is the laughingstock of her class. For an English class paper on conflict, Dicey writes about her mother, and the teacher accuses her of plagiarism. Mina defends her in front of the class, and the teacher realizes his mistake and changes the grade.

   Dicey has a hard time opening up to people, feeling that others control you when they know you. From Gram she learns that a person has to keep reaching out even when others do not respond to this. When Gram receives word that her daughter, Dicey's mother, is dying, Gram and Dicey travel to Boston. They tell the dying woman about their life together and realize that they have to let go of her and let her die. Mina persists in trying to befriend Dicey; she really has Dicey's attitude figured out, and they do become friends. Jeff also becomes her friend, and even though Dicey is not ready to go to a school dance with anyone, including Jeff, she knows their friendship will continue.

Questions for Discussion

   1. Does Dicey have any admirable qualities? Have you ever met anyone like her? Do you think she is a realistic character?
   2. Why is Gram considered odd? How does Millie remember her? What admirable qualities does Gram have? Do you think she handles the changes in her life effectively? Why doesn't she like welfare? Why does she find it difficult to accept the box from the shopkeeper? Why does she eventually accept it?
   3. Do you think that Dicey and Gram are alike in any way? Are they not alike in some ways?
   4. How does Dicey change as the book progresses? How does Gram change?
   5. How does Mr. Lingerle become a family friend? Why do the students laugh at him? Do you admire this? What surprises the Tillerman family as they get to know Mr. Lingerle better? Have you ever shared this experience as you got to know someone better?
   6. Gram says that even though Millie Tydings cannot read, she is not stupid. Why does Gram say this?
   7. Does Dicey learn anything about friends from both Mr. Lingerle and Millie?
   8. Gram tells Dicey to both hold on and to reach out. How does Dicey make sense of both of these things? How does Gram follow her own advice?
   9. What are some of Mina's admirable qualities? Would you like her for a friend? Mina tries very hard to be Dicey's friend. Why does she persist? How does she eventually succeed? If Dicey were new in your class, would you befriend her? How?
  10. What qualities are important to Mina and Dicey in choosing friends? Do you agree with their criteria?
  11. How important is family to Dicey?
  12. By some standards the Christmas gifts Dicey bought for her family are modest. Will everyone appreciate the gifts? Why or why not? If elaborate gifts are not important to the Tillermans, what is important?

Projects

1. In her English class, Dicey has to write a character sketch about a person she knows who has a conflict in his or her life. Dicey chooses to write about her mother while Mina writes about herself. Do this assignment as if you were in Dicey's class, and write a character sketch about someone you know who has experienced conflict.
2. Put together a memory album for the Tillerman family for their first year together. Include clipped pictures or drawings and enough written captions and descriptions to make an album a thorough record of their year.
3. In her home economics class Dicey is assigned the project of using $50 to plan meals for a family of four. Using an advertisement from your local grocery store, plan meals for a family of four with that amount of money.
4. Gram tells the children that their ancestors were bootleggers. Write a brief report of what bootleggers were and how they became important in American history.
5. Dicey buys some of the family's Christmas presents in the shop that sells carved animals, chess sets, and boxes of wood. There she buys a carving of a chicken for Sammy. Carve a small animal either from a piece of wood or a bar of soap.

Vocabulary

Each of the following quotations chosen from *Dicey's Song* includes one or more vocabulary words in **bold print**.

1. "There were still things to worry about here, but nothing **crucial**."
2. "Dicey stared at the woman, at the heavy **mottled** flesh of her face."
3. "Dicey hurried through them, but Maybeth **lingered**, humming."
4. "But even here, in Gram's house, with its big, boxy rooms, Dicey **preferred** outside."
5. "The voices **petered** out around her as she continued with her own thoughts."
6. "Dicey couldn't mistake that high carriage of the chin, or the **unkempt** curly gray hair."
7. "Dicey, leaning her weight into her work, trying to find just the right amount of pressure so that she would scrape off the paint without **gouging** the wood beneath, forgot he was there."
8. "When she felt someone standing beside her, she thought probably it was the teacher and didn't look up, as if she was too **engrossed** to notice."
9. "Did she think that just because Dicey was **scrawny** and small, and she was so large and strong-looking, that Dicey would be scared of her?"
10. "He was as **massive** as a mountain, Dicey thought."
11. "Others were **meandering** about, stopping at store windows, as if they had a whole day to kill."
12. "Dicey knew she shouldn't have been surprised at his quick **perception** of what Gram was saying; but she was."
13. "He hesitated, rocking up and back to get out of the chair, then sitting back, then **lurching** forward again."

14. "Sammy worked like Dicey did, without hurrying, without **dawdling**."
15. "Her eyes were red and swollen, her cheeks were wet, her mouth **quivered**."
16. "She could ask him right away, she supposed, but the class had been **pestering** him so much about how long it took to get the essays back that Dicey was starting to feel sorry for him."
17. "In the first place, her tongue felt like it was frozen solid, and her head was a block of ice, and all the blood in her body had chilled and **congealed**."
18. ". . . her stomach stretch **taut**. . . ."
19. ". . . he became **flustered** and embarrassed. . . ."
20. "Gram's face **swiveled** around to look at Dicey."

About the Author

Cynthia Voigt was born in Boston, graduated from Smith College, and studied education at St. Michael's College in Santa Fe. Her favorite job has been teaching, and she has taught students from elementary through high school. She discovered children's literature when she was teaching and assigned her fifth graders to write book reports. She now lives in Annapolis, Maryland, where she writes and teaches. *Dicey's Song* is a sequel to *Homecoming*, which was her first book.

Ella Enchanted
Author: Gail Clark Levine
Publication date: 1997

Awards

Newbery Honor Book
ALA Best Books for Young Adults
ALA Quick Picks for Young Adults

Characters

Eleanor "Ella" of Frell
Prince Charmont "Char"
Mandy, Ella's fairy godmother
Sir Peter of Frell, Ella's father
Dame Olga
Hattie and Olive
Lucinda

Setting

Fantasy time—Kyrria

Plot

The fairy tale, Cinderella, has enchanted children for centuries but *Ella Enchanted* adds the spice of humor and the thrill of adventure. Gone are the flat one-dimensional characters; they are replaced by people with virtues and vices, who love and hate, who laugh and feel pain, and who succeed and fail in the mythic kingdom of Kyrria.

Ella, the daughter of a selfish and avaricious father and a beautiful and fun-loving mother, is cursed at birth with the gift of obedience from the fairy, Lucinda. Each time Ella is given an order, she must obey, even if the order is harmful to her or others. Protected by her mother and cautious not to let people know her weakness, Ella's early years pass almost uneventfully. When she is fifteen, her mother dies. She encounters Prince Charmont at her mother's funeral, and the two find that they can make each other laugh and that they enjoy similar things. Soon after, she learns that Mandy, the cook, is her fairy godmother, but a fairy who will not perform big magic like lifting the gift.

Ella's idyllic life is soon over for her father, plagued by her clumsiness, sends her off to the same finishing school as Dame Olga's daughters, Hattie and Olive. Hattie soon surmises Ella's secret and makes her life miserable with her mean commands. In her time at finishing school, Ella makes friends, learns to sew with tiny stitches, loses her clumsiness, and improves her skill with languages. One of her saving graces at school is her magic fairy tale book given her by Mandy. Through it she sees that her father is going to the wedding of a giantess and that fairies usually attend such ceremonies. Ella hopes to make Lucinda take back her gift. On her way to the wedding, Ella befriends some elves and is captured by the dreaded ogres who feast on humans. With her language ability, Ella lulls them to sleep using their own slithery words until Prince Charmont rescues her. At the wedding, Lucinda does not take back her gift, but orders Ella to be happy obeying everybody's orders.

At home she learns that her father has lost all his money and has wed the wealthy Dame Olga for hers. Ella now has the wicked stepmother and the mean and stupid stepsisters of the original story. Her friendship with Char grows into love but she realizes that she cannot marry him. Her gift of obedience could well destroy him and his kingdom. Reduced to a drudge, she schemes to attend the balls in honor of the prince just to see and be near him. When discovered by Char, she refuses to obey his order to marry him, thus breaking Lucinda's spell. As all good fairy tales end, they live happily ever after.

Questions for Discussion

1. When Ella was eight, she told a friend, Pamela, about her gift. What was the result? Do you think you would feel frustrated as Ella was by Pamela's orders? Why did Ella's mother secure a position for Pamela's mother far from Frell?

2. Ella's father shows her a pottery made by a student of the elf, Agulen, and says that perhaps he can pass it off as a genuine Agulen. Would you like to deal with a merchant such as Sir Peter?

3. Why does Ella's father decide to send her to finishing school? Is he looking out for her best interests or his? Why is Ella frightened of him? Do you see any good qualities in him? What does this tell you about people?

4. What is it about the ogres besides their size and cruelty that makes them so dangerous? When Ella first meets the ogre in the king's garden, how does Char save her from being eaten?

5. Ella, Hattie, and Olive travel to school in the same coach. What traits of Hattie and Olive make them unpleasant? Do you know any people like them? What does Hattie discover about Ella? What are some of the unkind orders she gives Ella? How would you have felt if you were Ella?

6. Why does Hattie order Ella to end her friendship with Areida? Have you ever been jealous when you see others having a good time? What could you do that might help change the situation?

7. When Ella cannot disobey the ogre, NiSSh's, order not to run away, how does she escape being eaten? Does this example show you that you may solve a problem with different solutions? When Char captures the ogres, he does not respond to their entreaties. Why? Is this another solution to the problem? Think of a problem that you face and various solutions for it.

8. Sir Peter loses all his money in a fraudulent scheme. What is his first solution to the problem? How do you feel about a father who would sell his daughter? When this does not work, what is his second solution? Do you admire a man who would marry for his wife's money?

9. What does Mum Olga do as soon as Ella's father leaves? Why do you think Olga and her daughters are so unkind?
10. When Ella asks her father for help he does not hurry to respond, but when he does, what does he say? Is there anything likable in Sir Peter?
11. Ella and Char have written to each other through the years, and their friendship has turned into love. When he proposes to her, what is her first reaction? Why does she change her mind, and what is her response to Char? Could you have been this brave?
12. How does Char react to her response? Is his a normal reaction to rejection? Has a friend ever rejected you? How did you feel?
13. How does Ella finally break Lucinda's curse? Why was she able to do it now but never before?
14. Are you glad that you have never been given the gift of obedience? Can you see that a good thing can be misused?

Projects
1. Select a favorite fairy tale, and rewrite it with ideas of your own.
2. Select a favorite fairy tale, and illustrate it with drawings or paintings.
3. Research the life of Charles Perrault, who is credited with writing *Cinderella*. Report on your findings in a multimedia presentation.
4. Create an advertising poster for the king's menagerie; be sure to include all the creatures found there.
5. Research the dances performed at Sir Peter and Dame Olga's wedding. Write a report on their origin and when and where they were performed.
6. Research the dances, and perform one of them before an audience.
7. Illustrate the story of the Pheonix.

Vocabulary
Each of the following quotations chosen from *Ella Enchanted* includes one or more vocabulary words in **bold print**.
1. "We played princess and **ogres**."
2. "I followed it to the **spiral** staircase and walked down, remembering the times, Mother and I had slid down the banister."
3. "Part of the speech had been about dying, but more about giving **allegiance** to Kyrria and its rulers, King Jerrold, Prince Charmont, and the entire royal family."
4. "The tears I had swallowed all day **erupted**."
5. " 'The older one is an unpleasant **conniver** like her mother and the younger one is a **simpleton**.' "
6. "A red stain spread across the tablecloth, and Father's **doublet** was dotted with wine."
7. "I started for the royal **menagerie** just outside the walls of the king's palace."
8. "Hattie fastened it around her neck and patted it **complacently**."
9. "Then you may do without breakfast as well, for your **impertinence**."
10. "In two swallows I ate the soft white roll, more air than **sustenance**."

11. "Her face was changing, resuming its usual expression of gleeful **malice**."
12. "Hattie issued commands and I **retaliated**."
13. "**Frantically, I riffled** the pages of my book, hoping to be **vouchsafed** a map."
14. "On the **verso** was a letter from Hattie to her mother. On the **recto**, one to the same lady from Olive."
15. "I've never seen Ella so **solicitous**."
16. "She was **besotted** with him."
17. "I **extol** your virtues endlessly."
18. "I urge you to be, as always, my **stalwart** daughter."
19. "They wouldn't be **minxes** if they weren't masters of **artifice** and fraud."
20. My mouth filled with liquid, bile and blood from biting my tongue, salty and **corrosive** and sweet."

About the Author

Born in New York City, Ms. Levine received her bachelor of arts and worked for the Department of Labor for many years. She had an early interest in both acting and painting. Her interest in the theater led to her first writing experience. In collaboration with her husband, she wrote *Spacenapped*, a musical for children. Now living in Brewster, New York, she devotes time to volunteer work and her writing.

From the Author

"Growing up I wanted to be a painter or an actor. I gave up the acting early on, but I stuck with the painting. However, I was terribly, horribly self-critical about my art. If I didn't create a Van Gogh or a Rembrandt, my work wasn't good enough. A mental tape full of criticisms was always playing when I painted, and this robbed the activity of its pleasure. I kept at it, though, until around 1988, when I took a class in writing and illustrating for children. I discovered there how much I liked writing and how much I loathed illustrating. And I discovered that the negative voice in my head when I painted was silent when I wrote. I'm not sure why. It wasn't because my writing was better than my painting—I didn't know beans about writing fiction when I began. I'm just freer in the medium of words, I guess. I've learned since that lots of people have a negative tape running when they try to do something creative, and I know that the negative tape is the enemy of creativity. It doesn't speak the truth, it only gets in the way, and we need to silence it as much as we can so that we can enjoy our gifts."

The Face on the Milk Carton
Author: Caroline B. Cooney
Publishing date: 1990

Characters
Janie Johnson
Mr. and Mrs. Johnson
Reeve Shields
Sarah-Charlotte Sherwood

Setting
Present day—Connecticut

Plot
Janie Johnson is a happy fifteen-year-old who considers her big problems to be her lactose intolerance and her boring name. Then one day in the school cafeteria, she notices the little girl on her friend's milk carton. Janie remembers the polka-dot dress the little girl is wearing. She realizes that she is the little girl, Jennie Spring, who was abducted from a mall when she was three years old.

From this point on, she interprets many things as clues to support the idea of kidnapping. For example, with wild, red hair, she looks nothing like her parents. There are no baby pictures of her in their house, and her parents are reluctant to produce her birth certificate. Furthermore, she experiences flashes of memory from another life, like shopping and walking away alone when she couldn't have what she wanted, sitting in an ice cream store next to a woman with long hair before she went for a ride, a woman wearing a white apron with hard candies in the pocket, and a messy kitchen with two babies in high chairs. In the attic, she finds a trunk with school papers and quizzes belonging to a girl named Hannah and the dress Jennie Spring was wearing in the picture on the milk carton.

Janie confronts her parents, and they admit that they are her grandparents and not her parents. They tell her about their daughter Hannah who decided when she was sixteen years old that she wanted to join a cult. They rarely heard from her but received a letter telling them she had been married. One day she appeared on their doorstep with her little girl; she had escaped to bring her daughter to a better life. They moved around and changed their name from Javensen to Johnson, all to avoid being tracked down by the cult to which Hannah eventually returned.

Janie doesn't know if her parents are telling her the truth or if they really kidnapped her themselves. She finds the *New York Times* story of her kidnapping on microfilm but cannot make herself read the names of the members of the Spring family. She wants to keep her life as it is with her parents, but wonders how she can neglect to tell the Springs that their daughter is alive. She feels guilty that she went away with a stranger for an ice cream sundae and attention.

Janie gets her boyfriend and next-door-neighbor Reeve to drive her to New Jersey. They find the Springs' house and watch red-haired twins and a red-haired boy go into the house after school. A woman welcomes them at the door, a woman who has red hair, too. Janie writes a letter to the Springs, apologizing to them for not remembering them and telling them she is all right and wants to stay with her parents. The letter accidentally gets mailed. Reeve's sister, Lizzie, a law student, believes it is Hannah who kidnapped Jenny. When Janie's parents hear this and learn about the letter the Springs will be receiving, her mother phones the Springs. She hands the phone to Janie, who introduces herself to her mother on the other end.

Questions for Discussion

1. How does Janie react to the memory of her dress on the milk carton? At what point is she sure that the people who she has thought of as her parents are not so?
2. What emotions does Janie feel as she struggles with the emerging truth? Do you think the emotions she feels are realistic?
3. In what ways is Janie concerned for both sets of parents? What does this concern show you about Janie's character and compassion?
4. Why does Janie feel guilty about the kidnapping? Do you think she is right to feel this way? Why does she hate the little girl who was kidnapped?
5. At what point does Janie confront her parents about her suspicions? Do you think she handles this in the right way? How might you handle this situation differently?
6. Do you think the Johnsons did the right thing in not telling Janie that they were not her parents? Should they have told her earlier?
7. Why does Janie hang up on the phone calls to the Springs and avoid meeting them when she goes to their house?
8. How does Reeve see himself within his family? Do you think he is treated fairly by them? Do you think Reeve is a good friend to Janie?
9. How does Janie react to what her grandparents tell her about Hannah? How does she deal with the knowledge that they have not told her the truth? What impact can lying or not telling the whole truth have on a relationship?
10. Why does Janie's grandmother make the phone call at the end of the novel? Do you admire what she is doing?

Projects

1. Reeve tells Janie that, like the myth, she is opening up a Pandora's box. Read the myth, and write a letter to Janie explaining how this myth relates to what she is doing.
2. The Internet has become an important way for missing children to be tracked down, and several Web sites exist for this purpose. At the Web site for the National Center for Missing and Exploited Children (www.missing kids.org), select Education and Resources/Child Safety Tips for School.

Summarize these tips on a poster that would have appeal for young children.

3. Another Web site that exists to find missing children is the Missing Children Help Center (www.800usakids.org); select Posters of Missing Children\View Pictures of Recently Missing Children. Label a map of the United States at the places from which these children disappeared.

4. Locate information on the local, state, and federal agencies involved in finding missing children. Compile your information into a report.

Vocabulary

Each of the following quotations chosen from *The Face on the Milk Carton* includes one or more vocabulary words in **bold print**.

1. ". . . in the **infuriating**, affectionate way of fathers."
2. ". . . a wild, **chaotic** mane of red curls glinting gold."
3. ". . . **filching** each other's potato chips. . . ."
4. "I want to live in a city, he'd said last night, and be **anonymous**."
5. "She **slithered** backward into her mind."
6. "Now he was making terrible faces, **flexing** his forehead and lips. . . ."
7. "Her mind **plummeted** down into the nightmare."
8. "Janie **panted** like a child having an asthma attack."
9. ". . . full of victory or **deflated** by loss."
10. ". . . he leaped around like a **demented** boy cheerleader. . . ."
11. ". . . she could **extricate** herself from this dumb idea."
12. ". . . **wended** her way from hall to class."
13. "But it was too **preposterous** to say."
14. "Her body was **drenched** in sweat. . . ."
15. "For a moment they were as **isolated** as if they were trapped in a tin can."
16. ". . . put it over her own mouth to **stifle** hysterical laughter."
17. "Her mother's face, **taut** with worry and rage . . ."
18. "Nobody had expected it to **flourish** in the dry library. . . ."
19. "She was already protecting herself from the **penetrating** eyes of friends and parents."
20. "Janie was so **lethargic** she could not imagine moving again."

About the Author

Caroline B. Cooney's education has come from reading. She attended college and nursing school but received no degree. Because she enjoys being with teenagers, she volunteers in school and church. She writes for several hours each day and looks forward to letters from her readers. She has received the Romantic Book award for her body of work in the teen romance category.

The Giver
Author: Lois Lowry
Publication date: 1993

Awards

Newbery Medal
ALA Best Book for Young Adults
ALA Notable Book for Children
Regina Medal
Booklist Editors' Choice
School Library Journal Best Book of the Year
Boston Globe/Horn Book Honor Book

Characters

Jonas
The Giver
Jonas' parents
Jonas' sister, Lily
Gabriel

Setting

The future—The Community

Plot

Jonas lives in a perfect world. Each December until their Twelfth, the children are acknowledged as entering a new stage of development. For example, the newchildren born during the year and who have been cared for by the Nurturers become Ones, are named, and are given to sets of parents. Nines receive bicycles, and female Nines take their hair ribbons from their hair. At the Ceremony of the Twelve, the last of the ceremonies, each is given an assignment by the Committee of Elders in keeping with his or her talents and abilities. After this ceremony, the children will no longer spend time with others of their age, even their friends; instead they will be with those having the same assignment.

After all other Twelves have received their assignment, Jonas is given his. He is to be the Receiver of Memory. In the opinion of the Elders, Jonas has exhibited the qualities necessary for this exalted position—intelligence, integrity, courage, wisdom, and the capacity to see beyond. This is a great and rare honor because there is only one Receiver. Jonas will be trained by the man whom he is succeeding, The Giver, who tells Jonas that basically his job will be to transmit the memories he has of all time and of all the world to Jonas. By reexperiencing these memories, The Giver has achieved wisdom. As the new Receiver, Jonas will follow rules that the others do not; for example, he can lie, and he cannot participate in the dream-telling ritual that everyone participates in each morning.

The first memory that The Giver transmits to Jonas is of snow and going downhill on a sled. Jonas had no knowledge of snow because of Climate Control in the Community. With Sameness, unpredictable weather was eliminated. Subsequently, he gives Jonas other memories such as color, pain, war, birthday parties, museums, and Christmas. When Jonas becomes angry that all people do not have choices, The Giver tells him that color, sunshine, and differences were all given up when the people chose Sameness.

The Giver admits that the worst part of holding the memories is the loneliness, because memories are meant to be shared. He gives Jonas his favorite memory, of a family at Christmas, and Jonas experiences love for the first time. However, his parents tell him that love is an obsolete term. In fact, Jonas, his parents, and his sister must all pledge that they will not become attached to Gabriel, a baby that his father brings home from the Nurturing Center in an effort to help him develop so he can be named and placed. Jonas does become attached to Gabriel and even gives the baby memories to calm him when he is fretful.

The sharing that Jonas and The Giver have experienced makes The Giver realize that things have to change so that everyone experiences feelings again. He devises a plan for Jonas to escape, but he will stay to help the people deal with the memories Jonas has been holding for them. The Giver transmits memories of courage and strength to Jonas. However, when Jonas's father announces that Gabriel is going to be released the next day, the plan that The Giver has devised is not implemented. Jonas knows that releasing Gabriel means that the baby will be killed, so he flees with the baby. Jonas uses his memories and transmits some to Gabriel so that they can reach Elsewhere.

Questions for Discussion

1. At the December ceremony, all children in the same age group experience the same changes and new routines. What does this system ignore? Are there any ways in which you think this system is effective?
2. Rules are very important to the Community. Which rules do you think are good ones? Which are not good? Are any rules ever broken? Why are rules important to any community?
3. How are the Twelves given their assignments? Do you think this is an effective system? Would you like to be given an assignment like the Twelves are?
4. What qualities does Jonas exhibit that qualify him to be the Receiver? How are these qualities appropriate for any leader to possess? How can a person go about achieving these qualities?
5. What surprises Jonas in the rules for his training? Why is he especially surprised about the rule about lying?
6. How are the Old treated in the Community? Is there anything admirable or not admirable in the way they are treated?

7. Jonas says at one point that people have to be helped not to make wrong choices. Do you agree? How do people learn to make good choices?
8. The Giver says that nothing has meaning without memories. Do you agree? What memories do you have that make your life more meaningful?
9. The Giver tells Jonas that the memories he holds bring him wisdom. Do you agree? Do you have any memories that have made you more wise?
10. What emotions does Jonas see exhibited within his family unit? Are these strong emotions? If his parents think that love is obsolete, what feelings do they show toward each other and their children? How can you explain Jonas's father bringing Gabriel home for special nurturing and then voting to release him?

Projects

1. When The Giver transmits the memory of color to him, Jonas wonders why everyone cannot experience color, and Jonas sees color when he reaches Elsewhere. Make a book of colors for Jonas including examples of the use of the individual colors in everyday life and nature. Use drawings, clippings, and lots of color to create your book.
2. As The Giver tells Jonas that memories bring wisdom, current national and international events should bring us wisdom for our future. Look in your local newspaper for the last week, and select one national and one international story that you think should bring us wisdom. Write a paragraph about each of these events.
3. Children in the community volunteer before they are assigned. What kind of volunteer activities are you interested in? What opportunities exist in your community to pursue these volunteer interests? Contact these agencies for specific requirements of volunteers. Compile this information on a poster.
4. Jonas would find it difficult if not impossible to describe the sensations he feels as he receives memories, like riding on a sled. Write a letter to Jonas describing a physical activity that you enjoy. Be sure to tell him how each of your senses is affected by this activity.

Vocabulary

Each of the following quotations chosen from *The Giver* includes one or more vocabulary words in **bold print**.

1. ". . . the children rode their bicycles to the riverbank and watched, **intrigued**, the unloading and then the takeoff directly to the west. . . ."
2. "For the contributing citizen to be released from the community was a final decision, a terrible punishment, an **overwhelming** statement of failure."
3. "Even the children were scolded if they used the term lightly at play, **jeering** at a teammate who missed a catch or stumbled in a race."
4. ". . . as if one were looking into the clear water of the river, down to the bottom, where things might **lurk** which hadn't been discovered yet."
5. "There was no doubt that Benjamin would receive his Assignment to that field and would probably be permitted to **bypass** most of the training."

6. "At every other public ceremony, the audience was silent and **attentive**. But once a year, they all smiled **indulgently** at the **commotion** from the little ones waiting to receive their names and families."
7. "Birthmother was an important job, if lacking in **prestige**."
8. "He saw the others in his group glance at him, embarrassed, and then **avert** their eyes quickly."
9. ". . . he pushed with his body, moving it forward, not wanting the exhilarating ride to end."
10. "It wasn't a practical thing, so it became **obsolete** when we went to Sameness."
11. "Jonas glanced around at the **astonishing array** of volumes."
12. ". . . looking forward to the breathtaking slide down through the **invigorating** air."
13. ". . . Jonas **mimicked** in a cruel, **sarcastic** voice."
14. ". . . he was constantly **vigilant**, looking for the next nearest hiding place should the sound of engines come."

About the Author

Born in Hawaii, Lois Lowry lived all over the world because her father was in the Army. She attended Brown University and graduated from the University of Southern Maine after she married. Lois Lowry begain writing when she was in her forties, and she has written more than twenty novels. Among them are two novels that have won the Newbery Medal, *Number the Stars* and *The Giver*.

Harry Potter and the Sorcerer's Stone
Author: J. K. Rowling
Publication date: 1998

Award

British Book Award
Children's Book of the Year, Child Study Association
Smarties Prize
ALA Notable Books for Children

Characters

Harry Potter
The Dursleys, Vernon, Petunia, Dudley
Professor Albus Dumbledore
Professor McGongall
Hagrid
Classmates—Ron Weasley, Hermione Granger, Neville Longbottom, and
   Draco Malfoy
Professors Quirrell, Snape, and Flitwich
Voldemort or "You Know Who"

Setting

Present day—Little Whinging, Surrey

Plot

A rollicking romp is Harry Potter's introduction to wizardry. Orphaned at age one by his parent's death, Harry spends the next ten years living with his aunt, uncle, and cousin, the Dursleys. Sleeping in the cupboard under the stairs, Harry is mistreated by his aunt and uncle and persecuted by his cousin, Dudley. Just before his eleventh birthday, a letter arrives for Harry, but his uncle takes it before he can read it. In the succeeding days, more and more letters arrive until Uncle Vernon spirits the family away to a deserted shack on a lonely island.

It is there that the giant, Hagrid, comes with Harry's first birthday cake and his acceptance to Hogwarts School of Witchcraft and Wizardry. Much to the Dursleys' chagrin since they have spent ten years hiding the secret of Harry's heritage, he goes with Hagrid to shop for his school supplies: his owl, his wand, and his robes, but no personal broomstick. The Dursleys, on the other hand, head to the hospital with Dudley for the removal of the pig's tail wished upon him by Hagrid.

Before shopping, Harry and Hagrid stop at Gringotts', where they remove Harry's inheritance and a strange package from the vaults. On his way to the school, Harry meets some other first-year students: Draco Malfoy, who has the bullying personality of Dudley; Ron Weasley, the youngest son in a family of wizards; Hermione Granger, a prissy know-it-all; and Neville Longbottom, the smallest and most timid of the group. At Hogwarts there are four separate houses: Gryffindor, Hufflepuff, Ravenclaw, and Slytherein. Harry and his three friends are chosen for Gryffindor by the magic thinking cap, but Draco is sent to Slytherein. The school is headed by Professor Dumbledore, assisted by Professor McGonagall, teacher of Transfiguration; Professor Flitwich, Charms; Professor Quirrell, Defense against the Dark Arts; and Professor Snape, Potions.

Each year the houses at Hogwarts compete for the championship cup, which Slytherein has won for the past six years. An important part of the competitions is Quidditch, a game played on broomsticks. Harry becomes the greatest player and wins the championship but loses many points when he and his friends attempt to protect the Sorcerer's Stone from Voldemort or "You-Know-Who." In his final confrontation with Voldemort, Harry, assisted by his friends, Ron and Hermione, gets past the charms set to protect the stone, discovers that Professor Quirrell and Voldemort are one, and delays his getting the stone until the arrival of Professor Dumbledore. In the year-end awards ceremony, the ten points awarded to timid Neville for bravery break the tie between Gryffindor and Slytherein.

Questions for Discussion

1. On his birthday Dudley receives many presents but is not satisfied. Why? Are his parents responsible for his actions? Why? What could they have done differently?

2. Petunia and Vernon Dursley have never told Harry the truth about his parents' death. Why? How does Harry feel when he learns the truth about them and himself?

3. When Harry meets Draco Malfoy, he is reminded of Dudley. Why? Do you like either of the boys? Have you ever met people like them, and did you like them?

4. In Snape's Potions class, Harry receives two demerits. Does he deserve them? Do you think Snape holds a grudge against Harry?

5. What do you think it means when Hagrid does not meet Harry's eyes when he asks him about Snape's hatred?

6. Why is Harry concerned about Malfoy being in the broomstick flying class? Have you ever experienced similar feelings? How is Ron supportive?

7. What happens when Draco snatches Neville's Remembrall at their first broomstick lesson? Why is Professor McGonagall so excited about Harry's flying?

8. How do Ron and Harry help Hermione when she is trapped in the girl's bathroom with the troll? How does Hermione repay their kind bravery? Why does this incident make them friends?

9. Why does Harry suspect that Snape is Voldemort's confederate? Why are Ron and Harry worried about Professor Quirrell?

10. Why are Harry, Hermione, and Malfoy sent into the forest? What creatures do they meet in the forest? What else do they find there? Why is the cloaked

figure drinking the unicorn blood? Why is Harry frightened when Firenze talks about who might be desperate enough to kill a unicorn?

11. How does the stranger get Hagrid to tell him the secret to calming Fluffy? Why does Harry decide to use this information? Why do Ron and Hermione go with him? Who tries to stop them? Why?

12. What does Hermione say are more important than books and cleverness? Do you agree? How do Ron and Hermione demonstrate their friendship and bravery?

13. Does Voldemort's hiding place surprise you? How does the author keep you from knowing this secret? What is it about Harry that causes the defeat of Voldemort?

14. Why does Professor Dumbledore destroy the stone? Though Voldemort is defeated, he is not destroyed. What does this tell you about good versus evil?

15. Harry is going home to the Dursleys for summer vacation. Do you think he will have a good time? Do you think Dudley will be as cruel as he was previously? What is the reason for your answer?

Projects

1. Write the script for a sports announcer describing a game of Quidditch. Be sure to explain the various positions and their purpose in the description.

2. Trace the origin and evolution of the Halloween customs practiced today. Write a report on your findings.

3. Create a diorama or poster depicting Haigon Alley where Harry shops for his school supplies.

4. Many European legends relate tales of heroes slaying dragons. Find two of these heroes, and compare or contrast their exploits.

5. Illustrate a European legend of a hero slaying a dragon.

Vocabulary

Each of the following quotations chosen from *Harry Potter and the Sorcerer's Stone* includes one or more vocabulary words in **bold print**.

1. " 'All this "You Know Who" nonsense—for eleven years I have been trying to **persuade** people to call him by his proper name: Voldemort.' "

2. "'I know you haven't,' said Professor McGonagall, sounding half **exasperated**, half admiring."

3. "His Aunt Petunia was awake it was her **shrill** voice that made the first noise of the day."

4. "They ate in the zoo restaurant, and when Dudley had a **tantrum** because his knickerbocker glory did not have enough ice cream on top. . ."

5. "The snake nodded **vigorously**."

6. "The envelope was thick and heavy made of yellowish **parchment**, and the address was written in emerald-green ink."

7. ". . . and he took both Harry and Dudley by the **scruffs** of their necks. . . ."

8. "A braver man than Vernon Dudley would have **quailed** under the furious look Hagrid now gave him; when Hagrid spoke, his every **syllable** trembled with rage."

9. ". . . his fists were **clenched**."

10. " 'Spells—**enchantments**,' said Hagrid."

11. ". . . an archway onto a **cobbled** street that twisted and turned out of sight."

12. "Harry himself examined silver **unicorn** horns at twenty-one Galleons each. . . ."

13. ". . . and the three boys **clambered** onto the train."

14. ". . . and his work on **alchemy** with his partner, Nicholas Flamel."

15. "Perched atop a high mountain on the other side, its windows sparkling in a starry sky, was a vast castle with many **turrets** and towers."

16. " '**Transfiguration** is some of the most complex and dangerous magic you will learn at Hogwarts,' she said."

17. " 'You are here to learn the **subtle** science and exact art of potion making,' he began."

18. ". . . wide sweeping ones; narrow **rickety** ones . . . ."

19. "Harry mouthed to the others and, **petrified**, they began to creep down a long gallery. . . ."

20. "Snape was still ignoring Hermione's **quivering** hand."

About the Author

J. K. Rowling has written a first book that has taken the publishing world by storm. Published in England where it won several awards, the book spent many months on the *New York Times* best-seller list, a feat seldom achieved by a children's book. She was able to finish the book started in a café because of a monetary award by the Scottish Arts Council. Ms. Rowling lives in Scotland with her daughter. The sequels to her first book have also been enthusiastically received and have also been placed on the *New York Times* best-seller list.

Holes
Author: Louis Sachar
Publication date: 1998

Awards
Newbery Medal
National Book Award for Young People's Literature
New York Times Outstanding Book of the Year
School Library Journal Best Book of the Year

Characters
Stanley Yelnats
Mr. Sir
Mr. Pendanski
The Warden, Ms. Walker
Zero (Hector Zeroni)
Other boys in the camp including Magnet, Armpit, and Zigzag and X-Ray

Setting
Present day—Texas

Plot
The judge does not believe Stanley's story that the sneakers, valued at over five thousand dollars, fell out of the sky and landed on his head. Although Stanley is telling the truth, he is sent to Camp Green Lake for eighteen months to improve his character. To build his character, each boy at the camp is required to dig a hole each day, seven days a week. The hole has to be five feet deep and five feet in diameter, measured by the length of his shovel. The boys can get excused from their digging only when they find something interesting in the dirt. However, when Stanley digs up an engraved gold tube, he feels compelled to give it to X-Ray, the leader of the boys.

At the sight of this golden object, the camp directors, including the Warden, direct the boys to sift through the dirt even more carefully; obviously, the character of the boys is not the impetus for the digging; rather the directors are searching for something in the desert sand.

Among the boys, Stanley becomes closest to Zero, called this because everyone says his head is empty. While it is true that Zero cannot read, Stanley learns that he has a tremendous aptitude for mathematics and a desire to learn to read. Zero suggests that he will dig part of Stanley's hole each day in trade for Stanley teaching him to read. When the Warden finds out about this arrangement, she forbids it. Zero says he will not dig another hole, strikes Mr. Pendanski with his shovel, and leaves Camp Green Lake. After a few days, Stanley escapes from

the camp to find his friend. Stanley battles heat, fatigue, and thirst. He sees a
pool of water, which ends up being a mirage. However, he is encouraged by the
sight of a mountain shaped "like a fist, with its thumb sticking up." This is Big
Thumb, or the God's thumb that had given refuge to Stanley's great-grandfather.
Stanley finds Zero hiding under a boat, and they travel toward the mountain.
When they finally reach it, Zero confesses to Stanley that he took the shoes that
Stanley was convicted of stealing. The boys survive on dirty water and the on-
ions that are growing on the mountain and eventually return to the camp, where
they dig up the treasure for which the Warden and her cohorts had been searching. The treasure chest legally belongs to Stanley because it had been buried by
the bandit Kissin' Kate Barlow, who had robbed many people including Stanley's great-grandfather. Stanley shares the proceeds of stocks and trusts with
Zero. Both boys are released, and Camp Green Lake is shut down.

Questions for Discussion

1. What kind of family life does Stanley have? What kind of letters does he
   write to his parents from camp? What does this tell you about him? What
   do you learn about the relationship between Stanley and his parents?
2. What is Stanley's crime? What do you learn about him from the way he
   handles the accusation?
3. Why does the judge send Stanley to Camp Green Lake? How does the camp
   claim it will build character? Do you agree with this technique? Is the camp
   what it seems?
4. How does Stanley feel when he digs his first hole? Do you understand his
   feelings?
5. Describe the other boys at the camp. Why do you think they all use nick-
   names?
6. Why does Stanley take the blame for the sunflower seeds? Would you have
   done the same? How do the other boys treat him? Why does Zero dig the
   hole?
7. Why do you think the relationship develops between Stanley and Zero?
8. Do you think Stanley should have let Zero dig for him? Why do the other
   boys become annoyed that Zero is digging Stanley's holes? Do you agree
   with them? How does this develop into a fight?
9. Do you think Stanley is right when he says reading is better than digging for
   building character?
10. Why does Stanley go after Zero? What does this tell you about him?
11. When Stanley is in the desert with Zero, Stanley reaches a point that he can
    say he is happy and likes himself. Why does he feel this way? What has
    changed for him and why?
12. What coincidences are important in this story? What evidence does the
    book show of careful attention to detail on the part of the author?

Projects

1. Draw a map of Camp Green Lake and its surrounding areas, including
   God's Thumb.

2. Select a scene from the book that you think is especially dramatic or interesting. Write the scene as a play.

3. Stanley's father is an inventor. He tries for a long time to find a way to recycle old sneakers; by the end of the book, he is still working on this invention. Help Stanley's father find out what sneakers are made of; write a report that discusses other ways these products could be used. Be creative.

4. Stanley and Zero are forced to survive in the desert. What problems do they have? How do they survive? Find out if there are any other things they could have done to make their time in the desert easier. Present your information in the form of a poster or a multimedia presentation.

Vocabulary

Each of the following quotations chosen from *Holes* includes one or more vocabulary words in **bold print**.

1. "The town **shriveled** and dried up along with the lake. . . ."
2. "The bus wasn't air-conditioned, and the hot, heavy air was almost as **stifling** as the handcuffs."
3. "Stanley's father was smart and had a lot of **perseverance**. Once he started a project he would work on it for years. . . ."
4. "The land was barren and **desolate**."
5. "The judge called Stanley's crime **despicable**."
6. ". . . he felt a **throbbing** pain just above his neck. . . ."
7. ". . . his hands were tough and **callused**."
8. "Stanley was **drenched** in sweat."
9. ". . . they'd still have time to come back here, **eventually**."
10. "What if Zero was still alive, **desperately** crawling across the dirt searching for water?"
11. "Twitch **fidgeted**. His fingers drummed against the wooden shaft of his shovel, and his neck moved from side to side."
12. "The truck **lurched** forward."
13. "He was able to lift Zero high enough for him to grab the **protruding** slab of rock."
14. "As the ground flattened, a huge stone **precipice** rose up ahead of him. . . ."
15. "He wondered if he should try to scramble out of the hole before the lizards turned on him, but he didn't want to cause any **commotion**."
16. "The lizards **scurried** frantically across his very still body. He did not **flinch**."
17. "He felt as if he was walking in a dream, not quite able to **comprehend** what was going on around him."

About the Author

Louis Sachar became interested in writing children's books after he took a college class to become a teacher's aide. He continued writing even after he became a lawyer and was able to quit the law after eight years when his books started selling. He writes for about two hours every morning and completes a book in about a year and a half, rewriting it five or six times. He got the idea for *Holes*, a story about suffering in a hot place, when he moved to Texas.

The Indian in the Cupboard
Author: Lynne Reid Banks
Publication date: 1980

Awards
New York Times Best Book for Children
Association of Children's Librarians Distinguished Book of the Year
Pacific Northwest Library Association Young Reader's Choice Award
California Young Reader Medal
Association of Children's Librarians Distinguished Book
Arizona Young Readers Award

Characters
Omri
Patrick
Little Bear
Boone
Omri's mother
Adiel and Gillon, Omri's brothers

Setting
Present day—England

Plot
Omri starts his birthday with a disappointing gift from his best friend, Patrick, a plastic Indian that Patrick no longer wants. Truth be told, Omri does not want it either, since he has no cowboy to use with it and feels he is growing past playing with plastic toys. After school, however, from his parents, he receives his most wanted gift, a skateboard, and from his eldest brother, Adiel, a helmet. The other brother, Gillon, with no pocket money, presents him with a small white medicine cabinet that he has found, and his mother produces a pretty, old-fashioned key that works in the lock. The key had been a gift from her grand-mother, a gift that she treasures.

Just before Omri goes to bed, his mother suggests that he put his Indian on the shelf in the cupboard. This he does and locks the door. In the morning, "a pattering, a tapping, a scrabbling and—a high-pitched noise like—well almost like a tiny voice," emitting from the cupboard wakes him. Petrified, Omri opens the door to find the Indian not on the shelf but crouched in the corner of the cupboard. Alive!

Omri puts the Indian back in the cupboard, deciding to keep his existence a secret. At school, he arouses Patrick's curiosity when he wants to go home to play with the Indian rather than use his new skateboard. At home he starts to become acquainted with Little Bear, his rather demanding bad-tempered Indian. After some conversation with Little Bear, Omri realizes he is no longer a plastic toy but a tiny person who deserves respect.

In Omri's bedroom, the two create a world for Little Bear, with Omri supplying him with a bow and arrows, a tepee, and even a horse. Little Bear, being an Iroquois Indian has never ridden a horse nor lived in a tepee for Iroquois Indians walked, and they lived in longhouses. Little Bear begins to build his own longhouse.

Soon Patrick learns of Omri's secret and uses the cabinet to create Boone out of a plastic cowboy who is riding his horse and toting his gun. When Little Bear and Boone discover each other, they exhibit the animosity that was part of the history of the Indian and white man in America. Omri stops the ensuing battle and takes both men to school. While there, Patrick, frightened by the head master's threats to bring in his father, tells him the truth and shows him Boone. Unable to believe his eyes, Mr. Johnson leaves school, thinking he is having hallucinations.

After school, Omri purchases a plastic Indian woman who becomes Little Bear's wife, Bright Star. The adventures continue, but not all goes smoothly; Little Bear seriously wounds Boone, the magic key disappears, and Gillon's pet rat is loose beneath the floor of Omri's room. When Little Bear wants an Indian celebration for his wedding, Omri decides to send them all back to their own times. By putting them back in the cabinet, they again become plastic toys.

Questions for Discussion

1. Why is the key so valuable to Omri's mother? Do you have any possessions that you prize for reasons other than their value?
2. Why does Omri not tell anyone else about Little Bear? Have you ever had an experience that you did not want to share with others? What was your reason for wanting to keep it a secret? Can you understand how Omri felt?
3. When Omri mistakenly makes Little Bear plastic again, how does he feel? What made him feel better? Has your family ever comforted you in this way?
4. What does Omri feel about adults that kept him from telling someone about Little Bear? Do you agree with his estimation? Why?
5. Why does Omri, who is not a reader, look for a book about Indians? Does he become interested in the information? What does this tell you about readers and books?
6. Why does Patrick become annoyed with Omri's intense interest in playing with Little Bear? Though Omri lies to Patrick about why he cannot come home with him, he has serious reservations about lying to his mother. Why do you think Omri felt there was a difference?
7. Why was his father angry with Omri? Was his anger justified?
8. Why does Omri's refusal of the plastic cowboy pique Patrick's interest? Why does Omri finally decide to show Little Bear to Patrick? Was it a wise decision?

9. When Omri's brothers find Little Bear's longhouse, who do they think made it? Why does Omri let them believe that rather than tell them the truth? Do you have you brothers and sisters from whom you keep secrets? Why?

10. Does Patrick understand Omri's unwillingness to create whole armies of little people? What partially convinces him that it is not game playing? What does he do when Omri leaves the room? How does Patrick's treatment of the cowboy and his horse show that he does not understand that they are real live creatures?

11. When Boone and Little Bear discover each other, what ensues? Do their feelings and actions reflect the attitudes of the real cowboys and Indians in United States history?

12. When Omri and Patrick are questioned by the head master, they begin to giggle. Patrick cannot control himself and continues to giggle. Why do you think he does this? Have you ever reacted in this way to a situation? What made you react in this manner? What happens when Mr. Johnson sees the little men? Is this a natural reaction?

13. What reason does Omri give Patrick when he takes Boone and Little Bear back from him? Do you agree with Omri?

14. Why does Little Bear think Boone's town is not a real place? Approximately how many years later is Boone's time from Little Bear's? Can you think of some important events in United States history that happened in the years between their times?

15. Why does Omri decide to send Little Bear, Bright Star, and Boone back to their own time? Do you think it was a wise decision? What would you have done?

Projects

1. Build a model of an Iroquois Indian longhouse.
2. Research the French and Indian War alluded to by Little Bear. Write a report on your findings.
3. Re-create the drawing of the 1880s western town drawn by Boone.
4. A television program incites Little Bear's wounding of Boone. Do you think television causes people to do evil things? Write a paper defending your position on this issue.

Vocabulary

Each of the following quotations chosen from *The Indian in the Cupboard* includes one or more vocabulary words in **bold print**.

1. "So did the **minuscule** muscles of his tiny naked **torso**."
2. "He wore a kind of **bandolier** across his chest and his belt seemed to be made of several strands of some shiny white beads."
3. "It had occurred to Omri now that he had imagined the whole **incredible** episode this morning."
4. "Omri **gaped**."
5. " 'What?' he asked **suspiciously**."

6. "The dangling Indian twisted, **writhed**, kicked, made a number of **ferocious** and **hideous** faces. . . ."
7. ". . . but stared **haughtily** at him. . . ."
8. "The Indian rose **lithely** to his feet and jumped off onto the gray carpet."
9. "Just when his mind was **seething** with ideas. . . ."
10. ". . . he had **vaulted** over the bottom edge of the cupboard. . . ."
11. ". . . the lawn's edge an **escarpment** twice the height of a man."
12. " 'Is it a pony?' whispered Patrick, **agog**."
13. "He gazed up **imperiously** at Patrick. . . . "
14. ". . . making little **mock** jabs towards his face. . . ."
15. ". . . they rolled on the ground, **pummeling**, kicking, and butting with their heads."
16. "This was not as **outrageous** as it sounds."
17. "Omri had never arrived at school with more **apprehension** in his heart, not even on spelling-test days."
18. ". . . she asked in her **raucous** voice like a crow's."
19. ". . . for they were both **gesticulating** with their arms. . . "
20. "Mrs. Hunt was obviously **flummoxed**."

About the Author

The daughter of a Scottish doctor and an Irish actress Ms. Banks was born in 1929. She trained at The Royal Academy of Dramatic Art and spent her early years in the theater but could not make it financially. In 1953, she left the stage and began a career as a reporter, journalist, and then a scriptwriter. Her novels include works for adults as well as children, and she has written several sequels to *The Indian in the Cupboard*. Ms. Banks lives in England with her husband, whom she met while visiting Israel, and has three sons who oddly enough are named Adiel, Gillon, and Omri.

From the Author

The Indian in the Cupboard started life as a bedtime story told to my son Omri (all the boys in the book are my real-life sons). Later with his help, I wrote it as a novel, never thinking that it would go on to considerable success, and that I would write four sequels to it. The book has, of course, changed our lives for the better, and brought me, personally, much interesting travel and many encounters with readers. It and what came after it have taught me a great deal about native Americans and their history. I think I put this knowledge to best use in the fifth book, *Key to the Indian*."

Jacob Have I Loved
Author: Katherine Paterson
Publication date: 1980

Award

Newbery Medal
ALA Notable Book for Children
School Library Journal Best Book of the Year
CRABberry Honor Book
American Book Award Nominee

Characters

Sara Louise Bradshaw
Caroline Bradshaw
Mr. and Mrs. Bradshaw
Grandmother
McCall "Call" Purnell
Captain Hiram Wallace

Setting

Rass Island, Chesapeake Bay—1940s

Plot

Sara Louise and Caroline Bradshaw are twins, born only a few minutes apart. Louise, the elder, comes healthfully into the world, but Caroline has to be encouraged to breathe. As they grow older, Caroline's health is often precarious while Louise prospers. When a piano comes into the Bradshaw residence, it becomes apparent that Caroline is musically gifted, especially vocally. Because of her musical gift and her health problems, Caroline has become the focus of the family. In 1941, the twins are thirteen, and Louise often resents the feeling of being cast aside in favor of Caroline.

The advent of World War II brings changes to the life in the tiny island in the Chesapeake Bay. Another change is the return of Captain Wallace after being gone for fifty years. Call, Louise's chubby, homely crabbing buddy, convinces Louise that they should help the captain rebuild his family home and boat. Reluctantly, Louise becomes a part of the plan and soon develops an attachment to the old man. When the Captain's home is washed away by a hurricane, it is Caroline who thinks of a solution; the Captain should marry Trudy Braxton, a stroke victim soon to return from the hospital. Though Louise is appalled by the idea, Call and the Captain agree with Caroline. The Captain marries Trudy, and

Caroline becomes a part of the threesome, often singing for the ailing Trudy. Again Louise seems to be set aside in favor of Caroline. Her anger becomes greater when the Captain takes his inheritance from Trudy to send Caroline to school in Baltimore so she may continue her vocal training.

As the war progresses, Call, who has been helping Mr. Bradshaw on his boat, joins the Navy; Louise quits school to help her father. She is happy on the water, but with the end of the war, the men return to do the oystering and crabbing. Caroline is in New York with a scholarship to Julliard, and Call, returning from the service, joins her. Louise, heeding the words of the Captain and her mother, leaves home and begins to build a life for herself away from Rass Island.

Questions for Discussion

1. Throughout her childhood Louise feels she is constantly being put aside for her sister, Caroline. Enumerate some of these times, and analyze how you would feel in the circumstances. Do you empathize with her, or do you feel she is overreacting?

2. Why does Louise feel that they should cancel Christmas in the winter of 1941? How did her classmates react to her proposal? How does Mr. Rice treat the situation? What do you think he could have done to ease the situation for Louise? How does Caroline help Louise? Do you think she is a caring person?

3. Why does Louise feel alone when she is with Caroline? Why does she feel unimportant to her family? Can you understand why she would want them to worry about her? Does she equate worry with love? What do you think?

4. What is Louise's relationship with her grandmother? Is the grandmother a likable person? What are some of her qualities that make you dislike her? Do you know any elderly people with similar qualities? Do you think these qualities can be related to the aging process? Why?

5. Though Louise initiates contact with Captain Wallace, it is Call who pushes their relationship. Why do you think he does this? How does Louise feel about their friendship? Why is she afraid? Have you ever had similar fears about a friend?

6. How does Caroline solve the problem of Trudy Braxton's feral cats? When Call relates the story of Caroline's feat with the cats, Louise feels the same as when someone tells the story of her birth. Why? How do you think it feels to be always placed in the background?

7. When Captain Wallace loses his home in the hurricane, Caroline presents a solution to his problem. Louise is horrified with her solution, but Call and the Captain agree with Caroline. How do you feel about the Captain marrying Trudy Braxton?

8. How does Louise feel when the Captain solves the problem of Caroline's musical education? What does her grandmother say to her? Does this mean that the old lady sees into Louise's deepest thoughts? Why do you think Louise is so transparent to her grandmother?

9. How does Louise's mother attempt to soften the blow of Caroline's schooling for her? Why does Louise feel that this proves her mother hates her? Do you feel that Louise has telescoped her emotions so that she can see only her side of all issues concerning Caroline?

10. Louise is truly happy when she is on the water helping her father, but she knows that this work cannot be her life. Why? Do you think these gender barriers exist today? Can you give any examples of women in traditionally male professions?

11. When Call informs Louise that he is going to marry Caroline, he says to her, " 'You never did think I was much to brag about, now did you?' " What are some of Louise's descriptions of Call that make you agree with him?

12. What finally makes Louise decide to leave the island? What does her mother say to her that allows her to leave the island and build a life of her own?

13. Is the teenage Louise someone you admire and like? What are some of her qualities that you would like to emulate? What are some that you do not admire?

14. Select the character from this novel that you most admired. What are the person's qualities that determined your choice?

Projects

1. The novel *Jacob Have I Loved* receives part of its inspiration from a biblical quotation. Select a quotation from the Bible, and write a short story based on your interpretation of its meaning.

2. "Pleasant melancholy" is an example of an oxymoron. Find the meaning of this literary device, and create twenty sentences illustrating it.

3. The Chesapeake Bay is a unique ecosystem. Create a poster or a computer graphic illustrating some of the flora and fauna found there.

4. An example of an adage or a proverb is Grandma's quotation, " 'Whistling women and crowing hens never come to a no good end.' " Select ten such sayings, trace the origin of each, and orally report your findings to the class.

5. Louise and Caroline suffered from the many childhood diseases once prevalent in this country. Choose several of these diseases, and report why they are no longer a threat. Include the method of inoculation, the founder of the vaccine, and the date when it was developed.

6. Using the ideas presented in this novel, interview twins in your community to see if they have had some of the same ambivalent feelings as Louise. Deliver your findings in a taped or videotaped presentation.

7. Twins have been the source of a great of scientific research. Use the Internet or other research sources to locate articles concerning their feelings toward each other; report about your findings.

Vocabulary

Each of the following quotations chosen from *Jacob Have I Loved* includes one or more vocabulary words in **bold print**.

1. "There are only a few **spindly** trees."
2. "He, at fourteen, was pudgy, **bespectacled**, and totally unsentimental."
3. "The **terrapin** sensed the change in our direction."
4. "I smiled at my sister **benevolently**."
5. "But my mother was **undaunted**."
6. "Grandma had stopped her **litany**."
7. ". . . and **cajoled** the tiny chest to move."
8. "I was proud of my sister, but that year, something began to **rankle** beneath the pride."
9. ". . . was a distinction that neither of us bothered to **quibble** over."
10. "I expected a **reprimand** from my father. . . ."
11. ". . . with a certain pleasant **melancholy**."
12. ". . . and **flounced** around to the front door."
13. "I could feel a tiny **rivulet** of satisfaction invading the flood of my anger."
14. ". . . in which she and Caroline were little more than **parasites**."
15. "That was far more wonderful than being a **saboteur**. . . . "
16. ". . . so I just stood there on the **dilapidated** porch. . . . "
17. "But despite these **aberrations** he seemed to be accepted as an islander."
18. "Even Call was **flabbergasted**."
19. ". . . even before the **ominous** rust-colored sunset."
20. "The storm had been **capricious**."

About the Author

Born in China of missionary parents prior to the outbreak of World War II, Katherine Paterson returned to the United States to escape the invading Japanese. Her childhood was spent moving about the country, never settling in one place long enough to belong. Before becoming a full-time writer in 1966, Ms. Paterson taught school, and she did missionary work in Japan. Her earlier works were historical fiction set in Japan. Her novels for young adults have won many awards and often deal with serious topics such as death, sibling jealousy, and children in crisis.

From the Author

"In writing JACOB HAVE I LOVED, I was trying to discover what happens to a person who is so blinded by envy that she can't see her own worth much less the love that other people have for her. But I didn't want to leave her crippled by this childhood emotion. I wanted her somehow to come to love her Jacob and thus be free to love herself."

Lily's Crossing
Author: Patricia Reilly Giff
Publishing date: 1997

Awards
Newbery Honor Book

Characters
Lily Mollahan
Poppy, her father
Gram
Albert
Margaret

Setting
1944-1945—St. Albans and Rockaway

Plot
Lily is excited about spending another summer at Rockaway with Poppy, Gram, and her friend, Margaret. Soon after they arrive, she is disappointed to learn that Margaret and her family will be moving away so that Margaret's father can take a job in a factory that makes airplanes for the war. To make matters even worse, Lily learns that her father, an engineer, is being sent to Europe to help rebuild the countries ruined by the war. Lily is devastated and doesn't even say good-bye to him.

Soon she meets Albert, who is spending the summer with his aunt and uncle. Albert had escaped from Hungary two years earlier. His parents were killed by the Nazis because they wrote a newspaper article critical of Hitler, and his sister, who escaped with him, was detained in France because she was sick. Just as Lily feels guilty about not saying good-bye to her father, Albert feels guilty about not going with his sister and not saying good-bye to her.

Lily believes that her main problem is that she lies. Although she decides she will not tell any more lies, she tells Albert that she is planning to row and swim to a ship convoy and go to Europe to be with her father. Albert, in turn, decides he will go to Europe with her to find his sister. When Albert gets caught in a boat in a storm, Lily blames herself.

Lily realizes from clues that Poppy gives her about *Madeline* and *The Three Musketeers* that he is in France. Lily and Albert send him information about Ruth, and when he returns home, Lily finds out that he has located Ruth in a convent in France. When Lily, Poppy, and Gram return to Rockaway the next summer, Albert has also returned, but this year with his sister, Ruth.

Questions for Discussion

1. How does Lily react to the news that her piano will be shipped to Rockaway for the summer? What does this say about her?
2. Why does Lily take a star with her each year to Rockaway? How does this help her deal with the loss of her mother?
3. How does Lily react to her father's news that he is going overseas? Is this understandable? Is she being fair?
4. Lily lists lying as her number one problem. What kind of lies does she tell to Margaret? To Albert? What happens to make her stop lying?
5. How does Lily grow in understanding of her grandmother? What kind of relationship do you think they have?
6. How does Lily and Albert's friendship develop? What do they have in common?
7. Do you think Albert did the right thing to close his eyes when his sister was taken away? What about his grandmother's request that they stay together?
8. What qualities does Lily have that you admire? Does she do anything you do not admire? Would you want Lily as a friend?
9. Explain the significance of the book's title. Do you think it has more than one meaning?

Projects

1. Mrs. Sherman, the baker, has a hard time getting eggs, butter, and cheese. These products were rationed during the war. Also, people had blackout shades and painted their headlights. Find out about other conditions existing at home while the war was being fought elsewhere. Put these into a poster.
2. Lily's grandmother has a Victory garden. Why does it have this name? Why did people have them? What would have been planted in a Victory garden? Make a diagram for a Victory garden you might plant.
3. The characters in the book listen to radio for news, music, and stories. Find out what radio shows were popular. Write a brief report about the variety of shows on the radio, and give examples of specific shows.
4. This novel takes place at the end of World War II. Prepare a radio news show on what else was happening in this country and the world. Include segments on fashions, sports, and entertainment.
5. Lily "had written her way through the winter." Continue Lily's journal for the next summer with Ruth and Albert.

Vocabulary

Each of the following quotations chosen from *Lily's Crossing* includes one or more vocabulary words in **bold print**.

1. ". . . they were keeping the business going for the **duration** of the war."
2. "Gram was frowning, watching them **hoist** up the piano. . . ."
3. ". . . the **wrenching** sound of wood splitting . . . "
4. "She could feel the **vibration** of the motor. . . ."
5. ". . . not even a tiny little one, much less one of those **gigantic** ones . . ."

6. "Overhead, Lily could hear the **drone** of one of the trainer planes from the naval base."
7. "Lily dipped the oars into the water again, **veering** toward the railway station. . . ."
8. ". . . **apologizing** because it was made with margarine and not butter . . ."
9. "Lily stood there, hand on the screen door, **squinting** in the sun."
10. "She could see him **plodding** along across the street."
11. " '. . . but I have the key, and it really isn't **trespassing**.' "
12. ". . . opening the door less than an inch, **peering** out, then pushing it all the way."
13. "It was hot in the bedroom, **stifling**."
14. "The stairs were **rickety**, she had to admit."
15. ". . . she was walking on the sides of her feet, **hobbling** along."

About the Author

Patricia Reilly Giff is a native of Brooklyn and was educated at Marymount College, St. John's University, and Hofstra University. She got up early in the morning to write while she was working as a teacher and reading consultant. She is focused on writing for middle school readers and tries to handle situations familiar to them in a humorous way.

From the Author

"*Lily's Crossing* has to do with my own childhood. I too grew up in St. Albans during the Second World War, and it was a time of fear for most children. So in *Lily's Crossing*, I wanted to tell children that no matter how bad things are in life, if you have a friend, nothing is as terrible as it might be. Lily has Albert, and it enriches her life."

A Long Way from Chicago
Author: Richard Peck
Publication date: 1998

Awards
Newbery Honor Book
National Book Award Finalist

Characters
Grandma Dowdel
Joey Dowdel
Mary Alice Dowdel
Effie Wilcox

Setting
Depression years of the 1930s—Small town in Illinois

Plot
"You wouldn't believe we'd have to leave Chicago to see a dead body." So begins the nostalgic trips to Grandma Dowdel's for Joey and his little sister, Mary Alice. Reluctantly, Joey and Mary Alice, ages nine and seven, and city slickers from Chicago, board the train in Dearborn station for their first summer visit to Grandma. The year is 1929, and Grandma lives in one of the Midwest towns cut in half by the railroad and way behind in the modern conveniences found in the big city. Mary Alice does not look forward to using the privy in the backyard and being jumped at by the big snaggletoothed cat that lives in the cobhouse.

For seven summers in the Depression-ridden 1930s, the two visit Grandma. Starting in 1929 when Shotgun Cheatham dies and city newspapers pick up the obituary because of his strange first name, each year holds a new adventure, with Grandma as the central and larger-than-life figure. One of the newspapers sends a stringer to town to find the story behind the strange first name. Grandma knows that he has really come to poke fun at townsfolk, so when he appears at her front door she is ready for him with one of her whoppers. According to Grandma, Shotgun had received his name from Ulysses S. Grant at the Battle of Vicksburg when he shot rebels with his old Remington pump-action gun. And so Shotgun, who could not hit the side of a barn, is immortalized as a Civil War hero. More excitement follows before Shotgun is placed to rest, and each summer brings a new adventure. Though Grandma never changes, she becomes a different person to Joey and Mary Alice. By 1935, their last summer with Grandma, they have to pretend their reluctance for the visit.

Questions for Discussion

1. Why do Joey and Mary Alice dread going to Grandma Dowdel's? Have you ever experienced similar feelings? When?
2. On their first visit, Grandma tells a whopper to a reporter. Why does she do it? How does Grandma scare Mrs. Effie Wilcox, her worst enemy, and the big city reporter at Shotgun's wake? What is Mary Alice's reaction?
3. Who are the Cowgills? What do they do to Grandma and Effie Wilcox? How does Grandma stop their antics? Why is Grandma satisfied with the results?
4. After raiding the Piatt County Rod & Gun Club fishtraps, Grandma takes Mary Alice and Joey to visit Aunt Puss. Who is she? How did Grandma come to work for her? How does Aunt Puss treat Grandma? What does Grandma do for Aunt Puss? How does that make you feel about Grandma?
5. The Depression causes many people to be out of work, with many of them drifting around the country homeless. How do the people in Grandma's town treat the homeless hobos? What does Grandma do? What does this tell you about Grandma?
6. When Grandma enters her gooseberry pie in the baking competition at the fair, what does she do to win? How does Grandma get an airplane ride for Joey with Barnstorming Barnie Buchanan? Has Grandma acted admirably? Was she punished in any way for her deeds?
7. Mary Alice is eleven in 1933 when she meets Vandalia at the Coffee Pot Café. What is Vandalia's problem? What does Mary Alice do? What happens as a result of Mary Alice's action? How do you feel about Mrs. Eubanks and Mr. and Mrs. Stubbs? How does Grandma help Vandalia and Junior Stubbs? What do you think of Grandma's resourcefulness?
8. How does Grandma get the bank to return Mrs. Effie Wilcox's home to her? What do you think of her methods?
9. Grandma Dowdel is a complex human being with many virtues and some vices. What are some of her deeds that show her goodness? When does Grandma display character traits that are less than admirable? Do you like her? Why?
10. Mary Alice grows from an unhappy, uncertain seven-year-old to a self-assured thirteen-year-old during her summers with Grandma. What are some of her actions that illustrate the change?
11. How do you feel about Joey? Would you want to be like him? Why or why not?

Projects

1. Design a poster or a billboard to advertise Barnstorming Barnie Buchanan's air show. The poster must contain a picture or a drawing of the plane Barnie flew as well as pertinent information on the cost and the location of the demonstration and rides.
2. Build a model of one of the biplanes used in the barnstorming shows of the 1920s and 1930s.

3. Herbert Hoover, Franklin Roosevelt, and his wife, Eleanor, are famous people mentioned in this book. Pick one of them to research and write a biography of his or her life.
4. During the 1930s the United States was in the Great Depression. Research the causes, the effect on the people, the methods used to bring about economic recovery, and the important historic figures of this time. Report your findings in either a written or pictorial essay.
5. The Hupmobile, the Model A Ford, and the Terraplane are automobiles mentioned in this book. Discover the history of each; when and by whom it was developed, what it cost, how many were manufactured, and when it stopped being produced. Present your findings orally to the class. If possible, supply a picture of each car.
6. In the chapter titled "The Phantom Brakeman," two menu selections from the Coffee Pot Café are listed and priced. Obtain a menu from a local diner or café. Find comparable items and compute the percentage of increase in the cost. Select ten items from the menu, and create a poster for the Coffee Pot Café, listing the selections and the costs, as they would have been in 1933. For additional credit, find the average wage for a worker in 1933 and one today. Compute the percentage of increase. Were the food items more expensive for the worker in 1933 or for today's worker?

Vocabulary

Each of the following quotations chosen from *A Long Way from Chicago* includes one or more vocabulary words in **bold print**.

1. "A big old **snaggletooth** tomcat lived in the **cobhouse** and as soon as you'd come out of the **privy** he'd jump at you."
2. "One sent a **stringer** around the Coffee Pot Café for a human-interest story since it was August, a slow month for news."
3. "He was just an old **reprobate**. . . . "
4. "So now Mary Alice was **sulking** somewhere."
5. ". . . recalling the sound when Grandma's mailbox was blown to **smithereens**."
6. "The smell of breakfast **wafted** up from the kitchen."
7. "Mary Alice **glowered** but said nothing."
8. "Mary Alice stared up at her, **transfixed**."
9. "Of all the **invasions** of her privacy, this one took the cake."
10. ". . . everyone would say they'd seen the **cadaver**."
11. " 'But you'll have to confess you **falsified** those so-called Lincoln items.' "
12. "I put it in the crook of my arm, like we were an old **tintype** picture in a fancy frame."

About the Author

Born in Decatur, Illinois, Richard Peck, now living in New York City, is a prolific writer for children and young adults, with more than twenty novels to his credit. Each of his books offers something very special to the reader, from the humor of *The Ghosts I Have Been* to the excitement of *Lost in Cyberspace* and the depictions of teen life and problems in *Father Figure* and *Strays Like Us*. Many of his books have been selected by the American Library Association for its Best of the Best list and by *School Library Journal* for its Best Books list.

From the Author

"My novel in short stories, *A Long Way from Chicago*, has won a Newbery medal. You could knock me over with a feather because its looming central figure is a grandma who brews beer, fires a shotgun in her own parlor, and steals the sheriff's rowboat. To call her politically incorrect doesn't come near her. Yet her rough, midwestern façade conceals a woman who lives for the sight of her grandchildren and who loves the community she scorns. We need more novels that do not patronize the elderly. We need more novels about extended family for the young suburban reader. We need to provide grandparents on the page for a generation of young readers who no longer even have to write thank-you notes for gifts from their grandparents."

The Maze
Author: Will Hobbs
Publication date: 1998

Awards
ALA Notable Books for Young Adults
ALA Best Books for Young Adults

Characters
Rick Walker
Judge Samuel Bendix
Mr. B.
Lon Peregrino
Carlisle Carlisle
Gunderson

Setting
Modern day—Utah, Nevada, Arizona

Plot
Rick Walker, a fourteen year-old orphan, is mad at the world, mad at his mother who deserted him, mad at the father he never saw, mad at his grandmother who died when he was ten, mad at the foster homes and the group homes where he has lived since then, just plain mad at the world. It is this anger and frustration that he unleashes against the stop sign by hurling rocks at it. When he appears before Judge Bendix, it is this anger that he shows rather than the confusion and despair he feels in his present situation. Judge Bendix sentences him to six months in the Blue Canyon Youth Detention Center, a facility for hardened youthful offenders. While there, Rick spends time in the library, where he reads the story of Daedalus fashioning wings so that he and his son, Icarus, can fly out of the maze they are imprisoned in.

By the time he has been at the facility for four and a half months, Rick has learned that some of the guards are as incorrigible as the inmates and makes the mistake of reporting this to his social worker. From Killian, a boy so mistreated by his parents that his mind is gone, he learns that he has been set up for a beating and knows that he must escape. After going over the wall, he hitches a ride and winds up at a gas station where there are several men and a rust-colored pit bull. There he hides in the back of a Ford pickup with a camper shell on the back. The truck is filled with provisions and two large white coolers containing partially frozen dead calves. For five hours he is bumped around as the Ford travels over rough roads, getting farther and farther from civilization. When the truck finally stops at a campsite, Rick sneaks off into the rocks. Frightened by the dead calves, he is wary of these people and tries to escape, but the bearded inhabitant of the camp, Lon Peregrino, forestalls him. From him, Rick learns that he is in Utah in Canyonlands National Park at the edge of the Maze. The Maze is a network of canyons, "a thirty-square-mile puzzle in sandstone." Lon does not question why Rick was hiding in the supply truck, and gradually the two build a measure of trust. Rick learns that Lon is monitoring the fledgling condors that have been released into the area. When Lon goes hang gliding, they learn that they have the love of flying and dreams of flying in common. Lon teaches Rick how to hang glide.

Danger for the two of them appears in the persons of Carlisle and Gunderson, who have reasons for not wanting Lon and Rick to be in this part of the park. When they drive Lon into the Maze where he is in danger of drowning, Rick puts his novice flying skills to work and rescues Lon. Carlisle and Gunderson are arrested for possession of illegal weapons and bombs, and Rick is sent to a group home in Arizona, with school vacations to be spent with Lon.

Questions for Discussion
1. When Rick Walker appears in court, he realizes that he is filled with anger. At what is he angry? How would you feel if you were Rick?
2. The judge makes a general statement about young people. He says, " 'So many of them seem to be bundles of attitude with no substance inside, nothing they really care about. No conscience, no remorse.' " Does this attitude affect his decision to send Rick to Blue Canyon Youth Detention Center? Does Rick's attitude also color his decision? Do you think he acted fairly?
3. While at the detention facility, Rick makes the observation that, like him, many of the kids were raised by their grandmothers. Have you any thoughts on why this might be?
4. Rick and many of the kids had worked on a garden that supplied fresh food to the cafeteria, but one day it is ripped out by the maintenance men. Why does Rick think this is one more thing to be shrugged off? Why can't he do it?
5. Why does Rick identify with Icarus in the myth, "Escape from the Maze"? Why does Mr. B. disagree with him? Who do you feel is right?
6. Rick has always had flying dreams, and in them people are always beckoning him to come down, but he flies out of reach. This makes him both happy and sad. Why? Is it common to have conflicting emotions over an event or happening in your life? Can you recall an incident that has caused such feeling in you?
7. Why does Rick feel his life is a succession of dead ends? Do you think he has cause to feel this way? Have you ever felt this way? Why?
8. Why do Carlisle and Gunderson come to Lon's camp? What does Rick learn about them? When he tells Lon, what does he think they are up to?

9. Why does Carlisle hate the government? Is he justified in holding a grudge?
10. What does Lon mean by the statement, " 'Less is more' "? Do you agree with him?
11. Why does Rick start to care about the condors? Do you understand why he identifies with them and Lon? What do you think it feels like to be an outcast? Have you ever felt that way?
12. After they capture Maverick, Rick tells Lon the truth about himself. What is Lon's reaction? Why does he understand? Does it help with problems if you know someone with similar experiences who has conquered them?
13. What does Lon say when Rick agrees with his sentiment about closed doors? Lon disagrees with Rick when he says, " 'Some things shouldn't be forgiven or forgotten.' " What does he say? With whom do you agree?
14. What is Lon's advice about anger? Is it easy to do?
15. Maverick, the most precocious of the condors, is killed by an eagle and Carlisle's pit bull. What does Lon say is the reason? Do you agree with the comparison to Icarus?
16. When Rick flies tandem with Lon, he realizes he trusts him. Why is that an important accomplishment for him? Is it easy for you to trust? Why?
17. Why does Lon offer to speak to the judge? What does this do for Rick's well-being?
18. What does Rick discover when he is exploring the Maze? What happens when he is in the canyons? Why do you think Carlisle and Gunderson will not help him? How does Rick get out of the canyon?
19. When Rick tells Lon of the guns and bombs, what does Lon decide to do? He does not want Carlisle and Gunderson to feel threatened. Why? What is a common reaction when someone feels trapped or threatened? Do you think Carlisle and Gunderson would become violent? What is the reason for your answer?
20. How does Rick rescue Lon from the canyons? What qualities does he show by doing this?
21. What changes in behavior are evident in Rick when he appears before Judge Bendix? How does the judge's attitude differ from the first time? How do you account for the changes? What is a lesson you can learn from this?

Projects

1. In December 1996, California condors were released from the Vermilion Cliffs near the Grand Canyon. Research this news item, and write an indepth magazine article reporting the facts and the background of the incident.
2. Obtain and view a copy of the National Audubon Video, *California Condor*. Present the information in a brief oral report to the class.
3. Locate the Peregrine Fund, www.peregrinefund.org, on the Internet. On a world map, locate five sites of the International Conservation Program, and describe the work of each.

4. Find a design of a hang glider, and build a scale model.
5. Locate the agency in your community that regulates the management of foster homes, and obtain information on how they are evaluated. Report your findings orally to the class.
6. Read the myth of Daedalus and Icarus; prepare an illustrated booklet of the story.

Vocabulary

Each of the following quotations chosen from *The Maze* includes one or more vocabulary words in **bold print**.

1. " 'Just this morning over coffee, I read about two juveniles no older than you **bludgeoning** a nine-year-old to death with a baseball bat.' "
2. "Rick **recoiled** at the world *orphan*."
3. "He looked **frantically** around his social worker to Mike Brown."
4. ". . . and studying him with that **habitual** look of scornful amusement."
5. "He couldn't let himself get **paranoid**."
6. "Breaks were **inherently** unstable and dangerous."
7. "In the dream he had always had a **miraculous, inexplicable** power inside himself."
8. "In the dream all he had to do was spread his arms and he'd begin to **levitate** higher and higher until he was **hovering** above the earth."
9. "Killian was **scuttling** away like a crab."
10. "A five-minute run down the trail that led from the roads end brought him to the edge of an **abyss**."
11. "There was no mistaking the **magnitude** of the man's anger."
12. ". . . walked out onto a rolling sea of smooth white rock that **undulated** from the edge of the camp."
13. " 'A guy named Ernie,' he said **whimsically**."
14. "He screwed the **carabiner's** locking mechanism down tight."
15. " 'Jasper's the closest thing we have to a **pristine** canyon **ecosystem**.' "
16. " 'He's the most **precocious** flyer of any condor fledging I've ever seen.' "
17. "On foot no, they followed the signal from Lon's electronic bloodhound north toward the **confluence** of the two rivers."
18. " 'No point in keeping him **incarcerated**.' "
19. "Each time a side canyon came in, he marked his path with a **cairn** of stones."
20. ". . . he could give himself over to the **exhilaration**."

About the Author

Born in Pittsburgh, Pennsylvania, in 1947, Will Hobbs has a bachelor of arts and a master of arts from Stanford University. Mr. Hobbs's interests include hiking, archaeology, and natural history, themes that frequently appear in his novels. As he addresses the problems of choice and the struggle for identity in young people, he places them in an environment dealing with wildlife and wild places in hopes that this will increase the awareness of his readers concerning the natural world.

From the Author

"In December, 1996 my wife and I read that six young California condors had just been released at Vermilion Cliffs close to where we begin our Grand Canyon river trips. . . I should write a story in which a kid gets involved with the condors. . . My main character could be a boy in a lot of trouble, who considers his whole life to be nothing but dead ends—a maze."

.

The Midwife's Apprentice
Author: Karen Cushman
Publication date: 1995

Awards
Newbery Medal

Characters
Brat, called Beetle, and finally Alyce
Jane the Midwife
Town boys including Will, whom Alyce saves
Runt, called Edward by Alyce
Magister Reese

Setting
Fourteenth century—England

Plot
Brat is a homeless girl with no family; she doesn't even know her exact age. To survive she both steals and works for food and sleeps on a dung pile because compost emits a warmth as it rots. When Jane the Midwife finds her on a dung heap, she calls her Beetle, for the dung beetle, and takes her in as an apprentice. Soon Beetle christens herself Alyce when she is mistaken for someone by that name; she also believes Alyce is a better name for a person than Beetle. Alyce has become accustomed to the teasing and ridicule of the town boys. When a group of boys chases her into a tree, she sees that one of them, Will, has lost his footing and fallen into the river. All of the boys run away, but Alyce saves Will's life.

Alyce learns a great deal about the people of the town and their transgressions in the course of delivering messages at night. She puts the town into an uproar when she uses carved blocks of wood to make prints in the dirt leading directly to those doing wrong. The townspeole think these are the Devil's footprints. Alyce protects Runt, whom she calls Edward, from the teasing boys, and sends him to the manor where he can find work, food, and shelter.

Alyce learns about gathering and preparing herbs and plants that can be used for medicinal purposes, and she also learns about delivering babies. When the greedy Jane leaves the bailiff's wife to deliver the baby of the Lady of the Manor, Alyce delivers the bailiff's baby herself. She is not always so successful as a midwife and loses her confidence. She runs away and works in an inn where she meets Magister Reese and learns about letters and words. When she over-hears Jane the Midwife say she needs an apprentice " 'who can try and risk and fail and try again and not give up,' " she returns to Jane.

Questions for Discussion

1. How do the village boys treat Beetle at the beginning of the story? How does Beetle react to the boys? What qualities does she show? Do the boys ever change their behavior toward her?
2. Why does Beetle save Will? What does this show you about her character?
3. What qualities does Jane the Midwife have? Why do you think she takes Beetle in?
4. When Alyce acts as a night messenger, what does she learn about some people? What plan does she devise? What do you learn about her character from this?
5. Why are the boys tormenting Edward? How does Alyce protect him?
6. Why does Alyce run away when she cannot deliver Emma's baby? What does the Midwife think about this? Does Alyce ever take the Midwife's advice?
7. What do you learn about bullies from this story?
8. What outstanding qualities does Alyce have? Would you like to have her for a friend?
9. What characters do you admire? Why? What characters don't you admire? Why?
10. What do you learn about life in the Middle Ages from this novel?

Projects

1. Alyce learns about using herbs, such as sorrel, anise, milkwort, and sage, for medicinal purposes. Find out about other herbs used medicinally, and make a catalog of these with descriptions, pictures, and uses. The catalog may be done as a booklet or as a multimedia presentation.
2. Through Magister Reese, Alyce learns about letters and words. Make an alphabet poster with the letters drawn in the medieval illuminated style.
3. Compare and contrast Alyce and Edward to children today. Do you know of any children whose lives are similar to theirs? What would happen to Alyce and Edward if they lived today?
4. Several different occupations are mentioned in this book, such as miller, bailiff, and weaver. Find out about these and other occupations and trades common in the Middle Ages. Write want ads for people to hold these jobs, including qualifications and working conditions.
5. Alyce sends Edward to the manor to work. Find out about life in a medieval English manor. Build a model of the manor.

Vocabulary

Each of the following quotations chosen from *The Midwife's Apprentice* includes one or more vocabulary words in **bold print**.

1. "Beetle soon acquired a new name, the midwife's **apprentice**."
2. "She did her job with energy and some skill, but without care, **compassion**, or joy."
3. "Beetle endured their anger and their **taunts** in silence and complained only to the cat. . . ."

4. "... for never had she been in such a **luxurious** dwelling, with two rooms downstairs and a loft above and a high soft bed all enclosed by curtains. . . ."

5. "She dearly longed to **accompany** the midwife, but still being Brainless Brat, she was afraid to ask."

6. "... the midwife's **ranting** about lack of wit and the **dire consequences** if she were to lose the silver pennies . . ."

7. "Beetle took advantage of Will's **distraction** to duck beneath his arm, loop her skirts between her legs, and take off down the road to the river."

8. "She took a handful of nuts, the biggest and hardest and heaviest in her basket, and **heaved** them at the boys."

9. "And the boys moved off to **torment** someone else until they were found, slapped, and sent to work."

10. "Alyce stood outside for a minute, surprised at having been asked for and not knowing whether to be pleased, until the boy **nudged** and pushed her to the door."

11. "Just then a party of riders rode into the inn yard—a **prosperous**-looking man wearing too much jewelry."

12. " 'I am sure God does not **begrudge** me my little economies.' "

About the Author

Karen Cushman was fifty years old when she wrote her first book, *Catherine, Called Birdy.* An avid reader from her childhood, Cushman still enjoys the reading and research that are necessary for her writing. She holds master's degrees in human behavior and museum studies and works at John F. Kennedy University in San Francisco as the assistant director of the Museum Studies Department.

Missing May
Author: Cynthia Rylant
Publication date: 1992

Awards

Newbery Medal
Booklist Top of the List
Boston Globe/Horn Book Award
ALA Notable Books for Children
ALA Best Books for Young Adults
School Library Journal Best Book of the Year

Characters

Summer
May
Ob
Cletus
Mr. and Mrs. Underwood, Cletus's parents

Setting

Present day—West Virginia

Plot

Aunt May and Uncle Ob brought the motherless Summer home to West Virginia with them when she was six years old. For six years, Summer's life is idyllic. Their home might be a rusty trailer, but they fill it with love. As Summer says, "That first night in it with Ob and May was as close to paradise as I may ever come in my life." Furthermore, Ob makes magical whirligigs, not ordinary animals or cartoon figures, but *The Mysteries* like Dreams, Love, and Fire.

Then May dies while she is gardening in her friendly and substantial garden. Summer and Ob find their lives empty. Summer says, "I never would have thought us to be so lost." Ob tells Summer that May is trying to contact him, but after two visits from her, he is having trouble communicating with his dead wife. He enlists the help of Cletus Underwood, whom Summer knows from the school bus, to help him. Summer thinks that Cletus is a lunatic. He collects pictures that tell stories from anywhere he can and carries his collection around in an old suitcase. Cletus tells them that he has been to the afterlife, where he saw his deceased grandfather and dog. However, Cletus's presence when Ob stands in May's garden and extols her virtues fails to result in May's appearance.

Ob is discouraged and doesn't know if he can go on until Cletus suggests they go to see Reverend Mariam B. Conklin of the Spiritualist Church of Glen Meadows, who can communicate with the dead. When they get to the Spiritualist

Church, they find that the reverend herself has died. Ob is discouraged, but after they pass the West Virginia State Capitol, which Ob had promised Summer and Cletus they would visit for the whole day on their return trip, Ob suddenly has a change of heart. They return to the Capitol and spend the day there.

When they return home, an owl flies over them, reminding Summer of May and precipitating the tears she has not yet shed for May's death. As Summer sleeps, May talks to her about their lives together and the owl that passed over May and Summer's heads a few weeks after Summer came to live with them. To May the owl represented the good things Summer would bring into their lives.

The next day, Ob is himself again. He decides to fill May's empty garden with his enchanting whirligigs. "And then a big wind came and set everything free."

Questions for Discussion

1. How do Ob and May make Summer feel at home immediately? How is this different from the way other relatives have treated her?
2. What qualities do you admire in May? Have you ever known anyone who shared those qualities?
3. What does Summer mean when she says, "Nobody ever disappointed May"? How is this important for the people whom May deals with? Have you ever shown this quality when dealing with another person?
4. What do Ob's whirligigs represent? What makes them more special than ordinary whirligigs? What does this tell you about Ob?
5. Summer says she only expects one chance at happiness, and that is with Ob and May. How is this different from the attitude that May has? Which attitude do you admire?
6. What does Summer think of Cletus at the beginning? Does her attitude change? What does she learn about him from visiting his parents?
7. May tells Summer that the Lord brought them together when they all were "*just full of need*." Do you agree that they all appreciated each other more because they had waited a long time to be together?
8. Ob and May could not give Summer a lot of material things. What could they give her? What is more important?

Projects

1. Ob makes magical whirligigs. Locate information on how to make whirligigs. Construct a whirligig similar to those Ob made of *The Mysteries*, capturing your ideas of heaven, a thunderstorm, love, dreams, fire, or death.
2. Cletus collects all kinds of pictures that have potential stories to them. Make a collection of pictures that you think Cletus would have collected. Select two, and write a story about each.
3. Summer compares their trip to see Reverend Miriam B. Conklin to the journey to Oz. Read the story or view the movie version of the *Wizard of Oz*. Write an explanation for Summer's comparison of their trip to Dorothy's.
4. Have Summer continue her story in a journal. Write three or four journal entries including Cletus, Ob, and Summer in your writing.

Vocabulary

Each of the following quotations chosen from *Missing May* includes one or more vocabulary words in **bold print**.

1. "That first night in it with Ob and May was as close to **paradise** as I may ever come in my life."
2. ". . . as soon as she **hoisted** herself out of the front seat (May was a big woman) . . ."
3. "In place of roses it was full of thick pole beans and hard green cabbages and strong carrots. It was a **reliable** garden. . . ."
4. "Then he folded the cloth up neatly, gave his nose one more **confident swipe**, and jammed the hanky back in his pocket."
5. "I couldn't **fathom** May taking the trouble of dying just so she could go to Ohio."
6. "I hadn't seen Ob interested in one **solitary** thing since May left us last summer. . . ."
7. "But Cletus and Ob were as **enthralled** as cats in front of a fish tank. . . ."
8. ". . . and the only thing you saw was this child **hovering** in midair. . . ."
9. ". . . like her secretly saving up for three years in a row to buy him that expensive plane saw he was **coveting** over at Sears."
10. "He became the perfect **consoler**, because he listened to every word Ob said and kept his fat mouth shut."
11. "He was **humiliated**, I knew, and wanted to be left alone."
12. "But I've got too much to lose if this Bat Lady turns out to be a **hoax**."
13. "Then Ob and May would take turns trying to throw a blanket over the bat while it **swooped** around their heads. . . ."
14. ". . . afraid to let his parents see the way I barely **tolerated** their strange son."
15. "It was one of those rare occasions when he was too **flabbergasted** to speak."
16. "We were trying to **outwit** Death on this trip, rise above it, **penetrate** the **blockades** it put up between us and May."

About the Author

Cynthia Rylant was born in Virginia, and she received a bachelor of arts degree from Morris Harvey College, a master of arts from Marshall University, and a master of library science from Kent State University. She has taught English at the college level. The author of poetry, nonfiction, picture books, short stories, and novels, Cynthia Rylant has said that many of her books have their basis in her own life.

The Moves Make the Man
Author: Bruce Brooks
Publication date: 1984

Awards

Newbery Honor Book
School Library Journal Best Books of the Year
New York Times Notable Books
Boston Globe /Horn Book Award

Characters

Jerome Foxworthy
Braxton Rivers, "Bix"
Momma
Maurice and Henri Foxworthy, Jerome's brothers
Bix's mother and stepfather

Setting

1950s—Wilmington, North Carolina

Plot

Thirteen-year-old Bix Rivers has disappeared, and his friend, Jerome Fox-worthy, decides to write his story, or rather the story of their relationship, and to tell it truthfully.

Jerome, a black boy the same age as Bix, is a very lucky young man. He is a member of a loving but fatherless family. His mother is warm and understand-ing; his two brothers provide the proper proportion of teasing and support. An excellent student, Jerome is in all accelerated classes, loves to write, and has a passion for basketball. He first sees Bix during the summer at a baseball game and is awed by the white boy's athletic talent.

The fall brings changes for Jerome. He becomes the only black student in an all-white junior high school and must face the racial discrimination of some of the students and the basketball coach. His mother has been seriously injured in an elevator accident, and he and his brothers must share the domestic duties to run their home. To learn to cook, Jerome is placed in a home economics class where he meets Bix. Jerome does not learn until later that Bix is in the class be-cause his mother has been hospitalized following a nervous breakdown. As the only boys in the class, they form a friendship until the class is to make Mock-Apple Pie. Bix flips out at the deceit of pretending that it is a real apple pie, is removed from the class, and the two no longer see each other.

Jerome has a favorite basketball court on the other side of town but cannot get there during daylight because of his new chores at home. When he wins a railroad searchlight, he returns to the court to play ball and practice his moves, "reverse spin, triple pump, reverse dribble, stutter step into jumper, blind pass," For Jerome, these moves are him.

When Jerome arrives at the court, there is someone there playing in the dark. It is Bix. The friendship revives, and Jerome teaches Bix the basics of basketball, everything but the moves. Bix considers them falsehoods. When he has mastered the game, Bix challenges his stepfather to a game. For winning he gets to visit his mother in a mental hospital, but Bix finds he cannot win without the moves, so he gives into the lies in order to beat his stepfather.

When visiting his mother at the hospital, Bix makes the greatest move of all and then disappears.

Questions for Discussion
1. Jerome wonders why Bix's house has a pineapple over the door. Do you know the significance of this symbol? When and where was it used?
2. Why does Jerome think Bix's mother is weird? Why does he feel sorry for Bix? Why are the adults looking at her with pity and curiosity?
3. Why is Jerome so angry when Bix and his mother do not stay for the refreshments after the game? Is he justified in this reaction? After the baseball game Jerome begins to play basketball with an imaginary opponent. Who is it? Why has Jerome picked him for this role? What does Jerome think of his own actions? Do you agree with him?
4. How does the Wilmington School Board meet the desegregation ruling? What does Mama think of their action? How does she react? How would you have acted?
5. When Jerome enters Chestnut Junior High, he gets into a fight on the first day. What is the cause of the fight? What is the result? Does Jerome feel that it is a racial thing?
6. When Jerome goes to basketball tryouts, how does the coach treat him? Why does the coach act this way? How does Jerome react? Have you ever been treated in this manner? How did you feel and react?
7. In home ec class, the girls treat Bix unkindly. Why do you think they do this? Are there any children in your school who are treated this way? What can you do to help these people?
8. Bix is extremely agitated by Mr. Spearman's untruthful reaction to tasting the Mock-Apple Pie. Is his agitation normal under the circumstances? Why do you think he is so intense?
9. When Momma returns from the hospital, what worries Jerome? Do you think he was justified in this concern? How did Momma relieve his concern about her? What did she do to help Jerome and his brothers?
10. When Jerome finds Bix on his court he is afraid. "My reaction was, step back, tighten up, make sure of Jerome. Play basic defense until you see all the moves." What does he mean by this? How do you act when you are unsure of a situation?
11. Jerome fakes being from Saturn. Instead of laughing Bix thinks that it is not a big joke, but a lie. How do you feel about Jerome's teasing?

12. How does Bix answer Jerome when he asks if they are best friends? Does his reasoning make sense to you? Why do you think Jerome wants it said in words? Why does Bix not want words? Does Jerome see the wisdom in Bix's ideas about words?

13. Jerome and Bix argue about the best way to play basketball. What is Jerome's point of view? What is Bix's point of view? Who do you think is right? Why?

14. After the fight, the two boys do not see each other for a while. Though Jerome is used to being alone, he now feels something missing. What is he missing? What takes the place of being with Bix?

15. Where is Bix's mother? What kind of treatments had she received? Are these treatments used as often today? What has taken their place?

16. Why does Bix bet his stepfather that he can beat him in a game of one-on-one basketball? What happens when they play? Do you think this change was difficult for Bix?

17. What happens when Jerome invites Bix to his house for dinner? Why was Jerome so disappointed? What does Bix say that gets Jerome analyzing their friendship?

18. What happens when Jerome, Bix, and Bix's stepfather stop at the diner for hot dogs? Was the stepfather right in not wanting to stop? How does Bix react to the incident? How does Jerome react? Do you think things like this still happen today? Do you think racial discrimination has lessened since the 1950s of this book?

19. What do you think happens when Bix sees his mother? Why do you think he disappears? How do you think he is living in Washington, D.C. on his own?

20. "There are no moves you truly make alone." What does Jerome mean by this? Do you agree with him?

Projects

1. Phil Rizzuto of the New York Yankees and Bill Russell of the Boston Celtics are mentioned in this book. Select one of them, and investigate his life and professional career. Complete either a written or pictorial essay on your findings.

2. Investigate the integration of schools in the United States. Create a time line of important events in this process.

3. Write a synopsis of this story from Bix's point of view.

4. Make a Mock-Apple Pie from the ingredients in the book. Make a real apple pie. Write a critique of each, comparing flavor, texture, appearance, and so on. Ask tasters of the pies for their critical comments, and include them in your critique.

5. Create a basketball glossary, describing the terms used in this book.

6. During the Revolutionary War, the Swamp Fox was an American hero. Find out who he was, and write a report on his exploits.

Vocabulary

Each of the following quotations chosen from *The Moves Make the Man* includes one or more vocabulary words in **bold print**.

1. "About the second inning this **metallic** blue car came roaring up the street and screeched to a stop a way down the left field street line."
2. "I said to myself and felt all **righteous**, though lord knows why, though Lord knows why."
3. "... it was just so **humiliating** and nasty that I was screaming inside. . . ."
4. "I should not let her **agitate** me into a lack of confidence."
5. "What good did it do me to learn **quadratic equations**."
6. "You'll see, boy—the body will be avenged for its **servitude** to untruth."
7. "Momma was herself but very softly so, and plus she was wearing a **turban** of **gauze** bandaging. . . ."
8. "Momma just said very serious, she appreciated how **dedicated** we were and how good at our work too."
9. "Maurice told Henri not to be **chiding** me."
10. "... and probably people think their ghosts are there and **hogwash** like that."
11. "He pretended the word **philosopher** gave him all kinds of trouble."
12. "Bobo sort of **snarled**. . . ."
13. "All right, said the big sporting **enthusiast**, Bobo here will stand you for the ball."
14. "So he said, angry now, looking away and **gesturing** with the ball, starting to bounce it very **spastic** with the palm of his hand but stopped when he saw me watching him."
15. "But now I was hungry for some good old swift **deceit**. . . ."
16. "My feet were twisting to **gyrate**, and I knew if he got on the court it would be for some slow shooting."
17. "I kind of tagged along, **scuffing** through the grass."
18. "But Bix liked the idea of the man getting all **riled** and **flustered** by losing his way and stepping in marsh glop and getting bit by the skeeters and such things, just before the game."
19. "... he did not care a bit we were having an **unorthodox** kid over for supper, which made me a little suspicious."
20. "Counseling across the color line is **notoriously** fruitless, due to **preconditions** of distrust."

About the Author

Born in Washington, D.C., in 1950, Bruce Brooks received his bachelor of arts from the University of North Carolina and his master of fine arts from the University of Iowa. Now living in Maryland with his wife and son, he is a versatile writer whose books concentrate on important issues. Prior to writing his first book, *The Moves Make the Man*, he had worked as a newspaper and magazine reporter.

Nightjohn
Author: Gary Paulsen
Publication date: 1993

Awards
ALA Best Books for Young Adults
ALA Notable Books for Children
International Reading Association-Children's Book Council Choice

Characters
Sarny
John
Delie, "mammy"
Clel Waller
Alice

Setting
Pre-Civil War—The South

Plot
In a brief novel written in simple, realistic, stark language, Gary Paulsen portrays the evil of slavery in the United States. He exposes the inhumanity, cruelty, and abasement of the system and the courage and determination of some who sought to rise above it.

Sarny is a young, motherless child approaching womanhood. Her birthing mother has been sold for enough to buy four field hands. She is raised by Delie, the mammy, as are all the children birthed by breeders. One day Sarny's owner, Waller, brings in a new and costly slave, shackled around the neck and tied to his horse. The slave is naked and sweating from running; his back is covered with scars from previous whippings, and it is a wonder that Waller has spent so much money for him.

On his first night, the slave, named John, whispers for some tobacco and offers a trade. Sarny, who has some tobacco left over from chewing to spit on the roses, asks what the trade is and is told letters. " 'I'll trade you A, B, and C for a lip of tobacco.' " Reading is something slaves are not permitted to learn. They are whipped or dismembered if caught reading or writing. Despite her fear, Sarny bargains with John to learn to read, and that night she learns A.

Through some bad times on the plantation, Sarny continues her lessons until mammy finds out. It is then that they learn that John is a runaway slave who escaped to the North but has returned to the South to teach slaves to read and write. He does so in order that slaves will be able to record what is happening to them. Some crackers hunting bear caught him in the woods, and now he is a

107

slave again. After mammy hears his story, she does not interfere with his teaching.

When Sarny learns several letters she is careless, and Waller catches her scratching a word in the dirt. To find out who is teaching her, he attaches mammy to a wagon and makes her pull it, with him riding and cracking his whip. John steps forward and admits he is the one. Waller cuts off two of his toes with a hammer and a chisel. Though not recovered from the amputation, John escapes again, but true to his word to Sarny he secretly returns to the area to run a night school for the children.

Questions for Discussion
1. Sarny's mother was sold because she was a good breeder. What do you think that means? Why was this important to plantation owners?
2. As a child, what type of jobs does Sarny do? What does this leave her time to do? What does this tell you about Sarny? Do you think all the children on the plantation have her desire to learn? Do you think all the children you know have this desire?
3. What does mammy have to do to pray out loud? Why would the slave owners not want them to pray?
4. The slaves on this plantation eat out of a trough. How is a trough usually used? What effect do you think this would have on the slaves? How would you feel if you had to eat in this manner?
5. How does Waller bring Nightjohn onto the plantation? Why do you think he does this? Describe Nightjohn. Would John's appearance have an effect on the slaves who are watching?
6. What is Nightjohn's answer when Sarny asks, " 'Why they be cutting our thumbs off if we learn to read—if that's all it is?' " Is learning important to every person? What would the world be like if no one was allowed to read and write?
7. What happens when a slave tries to run away from Waller's farm? How does this discourage others from trying to escape? Is fear a deterrent that most people understand? Can you think of times in your life when fear has kept you from doing something that you wanted to do?
8. How do mammy and Sarny learn of John's escape from slavery? Where did he go? Why did he come back? What does he say to mammy that influences her to let him teach Sarny? Why is it important to record events?
9. How does Waller find out that Sarny is learning to read? Why did she become careless? What does he do to her? Why does he change his punishment from Sarny to mammy? What does he do to mammy?
10. When John confesses his guilt, what does Waller do to him? Does this deter John from teaching Sarny? Do you think their actions require a great deal of courage? What do you think you would do in this situation?
11. When John escapes again, does Sarny think he will return? If you were John what would you do?
12. What does Nightjohn use to teach the children reading in the pit school? Do you think this served another purpose besides teaching reading?

13. What qualities does Nightjohn have that make you admire him? What qualities does mammy have? And Sarny?
14. List some of the things that Waller did to make you dislike him. Do you think all plantation owners were as cruel as Waller was? Can you name some famous Americans who owned slaves?
15. Has this time of slavery in the United States had some lasting results that are still seen in America today? What can you do to help change this?

Projects

1. Research the history of slavery in the United States. Write an essay to record what you have learned.
2. Create a map of the United States as it was at the beginning of the Civil War, showing slave and free states. Display on each state the day it entered the Union.
3. Draw a picture of the slave quarters at mealtime.
4. Develop a picture book illustrating the average day in the life of a slave field hand.
5. John Brown was a leading abolitionist. What was an abolitionist? Find four other abolitionists, and create a poster depicting their contributions to the fight against slavery.

Vocabulary

Each of the following quotations chosen from *Nightjohn* includes one or more vocabulary words in **bold print**.

1. "I'm just quiet and they think because I don't make noise and go **twattering** all the time that I be dumb."
2. "When the day is coming on dark and we are all finished eating out of the **trough** in front of the quarters I get onto the **pallet**."
3. "Had a rope down and over to a **shackle** on Nightjohn's neck."
4. "I'm brown. Same as dark **sassafras** tea."
5. "He chuckled, low and **rippling**."
6. "During the day the young ones run and **scrabble** and fight or cry and they's always a **gaggle** of them."
7. "But I got slow and they got fast and some **crackers** caught me in the woods."
8. "But she was **addled** in the head, off dreaming sometimes, and mammy said one day that they would sell her."
9. "'Punishment according to the law, is the removal of an **extremity**.'"
10. ". . . be a good hell with fire and **brimstone**. . . ."

About the Author

Gary Paulsen, born in Minneapolis in 1939, has led a life as varied and exciting as the novels he writes. As well as being a writer of dynamic young adult fiction, he has been a teacher, field engineer, soldier, actor, farmer, rancher, trapper, migrant worker, and sailor to name some of his occupations. In addition, to well-researched historical fiction, he has written many adventure tales in which his protagonists are pitted against the forces of nature. Mr. Paulsen has an enthusiastic audience among children and young adult readers.

On My Honor
Author: Marion Dane Bauer
Publication date: 1986

Awards

Newbery Honor Book

Characters

Joel

Tony

Mr. and Mrs. Bates, Joel's parents

Mr. and Mrs. Zabrinsky, Tony's parents

Joel's brother, Bobby

Setting

Present day

Plot

Joel and Tony have been friends since they were babies, and Tony's mother was Joel's babysitter. At one point, Joel thinks, "When you were Tony, the outrageous seemed natural." Tony is always coming up with ideas for the two of them and often pokes fun at Joel, who is more cautious and whose parents often disapprove of the boys' plans. When Tony suggests that they bike to Starved Rock and climb the bluffs, Joel is reluctant and counts on his father to say no, as he has often done in the past. He feels shocked and betrayed when his father says that he can go. When Joel's father asks him to promise on his honor to go only where they plan and to be careful, Joel agrees, crosses his heart, and raises his right hand.

When they cross the bridge over the Vermillion River, Tony suggests that they swim in the river instead of going to Starved Rock. Joel's concerns about the pollution and dangerous currents, sink holes, and whirlpools in the river do not discourage Tony even though Joel finds out later that Tony cannot swim and is even afraid of the water. When Tony accuses Joel of being too scared to climb the bluffs, Joel challenges him to swim to a sandbar. When Joel reaches the sandbar, Tony is nowhere in sight. Joel goes back into the water but cannot find him; he enlists the help of a passerby, but he cannot find Tony either.

When he goes home, complicated emotions overwhelm Joel; he blames his father for letting him go, blames Tony for being a daredevil, and blames himself. He is also afraid of what his and Tony's parents and the police will say. Therefore, he doesn't tell anyone what happened until the police are called. Joel's father helps him sort through his emotions. Joel wants his father to punish him, but his father says Joel could learn nothing from a punishment. They all have to live with their choices.

Questions for Discussion

1. Describe the friendship that exists between Joel and Tony. What kinds of things do they enjoy together? Is there anything that causes tension between them?
2. What admirable qualities does Tony have? Does he have any qualities that you do not admire? Would you like to have him for a friend?
3. What admirable qualities does Joel have? Does he have any qualities that you do not admire? Would you like to have him for a friend?
4. Why is Joel angry with his father for letting him go on the bike ride to Starved Rock? Have you ever shared Joel's feelings?
5. What promise does Joel make to his father? What do you think the word *honor* means to both of them?
6. What efforts does Joel make to save Tony? Why can't he go back in the water when the boy is looking for Tony?
7. How does Joel behave when he gets home? Why is he mad at his brother? At Tony? Do you think he is behaving as he should?
8. Why doesn't he tell the truth immediately? Do you blame him for this?
9. After Joel tells the truth, he pounds his father's chest and tells him it is his father's fault. Why? Is this what Joel really believes?
10. Who do you think is responsible for this accident? Why?
11. What advice does Joel's father have that might make Joel come to terms with Tony's death? Do you think he makes Joel feel better? What would you have said to Joel if he were your friend or brother?
12. What is the significance of the river smell that Joel cannot get rid of?
13. Do you think Joel is an honorable boy?

Projects

1. Joel is concerned about swimming in the Vermillion River because of its whirlpools and currents. Write a brief report on whirlpools, sink holes, and currents in rivers. Why are they dangerous? If you can, find out if these phenomena exist in rivers close to you.
2. The boys set out to climb Starved Rock bluffs. What should a person know about equipment and safety before climbing a cliff or mountain? Put your information into a poster or a multimedia presentation.
3. Joel used his bicycle for fun and for delivering his newspapers. Look up information on bicycle maintenance and safety. Prepare an oral presentation outlining the basic techniques for keeping a bicycle running properly and for riding safely.
4. Joel's feelings after Tony's death are complicated. Writing about them in a journal might be a helpful way for Joel to sort out these feelings. Write three journal entries for Joel as he deals with the death of his friend.

Vocabulary

Each of the following quotations chosen from *On My Honor* includes one or more vocabulary words in **bold print**.

1. "His voice reminded Joel of the hovering **whine** of a mosquito."
2. "His father **surveyed** their bikes, frowning slightly."
3. "Joel watched his father drive away. He felt **betrayed**, trapped."
4. "As soon as the bike's **momentum** slowed enough that his legs could keep pace with the spinning wheels . . ."
5. ". . . Tony **mimicked**, his voice coming out high and girlish."
6. "Joel decided to ignore the **taunt**."
7. "Leaving Joel's Schwinn still perched **haphazardly** against the railing . . ."
8. "Joel watched Tony yelling and **flailing** his arms as he ran down the steep hill to the river."
9. "Tony's chest was **heaving**. He **gasped** for breath as if he had been swimming for miles."
10. ". . . **peering** back toward the riverbank . . ."
11. ". . . looking across the **deceptively** smooth surface of the river."
12. "The questions came at Joel in a barrage, leaving no space for answers. . . ."
13. "A shiver **convulsed** Joel. . . ."
14. ". . . his teeth chattering in **erratic** bursts . . ."
15. "Joel straightened up, freezing his features into what he hoped was an image of innocence, of **nonchalance**."
16. ". . . the wall of trees nearly **obscuring** the water."
17. "Looking tired and a little bit **frazzled** . . ."
18. "Joel shook his head, trying to **dispel** the red fog that had taken possession of his brain."
19. ". . . **teetering** on the edge of the porch."
20. "He wanted to push his father away, to **pummel** him again."

About the Author

Marion Dane Bauer grew up in a small town in Illinois and enjoyed writing even as a child. A former high school teacher and creative writing instructor, she began writing in earnest after her daughter started school. In her books she deals with traumatic events in the lives of young people and tries to show the importance of making good moral choices. She makes her home in Minnesota.

From the Author

"ON MY HONOR is the only one of my books to be based on something that really happened. The incident didn't happen to me, but to a friend of mine when we were both about thirteen. Only the surfaces of the story come from the real incident, however. Most of the story, the part that makes you feel as though it is happening to you, is written from inside Joel's thoughts and feelings, and of course, that is all imagined."

Out of the Dust
Author: Karen Hesse
Publication date: 1997

Awards
Newbery Medal
Publishers Weekly Best Book of the Year
School Library Journal Best Book of the Year
Booklist Editors' Choice

Characters
Billie Jo
Billie Jo's parents
Louise

Setting
1934-1935—Oklahoma

Plot
Billie Jo tells her story of growing up in the Oklahoma Dust Bowl in free-verse poems. Her father is a farmer trying to keep going against drought and dust. One joy that Billie and her mother have during the hard times is playing the piano.

When her mother picks up a pail of kerosene placed next to the stove by her father, a fire starts. Billie Joe throws the burning pail outside, and her mother runs into it. Trying to put out the flames, Billie Jo's hands are burned. Her mother and the baby she is carrying both die. It is physically and emotionally difficult for Billie Jo to play the piano, but she eventually enters a contest mostly to prove to herself that she can still play.

Billie Jo holds her father responsible for putting the kerosene near the stove. They find it difficult to communicate with each other and share their grief. Billie Jo says, "I don't know my father anymore." She leaves home but finds she does not feel better, just lonelier. On a train, she meets a man who has left his family because he cannot stand being unable to feed and care for them. Billie Jo realizes that her father has been able to stay at home even through his problems and grief. "My father was more like the sod. / Steady, silent, and deep." When she returns home, she calls her father "Daddy" for the first time since her mother died.

In case his farm fails, Billie Jo's father has been attending night school. There he meets Louise, who is his teacher. Billie Jo likes her and likes the way Louise makes her father happy. Louise and Billie Jo's father will marry, and Billie Jo is "waiting for the day when she stays for good." The book ends with Billie Jo at the piano.

Questions for Discussion
1. What kinds of things give Billie Jo pleasure during the hard times of the Dust Bowl? What does playing the piano mean to Billie Jo and her mother? How does it help the deal with the dust storms?
2. How does Billie Jo's mother stress the importance of school to her daughter?
3. Billie Jo says, "I look at Joe and know our future is drying up and blowing away with the dust." How important is it to know you have a future? What impact does this have on Billie Jo to think she does not have something to look forward to?
4. Do you hold anyone responsible for the accident that injured Billie Jo and her mother? Does Billie Jo blame anyone?
5. How does Billie Jo react to the piano soon after her mother's death? Do you understand this reaction?
6. How does Billie Jo show courage and strength in trying to play the piano again? What do you think of the way the losers act after the contest in which Billy Jo wins third prize?
7. How does Billie Jo's relationship with her father change after the accident? Why can't she forgive him?
8. How do Billie Jo and her father show they care about each other when she's out in the dust storm?
9. Why does Billie Jo leave home? What does she learn about herself and about home? What does she learn from the man on the train? Is he similar to or different from her father? How does her relationship with her father change when she returns home?
10. When Billie Jo returns home, the pond her father has been digging is finished. Why is this important to Billie Jo and her father?
11. Near the end of the book, Billie Jo says, "And I know now that all the time I was trying to get / out of the dust, / the fact is, / what I am, / I am because of the dust. / And what I am is good enough. / Even for me." What does she mean by this comment?
12. What kind of woman is Louise? What qualities does she have that make Billie Jo like her? Do you think Billie Jo is right in not letting Louise visit her mother's grave?
13. Do you think Billie Jo's father is a good parent? What qualities does he have that make him admirable?
14. What is Billie Jo thankful for? What do these things show about her character?
15. In her Newbery acceptance speech, Karen Hesse said, "It was about forgiveness. The whole book. Every relationship. Not only the relationships between people, but the relationship between the people and the land itself. It was all about forgiveness." Have you ever shared Billie Jo's difficulty in

granting forgiveness? Why is forgiveness important for both the person being forgiven and for the person granting the forgiveness?

Projects

1. Billie Jo's father thinks about applying for a loan from President Franklin Delano Roosevelt. Make a poster that shows the programs FDR started during the Depression. Find out if any local projects or buildings were part of these programs.
2. Billie Jo tells her story in free-verse poetry. Many of her poems, such as "On Stage," contain examples of similes, metaphors, and imagery. Select two poems that are especially meaningful to you, and, in a short essay, discuss the poetic devices used in them.
3. Select one poem that impresses you as particularly powerful. Create a multimedia presentation with the words of the poem and appropriate music and graphics.
4. Continue the story of Billie Jo by writing three or four poems of your own. Billie Jo's growing up, her piano playing, and her father's marriage to Louise are possible topics for your poems.
5. *Out of the Dust* is told from Billie Jo's point of view. Select one portion of the story, for example, the accident scene or Billie Jo's leaving and returning home, and tell this, in prose or poetry, from her father's point of view.
6. In two boxes in her closet Billie Jo keeps the important things of her life, from school papers to her baby teeth. Cover a shoe box, and place in the box several items that are particularly important to you. Describe their meaning to you on the inside cover of the box.

Vocabulary

Each of the following quotations chosen from *Out of the Dust* includes one or more vocabulary words in **bold print**.

1. "They pledged **revenge** on the rabbit population; / **wagering** who could kill more."
2. "She always gets **testy** about me playing, / even though she's the one who truly taught me."
3. "One quarter of the wheat is lost: / blown away or **withered** up."
4. "I **wince** at the sight of his rib-thin cattle."
5. ". . . in spite of the **drought**, / because of Ma's **stubborn** care, / these trees are / thick with blossoms. . . ."
6. ". . . and only if she didn't hear me **gripe** how I was tired . . ."
7. ". . . she cried for the water that / would not soothe her throat / and **quench** her thirst. . . ."
8. "My father, **hunched** over, said nothing."
9. "He doesn't stare at my **deformed** hands."
10. ". . . the frail stalks **revive**. . . ."
11. ". . . the family of **migrants** who have moved out from dust . . ."
12. ". . . all of them **crammed** inside that rusty old truck."
13. "I have practiced my best piece over and over / till my arms **throb**. . . ."

14. ". . . **assure** him that everything was all right . . ."
15. ". . . so you'd think it would have **smothered** the fire out. . . ."

About the Author

Karen Hesse was a teacher, librarian, secretary, and proofreader. John Hersey's book *Hiroshima*, which she read when she was about twelve, had a great effect on her because it dealt with real issues. Through her books, she hopes to show readers that they are not alone and that, like her characters, they can survive and grow because of difficult situations. Karen Hesse lives in Vermont.

From the Author

"In my research I discovered a poetry competition taking place in the Panhandle in the early 1930s. An advertisement in the newspaper from the period requested submissions of poetry from local residents. That is part of where the idea of doing the book as poetry began. I also wanted to convey to readers how spare Billie Jo's life was. How every word, every movement was considered. Nothing was wasted. These people didn't have the energy to go on and on. They were simply trying to survive. I thought this could best be expressed in paring down the words, and poetry felt like the natural form Billie Jo's voice would take."

Petey
Author: Ben Mikaelsen
Publication date: 1998

Awards
New York Public Library's One Hundred Titles for Reading and Sharing
ALA Best Books for Young Adults
Western Writers of America 1999 Award Winner

Characters
Petey Corbin
Calvin Anders
Trevor Ladd
Esteban Garcia
Joe
Cassie
Owen Marsh
Sissy Michael

Setting
1922-1990s—Montana

Plot
When Petey Corbin is born, his mother is told that he is deficient. For two years, his parents try to care for him at home, but medical bills wipe out all of their resources. They recognize the sacrifices their other two children are making, and they are drained from the physical care of the child, who suffers with seizures and shows no hope of improving. Therefore, they reluctantly decide to place Petey in the care of the state, and he is sent to the Warm Springs Insane Asylum.

Within the first three years of his residence at Warm Springs, Petey's physical condition deteriorates: his legs retract against his abdomen, his arms permanently bend at the elbows, his hands bend back, and his head tilts to one side. No one who cares for him realizes the thoughts within him that he cannot express; they only notice an occasional smile and interpret the smile as the reaction of an idiot. When he is eight years old, Esteban Garcia, a migrant worker, comes to work at the hospital. He begins to give Petey pieces of chocolate and teaches Petey to nod his head to indicate that he wants the candy. However, when a visitor to the hospital refers to the patients as freaks, Esteban leaves and does not return. When he is twelve, a new patient comes to the hospital. Nine-year-old Calvin Anders has club feet and is mildly retarded. As the only two children in a ward of adults, Calvin and Petey develop a bond. They learn to communicate with each other, Calvin asking simple questions and Petey gesturing and grunt-ing. Petey becomes attached to the mice that come to his bed and eat the crumbs from his sheets. Through his probing questions Calvin understands that Petey is pushing them away to save them from eating rat poison. When Calvin falls, Petey squeals and flails his arms until help comes. The two boys enjoy playing cowboys, and an aide gives them holsters and toy guns for Christmas. Another attendant, Cassie, suggests that Calvin assume responsibility for Petey, helping to feed him and communicating Petey's needs to the staff.

When Petey is in his forties, Owen Marsh, a retired man, comes to work at the hospital. He becomes fond of Petey and risks losing his job to have a wheel-chair rebuilt to accommodate Petey. He opens up the world of Petey and Calvin, taking them outside, to movies, to dances, to watch television. By the time Owen has to leave his work in the hospital, Petey is the most loved patient in the hospital because of his depth of feeling and his appreciation and delight in life.

Petey and Calvin are separated when the patients in the hospital are relocated to other facilities. Petey is moved to a nursing home in Bozeman, the city in which he was born. Petey does not want to make any close friends until young Trevor Ladd saves him from bullies who are pelting him with snowballs. He indicates to nurse Sissy Michaels that he wants to thank Trevor in person. She explains to Trevor that Petey was born with cerebral palsy that was misdiag-nosed, causing him to spend most of his life in an asylum. Trevor and Petey be-come friends. Trevor takes Petey for walks and even takes Petey fishing. When his wheelchair continually breaks, Trevor starts a fund drive to get Petey a new chair. They meet Owen on one of their walks, and Trevor searches until he finds Calvin and reunites the men. At the end of Petey's life, Trevor declares that he and Petey are grandfather and grandson, in spirit if not in lineage.

Questions for Discussion

1. Why do Petey's parents institutionalize him? Do you agree with what they did?

2. Why does Esteban fail to come to work after the incident in which the hos-pital visitors insult the children in Petey's ward? What does this tell you about Esteban?

3. What do you learn about Petey from his devotion to mice? What do these actions reveal about his emotional and intellectual capacity?

4. What special bond develops between Petey and Calvin? Why does Cassie put Calvin in charge of Petey?

5. Why do the bullies torment the defenseless Petey? How does Trevor handle the bullies? Do you think he handles them correctly?

6. What kind of boy is Trevor? Do you think he has an easy or a difficult life? What qualities does he have that you admire? Would you like him for a friend?

7. How are Trevor and Petey similar? What needs do they have in common? What do they gain from each other?

8. How do people react to Petey before they know him? Is this understandable or excusable? Are there people other than the handicapped who are treated this way? Have you ever met anyone and had this reaction?

9. Why do Trevor's parents feel as they do about Petey? How do you think they should feel about their son's friendship with Petey? Does Trevor deal with his parent's feelings in an appropriate and constructive way? What would you have done in Trevor's position?

10. Calvin tells Trevor that he and Petey are rocks, jewels that don't know how to shine. Do you agree?

11. Owen tells Petey and Calvin that he stopped coming to see them because it hurt not to be able to help them. Is this understandable? Should he have kept in touch? How is he a special part of Calvin and Petey's lives?

12. What qualities does Trevor display in getting a wheelchair for Petey? Do you admire his actions? In what other situations does he exhibit these qualities?

13. When Trevor tells Petey they will be grandson and grandfather, he says that family is in a person's heart forever. Why is this important for both of them? Have you ever felt about a friend as you do about family?

14. What are the messages of Petey's life? Why is he special?

15. Does the message of Petey's life have more impact because you know the character is based on a man who really lived?

Projects

1. Petey communicates through gestures, facial expressions, and sounds that carry meaning for him and his listeners. Find out what devices have been developed to help the handicapped communicate. Present your information in the form of a poster.

2. Petey is returned to the community in which he lived as a baby. Write a chapter for this novel in which Petey meets his brother or sister again.

3. Trevor sees Petey's need for a new wheelchair and puts a plan into action to get Petey a new chair. Contact your local agency that serves disabled persons, including those with cerebral palsy, and find out what needs might exist there, such as volunteers, recreational activities, or personal items. Develop a plan to fulfill these needs. Share your written plan with the agency, and, if it is approved, implement your plan.

4. Petey's cerebral palsy was misdiagnosed. Locate information on cerebral palsy, including causes, resulting disabilities, treatments, and life expectancy. Present your information in the form of a report.

5. Esteban Garcia, the first person to see what lies inside Petey, was a migrant worker. Research the life of migrant workers. What is their daily life like? How did the efforts of Cesar Chavez improve the life of migrant workers? Use this information to write a feature story for your local newspaper.

Vocabulary

Each of the following quotations chosen from *Petey* includes one or more vocabulary words in **bold print**.

1. ". . . as the Model T **careene**d over the track seconds ahead of the rushing locomotive."
2. "Then a sob broke through her **composur**e. . . ."
3. "**Pungent** smells of sagebrush and an occasional **whiff** of coal smoke from the locomotive drifted through the open windows."
4. "An examination table **dominated** one end."
5. "The sharp, **caustic** odor of cleaning fluid greeted newcomers rudely."
6. ". . . exposing a **gaudy** yellow undercoat that contrasted with the bright white uniforms . . ."
7. "Of those allowed in the play area, nearly half sat **morosely**, like **banished** souls."
8. "Esteban stared up at the **immense** man with a pleading look."
9. "Petey **skewed** his face into a frown. . . ."
10. ". . . they **converged** as a **horde** on the helpless sixty-pound boy."
11. "Mildly retarded, with severe club feet, Calvin **cowered** from everyone."
12. "Never taking no for an answer, he **badgered** every attendant or nurse who worked the ward."
13. "Petey's arms **pummeled** him, sending him tumbling to the floor."
14. "**Docile** patients staring out windows . . ."
15. "**Devouring** the fastest meal ever **consumed** on the ward . . ."
16. "Now the slow arrival of morning **taunted** him."
17. "How could such small **glitches** in a human body **wreak** such **havoc** on a life?"
18. "His depression locked him in a **lethargic apathy**. Owen wondered what key could ever open Calvin's closed world."
19. "Owen knew that **blatant** disobedience might cost him his job. . . ."
20. "A **blissful** smile **betrayed** his thoughts."
21. "Just touching the **gnarled** old lady's frail arm might break it."
22. "Trevor's thoughts raced as the three boys **sauntered** toward them."
23. ". . . he rolled from bed and **traipsed** downstairs."
24. "Calvin was so **engrossed** with dressing that he didn't notice Trevor return to the kitchen."

About the Author

Ben Mikaelsen has won numerous awards for his writings. He lives in Bozeman, Montana, with his wife and a black bear they have had for thirteen years. He knew the real-life Petey, Clyde Cothern, who became his "grandfather."

From the Author

"*Petey* was more than a story. This was a real-life person who captivated me and became one of my best real-life friends. He has changed me in ways that have left me forever indebted."

The Pigman
Author: Paul Zindel
Publication date: 1968

Awards

Horn Book/Boston Globe Award

Children's Book of the Year, Child Study Association of America

Characters

Angelo Pignati

John Conlon

Lorraine Jensen

Mr. and Mrs. Conlon, John's parents

Mrs. Jensen, Lorraine's mother

Dennis Kobin

Norton Kelly

Setting

Present day—Staten Island, New York

Plot

Written in alternate chapters by John and Lorraine, *The Pigman* is the story of their experiences with Angelo Pignati. John and Lorraine are high school sophomores who form a friendship based on their acceptance of each other's uniqueness. Neither John nor Lorraine is happy at home. Lorraine's mother, who was deserted by her husband, works as a private duty nurse. She spends much of her time complaining about her lot in life and harping on Lorraine about her behavior and boys. John feels that his parents have lost interest in raising a child and have no understanding of his wants and needs. He and his father have a definite adversarial relationship.

Like many teenagers with too much time on their hands, Lorraine and John, with their friends Dennis and Norton, are given to practical jokes. One is to make phone calls to randomly selected people to see how long they can keep them on the line. In calling Mr. Pignati, they solicit a donation for a phony charity and the next day go to his home to collect the money. Though Lorraine is against the idea, John wants the money to buy beer and finally convinces Lorraine to accompany him.

Mr. Pignati is a big man in his late fifties who greets them warmly. He is so happy to see them that his eyes and mouth are alive with a twinkle and a huge smile. On their first visit, Mr. Pignati, thinking they are adults, offers John and

Lorraine some homemade wine. He tells them that he goes to the zoo every day, usually accompanied by his wife, but she is presently in California. On the same day, he proudly shows them his wife's collection of pigs.

The next day John and Lorraine cut school to meet Mr. Pignati at the zoo, where he introduces them to Bobo, a baboon. Mr. Pignati favors Bobo above all the creatures in the zoo. A friendship among the three lonely people develops with Mr. Pignati buying them gifts and special foods. John and Lorraine, feeling some guilt, admit to Mr. Pignati that they are high school students and not working people. In turn, Mr. Pignati tells them that he has lied about his wife being in California; she is really dead.

After a vigorous game on the roller skates Mr. Pignati bought for them, he has a heart attack. While he is recovering in the hospital, John and Lorraine have the run of his house. Just before he is supposed to come home, the two decide to have a party. As with most unchaperoned teenage parties, things get out of hand. When Norton arrives, he starts to steal things and then destroys Mrs. Pignati's pig collection. In the midst of the chaos, Mr. Pignati arrives home and calls the police. Though devastated by their disloyalty, Mr. Pignati agrees to meet them at the zoo the next day. When they reach Bobo's cage, it is empty, and the attendant tells them that Bobo has died. With a cry Mr. Pignati falls to the ground dead. John and Lorraine are left with their guilt and remorse.

Questions for Discussion

1. Lorraine, in speaking of John's behavior, states that an ugly boy would have been sent to reform school by now. Do you agree with her that looks play a part in how behavior is judged? Do you think this is true in the classroom as well?

2. John is a sophomore in high school who both drinks and smokes. What do you think of these practices? Do you think many people at that age drink and smoke? What do you think are the reasons for these practices?

3. In explaining the difference between John and herself, Lorraine says that she has compassion because she is a girl and he does not because he is a boy. Do you agree with this conclusion? Why do you think boys are judged to have little or no compassion?

4. Lorraine's mother criticizes her daughter's appearance frequently. How do you think this affects Lorraine's self-esteem? What do you think Lorraine could have done to improve this situation? Do you sometimes feel that your parents are too critical of your appearance and behavior? Have you ever tried to discuss this with them?

5. Why does Lorraine think John drinks? Do you agree with her? Why do you think he drinks?

6. John states that he and his father have been having a lot of trouble communicating. Is it common for young people to find it hard to make adults understand their values, purposes, and behaviors? Do you think John's case is more exaggerated than most families? Why do you think John is so rude

when speaking of and to his parents? What do you think his parents could have done to help the situation?

7. John and Lorraine play phone games. Why is this an unacceptable practice? Can you think of some bad outcomes that might result from such pranks?

8. What happens when John and Lorraine go to Mr. Pignati's house? What is your impression of the man? How do you feel about John and Lorraine taking money from Mr. Pignati? What do you think of John's rationalization for cashing the check? Is Lorraine any more ethical about the money?

9. Mrs. Jensen removes food and other groceries from her clients' homes. What did you think of this behavior? Is she a good example for Lorraine?

10. How does John describe Norton? What does Norton want from John when he invites him to the cemetery? Is he the kind of person whom anyone should have for a friend?

11. Why does John call his parents "Bore" and "Old Lady"? How does he compare their attitude toward him with Mr. Pignati's? How does John feel about Mr. Pignati?

12. How do John and Lorraine react to Mr. Pignati's heart attack? Despite their feelings, what do they decide to do? Why is Mr. Pignati so upset by their actions and the result of the party? How would you feel if someone betrayed your friendship?

13. What do John and Lorraine feel when Mr. Pignati dies at the zoo? Do you agree that they are partially responsible for his death? What could they have done differently in their friendship with him?

14. What do they learn from this experience? Do you think they will be better people for having known the "Pigman"?

15. What are the qualities that you admire in the "Pigman"? What are the qualities in John and Lorraine that you admire or dislike?

Projects

1. Mr. Conlon works on the Coffee Exchange. Research what that is, its purpose, and its importance. Write a report of your findings.

2. Locate agencies in your community that concern themselves with the problem of teen drinking. Make a list of their locations and phone numbers for distribution to the class. In addition, contact them to request any free literature they may have on the subject, and make it available to interested classmates.

3. Do the assignment that Lorraine and John had to do for their "Problems in American Democracy" class.

4. The United States is an aging society. Research some physical problems that affect people as they get older, and design an aid to assist with this problem. Make a poster of your design illustrating its use.

Vocabulary

Each of the following quotations chosen from *The Pigman* includes one or more vocabulary words in **bold print**.

1. "I could curse only if it's **excruciatingly** necessary by going like this @#$%."
2. "If it's going to be a disgusting curse, I'll just put a three in front of it—like 3@#$%—and then you know it's the **raunchiest** curse you can think of."
3. "I should never have let John write the first chapter because he always has to twist things **subliminally**."
4. ". . . and I'm not about to have a **thrombosis**."
5. "And, you'll soon find out that John **distorts**."
6. "I think his father was a **compulsive** alcoholic."
7. ". . . at an age when John was **impressionable**."
8. "They call that **paranoia**."
9. "He **prevaricates** just for **prevaricating's** sake."
10. "It's a kind of **subconscious, schizophrenic** fibbing. . . ."
11. ". . . she'd need three years of **intensive psychoanalysis**.
12. " 'Be yourself. Be **individualistic**!' he called after me."
13. " 'Enjoy yourself, enjoy doing something absolutely **absurd**.' "
14. "She's what **psychologists** call **fixated** on the subject."
15. ". . . and couldn't devote her full energies to **interrogating**."
16. "If I didn't know how **maladjusted** John is at times."
17. ". . . and her voice had switched from **hysterical** to commanding. . . ."
18. ". . . the one Helen Kazinski had **demolished**."
19. "It was **pathetic**, that's what it was."
20. "Then came the tigers and bears, the two hippos who were inside for the season, and the eight-ton bull elephant, the only part of which we could see being the long trunk **protruding** from the doorway of his barn."

About the Author

If not the creator of the genre Paul Zindel is definitely a pioneer in the writing of realistic fiction for young adults. Born and educated on Staten Island, New York, Mr. Zindel spent ten years as a chemistry teacher there before becoming a full-time writer. In addition to the awards received for his novels, Mr. Zindel is the recipient of the Pulitzer Prize for his play, *The Effect of Gamma Rays on Man-in-the-Moon Marigolds*. Though often criticized for his harsh treatment of adults in his novels, children always enthusiastically receive his writing.

Pudd'nhead Wilson
Author: Mark Twain
Publication date: 1894

Characters
David "Pudd'nhead" Wilson
Roxy
Thomas à Becket Driscoll
Valet de Chambre, known as Chambers
Judge Driscoll
   Mr. and Mrs. Percy Driscoll
Luigi and Angelo Capello

Setting
Nineteenth century—Dawson's Landing, Missouri

Plot
Although he was trained as a lawyer, for most of his years in Dawson's Landing, David Wilson will never try a case. Remarks made on his first day in town and his inclination to explore every new fad he discovers contribute to the town's labeling him a fool, a "pudd'nhead." One of his hobbies is to collect the fingerprints of everyone in the town; he keeps these on meticulously labeled glass strips.

The Driscoll family, led by Judge Driscoll and his younger brother, Percy, is a prominent one in Dawson's Landing. Roxy, just one-sixteenth black, is a slave belonging to Percy and his wife. Both she and Mrs. Driscoll bear sons on the same day, Chambers to Roxy and Thomas to Mrs. Driscoll, who dies within a week of her son's birth. Roxy cares for both children and is the only person, including her master, who can tell them apart. Roxy becomes frightened when Driscoll threatens to sell his slaves down the river for stealing from him. This threat is a dire one, since to be sold down the river means being sold deeper into slave territory, a virtual hell on earth. Roxy is terrified at what could happen to her and her innocent son, who has the misfortune to be one-thirty-second black. She switches the children, and no one is the wiser.

Roxy's own son, who grows up as Tom, is obnoxious and spoiled, while the boy who grows up as Chambers is humble and kind. All the while they are growing up, Chambers protects Tom and endures his physical and mental punishment. Through the years, Tom treats Roxy only as his slave; any affection she displays for her real son is rejected. She vacillates between anger at his treatment of her and elation at his rare kindness. When Percy Driscoll dies, Roxy, who is thirty-five years old, is set free, and Judge Driscoll buys Chambers to save him from being sold down the river as Tom has threatened.

Roxy spends eight years as a chambermaid on a steamboat, but the bank loses the money she has saved, and she returns to Dawson's Landing hoping that her son's temperament has changed and that he will help support her. When Tom refuses, Roxy threatens to go to his uncle and tell him what she knows about Tom. Tom thinks she knows about his gambling debts; she tells him that he is her son. For a while, Tom is more humble, but before long he reverts to his usual arrogant ways. Furthermore, he is disguising himself as a girl and stealing from the homes in Dawson's Landing to support his gambling. When his plunder is stolen and Tom is especially desperate, Roxy volunteers to be sold into slavery to help him pay his debts. He sells her down the river. She escapes from a cruel overseer and demands that Tom ask his uncle for the money to buy her freedom.

Instead, Tom robs his uncle and in the course of the robbery stabs and kills the elderly man. Charged with the murder is Luigi Capello, who with his identical twin has come to town and become Tom's foe. Pudd'nhead defends Luigi. When Tom leaves his fingerprint on a glass strip, Pudd'nhead recognizes it as the identical print to the one left on the murder weapon. He also discovers that, between their seventh and eighth months, the fingerprints of Tom and Chambers were switched. The man brought up as Tom is sold down the river; the real Tom is free but unable to read, write, and function comfortably as a member of white society.

Questions for Discussion
1. Why do the people of Dawson's Landing label David Wilson as a fool? Do you think this is fair? Have you known people who have been unfairly labeled? What did you do about this? How do the people of Dawson's Landing change their opinion of Wilson?
2. Describe Roxy's personality and appearance. How does she act differently when she is with blacks and whites?
3. How does Driscoll treat his slaves? How does Twain describe the difference between Dawson's treatment of whites and blacks? What does Driscoll do when he believes a slave has stolen from him? Why do the slaves steal? What is Twain's attitude toward this stealing? Do you think it is right for them to steal?
4. Describe Roxy's feelings when the other slaves are almost sold down the river. How does this lead to her switching of the babies? How does she justify this switch? Do you support or criticize her action? Why?
5. What kind of boy is Tom? Do you think the adults in his life contribute to the way he behaves? Do other children like him? What kind of adult does he become?
6. What kind of boy is Chambers? How does he differ from Tom? Which boy would you rather have for a friend?

7. Describe the relationship between Tom and Chambers. How does Tom treat Chambers? What happens when Chambers saves Tom from drowning? Do you admire the way Tom treats Chambers?

8. Describe the relationship between Roxy and Tom. What is her attitude toward him? How does Tom treat Roxy? How does she feel about this treatment?

9. What kind of relationship does Roxy hope for with Tom when she returns to Dawson's Landing? Why does she tell him the truth? How does she bluff Tom? How does he change when Roxy tells him she is his mother? How does he have a better understanding of the slaves? Is the change permanent?

10. Why does Roxy volunteer to be sold back into slavery? How does Tom betray her?

11. Is justice served at the end of this novel? Explain the reasons for your opinion.

12. By using the literary device of foreshadowing, an author creates situations that prepare the reader for events to come. What events in this book foreshadow the conclusion of the story?

13. Dramatic irony is a literary device by which the reader has more information about the events of the story than do the characters. What are some examples of dramatic irony in this novel?

Projects

1. Twain describes Dawson's Landing as "a slaveholding town." Locate information on slavery, focusing either on the history of slavery in this country, the daily life of a slave, or a notable person of the antislavery movement, such as Nat Turner, Sojourner Truth, or Harriet Tubman. Compile your information into an essay.

2. Each chapter begins with at least one selection from *Pudd'nhead Wilson's Calendar*. Select a saying that you find to be especially meaningful, and write an essay of illustration giving specific examples of the truth of this saying.

3. Dawson's Landing is on the banks of the Mississippi River, which flows through nine climate zones. Draw a map of the Mississippi River including the rivers that flow into it and the major cities along its banks.

4. Pudd'nhead solves the murder of the judge and unravels the switching of Tom and Chambers through fingerprints. Locate information on the most common patterns of fingerprints. Using an ink pad and paper, collect fingerprints from ten people, and write brief descriptions of these to illustrate their unique nature.

5. When he discovers he is a free white man, the real Tom can neither read nor write and is uncomfortable in white society. Write another chapter to this novel continuing the story of the real Tom. What happens to him? How does he survive?

Vocabulary

Each of the following quotations chosen from *Pudd'nhead Wilson* includes one or more vocabulary words in **bold print**.

1. ". . . **opulently** stocked with hollyhocks, marigolds . . ."
2. ". . . his **fads** added to his reputation as a puddn'head. . . ."
3. "She was of **majestic** form and **stature**, her attitudes were **imposing** and **statuesque**. . . ."
4. ". . . they would go to church and shout and pray the loudest and sincerest with their **plunder** in their pockets."
5. "She gathered her baby to her bosom now, and began to **smother** it with **caresses**."
6. "She seemed in a **trance**. . . ."
7. ". . . and she went home **jubilant**, and dropped all concern about the matter **permanently** out of her mind."
8. "He was **indulged** in all his **caprices**, howsoever troublesome and **exasperating** they might be. . . ."
9. ". . . his **exposure** to the world as an **imposter** and a slave . . ."
10. "His estates were **confiscated**. . . ."
11. ". . . and then he **resolved** to **meddle** no more. . . ."
12. "One or two very important features of it were **altered**. . . ."
13. ". . . they felt sorrier for the **affront** put upon him by his guest's outburst of ill manners. . . ."
14. ". . . he **swerved** from it by so much as half a point of the compass. . . ."
15. ". . . he walked up and down the room, still grieving and **lamenting**."
16. "It made him **wince**. . . ."
17. ". . . he melted into the **throng** of people. . . ."
18. "A flash of lightening exposed Tom's **pallid** face. . . ."
19. ". . . for with all his tireless **diligence** he had discovered no sign or trace of the missing confederate."
20. ". . . he was comfortable once more, even **jubilant**."

About the Author

Mark Twain was born Samuel Langhorne Clemens in 1835 in Missouri. He grew up in Hannibal, on the banks of the Mississippi, a locale that he made famous in his writings. He worked as a journeyman printer, a steamboat river pilot, and a lecturer. By the time he became famous with the publication of *The Celebrated Jumping Frog of Calaveras County* in 1865, he had already adopted the pen name of Mark Twain, the term used by rivermen to denote safe water. Among his most popular works are *The Adventures of Tom Sawyer* and *The Adventures of Huckleberry Finn*, the latter considered to be a classic of American literature.

Save Queen of Sheba
Author: Louise Moeri
Publication date: 1981

Characters
King David
Queen of Sheba

Setting
Mid 1800s—Oregon Trail

Plot

Twelve-year-old King David and his six-year-old sister Queen of Sheba left St. Louis and are traveling with their parents in a wagon train to the west over the Oregon Trail. King David is walking ahead of a small group of seven wagons along with Mr. Skinner, the guide, when Sioux Indians attack. For a time, King David thinks he is the only survivor of the attack; then he finds his sister. His feelings of loneliness, with no one to turn to for help, are mixed with his sense of responsibility for Queen of Sheba. He can only hope that their parents, traveling in a group of fourteen wagons a short distance behind them, have survived and made a run for Fort Laramie. He is sure that they cannot come back to find him and his sister, so it is up to King David to find them. Among the devastation, King David finds a quilt, a box of matches, a knife, two coats, a tin pan, two canteens with some water in each, a small sack of cornmeal, some apples, a little piece of bacon, and a rifle with a box of caps and a pouch of bullets. These are all the provisions he can find for their journey. Luckily, he also finds one of the horses from the wagon train.

King David has not escaped unscathed from the attack. As a result of the Sioux attempt to scalp him, he has a jagged flap of skin on his head. This wound weakens him, and when the wound becomes infected, King David lances it with his knife. Furthermore, the willful and complaining Queen of Sheba complicates their chances of survival, but King David reminds himself that she is little and continually encourages her to eat and lets her ride on the horse.

King David relies on the knowledge of tracking that his father had taught him. When Queen of Sheba wanders off, he follows her tracks and finds her beside a pool of water cradling a piece of wood that she tells him is her doll. King David is horrified when she later attacks this doll with a stick and wants to scalp it in imitation of the Indians. King David believes he is making progress in following the tracks of the wagon train when Queen of Sheba disappears again. He backtracks, is unable to find her, and gives up the search. Later, overwhelmed with guilt and struggling to think of how he could ever make his parents understand why he had left her, King David remembers that Queen of

Sheba loves to play in the water. He begins to search for green vegetation. He then finds the water he so desperately needs and Queen of Sheba playing in the mud with an Indian boy. Before he can reach his sister, an Indian woman grabs her. As King David aims his rifle at the woman, she places her knife at Queen of Sheba's throat. He then turns his rifle to bring the boy into sight. Although the frightened Queen of Sheba tells him to shoot the Indians, King David thinks of what his father would do and lowers the rifle. The woman releases his sister.

They find the wagon trail again but have no provisions left. When King David shoots and kills a rabbit, the horse runs away. It stops at the top of a hill and whinnies, a signal that it has seen other horses. King David warns his sister that they might have to face more Indians, but three men ride over the hill, and one of them is their father.

Questions for Discussion

1. King David first thinks he is the only one alive. When he finds his sister, he asks himself for the first time if he is better off or not to have found Queen of Sheba. Why does he feel this way? Do you understand his feelings or are you critical of him for feeling this way?

2. Do you think King David acts clearly to plan for their survival? Is there anything else he could have done?

3. What kind of child is Queen of Sheba? Is her behavior understandable? How does King David treat her? Would you have acted differently toward her?

4. Queen of Sheba is not always an easy child to handle. What are some of the ways King David deals with her temper and obstinacy? Are there any ways in which her brother could have dealt with her more effectively?

5. How do thoughts of his parents inspire King David to fight for survival? How do they influence his actions throughout the novel?

6. When Queen of Sheba finds a piece of wood that resembles a baby, she first nurtures it, then attacks it. How do you explain her actions? How does her brother react to what she does?

7. Why does King David quit looking for Queen of Sheba? Explain the feelings of guilt he has after quitting. What would you have done in his situation? Why does he finally search for her again?

8. What does King David know about the Indians? Does he understand the feelings of the Indians whose land they are crossing?

9. Why does King David decide not to shoot the Indian woman? How do you feel about this decision?

10. Is King David the kind of boy you would like to have for a friend? What qualities would make him a good friend? Is there anything you do not admire about him?

Projects

1. The Oregon Trail was at the peak of its use as a road to the west in the 1840s and 1850s. Draw a map that includes the Oregon Trail and other trails that led to the west.

2. King David lances his wound because he does not have the poultices and hot water his mother would have used. Locate information on healing with natural means, including herbs and plants. Present these on a poster or in a multimedia presentation.
3. Select a wilderness environment, such as a desert in hot weather or the Arctic in the winter. Locate information on survival in this climate. Present your information on a poster.
4. King David has learned to track from his father. Locate information on tracking animals. Write a report on the essential elements of this skill.
5. King David mentions several Indian tribes, including the Sioux, the Blackfeet, the Cheyenne, the Arapaho, the Pawnee, and the Crow. Locate information on one of these tribes, including where they lived, their houses, their food, their customs, and their leaders. Pretend you are a reporter from the east who comes upon this tribe. Write a feature story for your paper about this tribe.

Vocabulary

Each of the following quotations chosen from *Save Queen of Sheba* includes one or more vocabulary words in **bold print**.

1. ". . . the **iridescent** wings flick, the big **bulbous** eyes."
2. ". . . still held in the **clenched** hand of a dead woman."
3. "He stared at Queen of Sheba, sitting dumpy and **defiant** with the plate of cornmeal untouched."
4. "The sun was very low and shadows were filling the hollows of the **desolate** sand hills."
5. ". . . the shallow gully that **meandered** northwards . . ."
6. ". . . the utter **desolation** of the overturned wagons . . ."
7. ". . . he **roused** himself and crept to the edge of the water."
8. "The bay mare was **tethered** downstream about thirty feet from where they lay. . . ."
9. "Queen of Sheba **devoured** her portion and picked the bones clean."
10. ". . . he had buried the bones of the rabbit so as to keep any wandering coyotes or wolves from smelling them and **venturing** too near the camp."
11. "He grabbed his sister and lifted her with one **convulsive surge** of energy. . . ."
12. "King David was surprised and pleased at his own **ingenuity** in **devising** a plan of such bloodless cruelty."
13. "For such a little girl she could **emit** an unbelievable volume of sound."
14. "King David was glad Pa had taught him a good deal about handling **fractious** horses."
15. ". . . she ate **ravenously** all the grass he could gather. . . ."
16. "Her shoes, he noted, were beginning to show heavy wear from the stony ground and **abrasive** sand. . . ."
17. "It was a spring, **replenished** and running from the recent rainstorms."
18. "He placed the shoes inside his shirt, like a **talisman**. . . ."

About the Author

Louise Moeri was born in Oregon, grew up during the Depression, and attended a one-room schoolhouse where she learned to read and write poetry. She received a degree from the University of California at Berkeley and worked for eighteen years as a librarian. She wrote all her life but it took her time to realize that she was best suited to write children's books. Although she would not characterize her life as exciting, she believes that the pleasures and pains of her ordinary existence have enabled her to expand her mind.

From the Author

"My grandfather drove a team and wagon the length of the Oregon Trail to the Wilamette Valley when he was twelve years old. His father expected nothing less of him. Our pioneers were sturdy people; it is my hope that my book, SAVE QUEEN OF SHEBA, reflects that courage and strength. Can we find that courage in ourselves today? I hope so. We need it."

The Séance
Author: Joan Lowery Nixon
Publication date: 1980

Awards

Edgar Allan Poe Award for Best Juvenile Novel

Characters

Lauren
Sara Martin
Aunt Melvamay
Roberta Campion
Sheriff Norvell
Ila Hughes
Carley Hughes

Setting

Present day—East Texas

Plot

Lauren, an orphan who lives with her mother's Aunt Melvamay, tells her own story. She is not happy when Sara Martin is placed in their home as a foster child. Although Aunt Mel thinks the two seventeen-year-olds should get along, they have little in common. Lauren watches Sara sneak home at night when Aunt Mel does not know she has left the house. Lauren is jealous of Sara's popularity with boys and her good looks and envies the relationship Sara says she enjoyed with her mother.

Sara and Lauren's friends convince Lauren to go to a séance at the home of another student, Roberta Campion. Lauren goes reluctantly. During the séance, Sara begins to shake, screams in terror, and falls on the candle, extinguishing it. When the lights are turned on, Sara is gone. Her body is later discovered by a hunter in the Thicket, a dense and swampy area.

When she learns that Sara in fact has a mother who had made the girl a ward of the court because she was uncontrollable, Lauren realizes that she never knew Sara. Sara had told her, however, that she was intending to feign an attack at the séance so she could slip out the door, meet someone, and leave town. Lauren had helped her in this plan by locking the door behind her. Because of this, Lauren is determined to find out whom Sara was meeting and who was responsible for her death.

To solve the crime, the sheriff asks that the girls re-create their séance, but Roberta never shows up. Two days later, her body is found in the Thicket. Several of the girls begin to get threatening phone calls. Lauren especially believes her life is in danger.

Ila Hughes, one of the women from the town and the grandmother of Carley Hughes, gives Lauren the impression that she is supportive of the girls. However, when Lauren visits Mrs. Hughes, the woman is very interested in what happened at the séance and says that the girls had unleashed evil forces on that night. Lauren is also taken aback by the bird skulls Mrs. Hughes has gathered from the Thicket and placed on her mantel and the cat that she has buried in her fireplace. Carley admits to Lauren that he was the one meeting Sara. In the end, Mrs. Hughes admits that she killed the girl so she could not go away with Carley and killed Roberta because she believed that she was helping Sara and was going to put a spell on Carley.

Questions for Discussion

1. Why is Lauren jealous of Sara? Do you think her reaction to the newcomer in her house is understandable? Have you ever shared the feelings Lauren experienced?
2. Why is Roberta not accepted in the school? Do you know of any situations like this that have occurred in your school? How do you feel about this? How can you change these occurrences?
3. Why does Lauren say that there are two Saras? How does she come to know Sara better?
4. Why does Sara tell stories about her past? Do you understand why she did this? How does this make you feel about Sara?
5. Why does Lauren go to the séance? Would you have reacted as Lauren did?
6. Is the trust between Lauren and her friends and between Lauren and Aunt Mel damaged by what happened? How important is trust between friends and between a teenager and an adult?
7. Do you think that the girls and Aunt Mel are all correct to feel guilty about what happened to Sara? Have you ever felt guilty about something you were involved in? How did you deal with your guilt?
8. How does Lauren's relationship with Aunt Mel change as the story progresses? Do you think the change is for the better?
9. Do you think that Lauren acted correctly in telling her part in Sara's disappearance? How would you have reacted if you were in Lauren's place?
10. Through the literary technique of foreshadowing, the author gives clues to the reader about what will happen in the story. Does Joan Lowery Nixon use this technique to give you clues about the identity of the murderer?

Projects

1. The Thicket is a place with dense foliage and a variety of animal life, from rattlers to wild hogs. Find out what plants and animals are common to east Texas. Create a poster with this information and illustrations of the plant and animal life.
2. When Lauren hears an owl hooting after midnight, she is afraid that someone is going to die. Find and write about ten common superstitions.

3. Sara is a foster child. Contact your local social service agency, and find out how a family could become a foster family. What is the need for foster families in your community? Write an advertisement for the foster parent program.

Vocabulary

Each of the following quotations chosen from *The Séance* includes one or more vocabulary words in **bold print**.

1. "I'm **gaunt**, and gauntness runs in our family."
2. "I **burrowed** my head into my goose-down pillow. . . ."
3. ". . . its seal **embedded** over the door . . ."
4. ". . . she seemed so small and plain and **nondescript**. . . ."
5. "I set out for the séance with a **queasy** feeling in the pit of my stomach."
6. "I crawled across the floor, getting my fingers stepped on, and **groped** for the candle. . . ."
7. ". . . while he **straddled** a hard-backed chair from the kitchen . . ."
8. "The knuckles were **distended** like punctuation marks along his fingers."
9. "Her lips turned up in a **tremulous** smile."
10. "She looked at me with the **antagonism** she'd show if I were accused of stealing a first grader's milk money. . . ."
11. "With the heel of one shoe she ground out her cigarette butt viciously, **pulverizing** it into the wooden step."
12. ". . . with the **persistence** of a **pesky** bottlefly."
13. "She was so **indignant** I could hear her voice vibrating from across the room."
14. ". . . a meat **concoction** that was anyone's guess."

About the Author

Joan Lowery Nixon was born in Los Angeles and received a bachelor's degree from the University of Southern California. She was an elementary school teacher and taught creative writing. She credits her training in journalism with teaching her to concentrate on writing. Her ideas for plots come from her own experiences into which she weaves her own sense of right and wrong and her own philosophy. She most enjoys writing fiction for children because of the challenge it presents in writing for a wide range of ages and interests.

From the Author

"Sometimes the setting of a story becomes almost as important as the characters. To me the piney backwoods of East Texas with dark, mysterious swamps and hidden settlements—from which residents rarely emerge—was a strong influence on the plot of *The Séance* and on the fictional people who inhabited the story. The superstitions, the suspicions, and the scary beliefs of the main character and secondary characters made *The Séance* happen.

"I do a great deal of research when I'm writing a book because I respect my readers and want the stories I give them to be accurate in every way. So I was happy when soon after *The Séance* was published, a bookseller who had grown up in East Texas said to me, 'Everything in your story was so true. I didn't know you had lived in East Texas.' "

The Secret Garden
Author: Frances Hodgson Burnett
Publication date: 1911

Characters

    Mary Lennox
    Dickon Sowerby
    Archibald Craven
    Colin Craven
    Martha Sowerby
    Mrs. Susan Sowerby
    Mrs. Medlock
    Ben Weatherstaff

Setting

    Early twentieth century—England

Plot

Until the age of ten, Mary Lennox has been brought up in India with servants to wait on her every move but with no one to give her love and companionship. She has become a stubborn, mean-spirited child whose nickname "Mary Quite Contrary" fits her accurately. When cholera strikes India, her parents die, and she is sent to live in England with her uncle, Archibald Craven.

At Misselthwaite Manor, Craven's home, Mary still is virtually without companionship, except for the maid whose job it is to wait on her. This young Yorkshire girl, Martha, opens Mary's perspective as she cajoles Mary into such independent endeavors as dressing herself. Martha also chatters about her large family including her twelve-year-old brother, Dickon, who spends his time on the moor and can communicate with animals. When Martha returns to the manor from an overnight at home, she brings Mary a jump rope from her mother. For the first time in her life, Mary wants to thank another person for something.

After weeks at the manor, Mary has not yet met Archibald, but she has learned that his wife died ten years earlier. With his wife, Archibald had created a secret garden on their property, and when she died, the garden was locked and the key thrown away. Mary does determine the location of the garden and sees a bird perched atop a tree that she believes is within the garden. A gardener Ben Weatherstaff will neither confirm nor deny that she is correct, but does tell Mary about the robin she has seen, a bird that demonstrates near-human qualities. One day while jumping rope along the garden paths and watching the robin, she discovers a key in a mound of freshly turned-over earth. The very next day, while again talking to the robin, a gust of wind blows aside the tendrils of ivy and reveals the door to the secret garden. Mary is immediately captivated by the mystery and beauty of the garden, especially when she notices sprouts of plants poking through the spring soil. She shares the garden with Dickon, who begins helping her care for it.

Mary is discouraged from venturing outside her own rooms in the manor, but she occasionally hears a youthful voice crying. Determined to find out who is crying, Mary follows the sound and finds a wailing boy in bed. This is Colin Craven, the son of Archibald, a boy as ornery and peevish as Mary. His ill temper is compounded by his belief that he is going to develop a hump on his back and die. He is the terror of the manor, and all the servants are frightened not to do his bidding. Mary's determined nature matches his obstinacy, and she eventually shares with him the fact that she has been in the garden. When he sees the garden for himself, he is overwhelmed with optimism for his health and future. With the outdoors, his friends, and new attitude, Colin flourishes and begins to walk in the garden. A letter from Mrs. Susan Sowerby brings Archibald home from his travels to find his son thriving and well.

Questions for Discussion

1. What are the circumstances of Mary's childhood in India? What effect does this upbringing have on Mary's personality and behavior?

2. Mary tells Martha that she doesn't like herself. Do you like her? What are her good qualities? What qualities do you not admire? Would you like her for a friend? How does she change as the story progresses?

3. What effect does her association with the simple country maid, Martha, have on Mary? Would Martha be a person Mary would have chosen to be a friend? Have you ever made a friend of an unlikely person? What does this tell you about true friendship?

4. How is the robin integral to the unfolding of the plot of this novel? What characters in the novel have a special bond with the robin? Have you ever shared a special bond with an animal or a pet?

5. In what ways is Dickon a special boy? How is his friendship important to Mary? What does he do for Mary? For Colin? Would you like him for a friend?

6. Why does Archibald shut himself off from his son? How does this affect Colin?

7. What is Colin's life like before Mary introduces him to the secret garden? How does he behave? How does he treat servants? How does he feel about his father? How does he change as the story progresses?

8. Why do Colin and Mary get along? Do you think they are good for each other? Why? What are the similarities between the early childhoods of Mary and Colin?

9. Why does the garden become important in Mary's life? How does it become important for Colin? How important is it that the garden be secret?

10. Colin says that when he grows up he is going to make scientific discoveries about magic. What kind of magic does this story hold? What does Susan Sowerby say about magic?

11. The Sowerby family is poor and uneducated and certainly does not share in the social advantages of Mary or Colin. However, their spirit and wisdom are important to this story and the characters in it. How? What can you learn from the Sowerbys?
12. What are the themes of this novel?
13. What parallels do you see between the children and the garden?
14. *The Secret Garden*, considered a classic and a masterpiece, has endured since 1911. Why do you think it has achieved this stature? What are the timeless qualities of this novel?

Projects

1. The robin in this novel has special qualities. Find out about the habits and traits of birds, especially robins. Make a poster that illustrates these qualities.
2. The secret garden is a magical place. Reread the descriptions of the garden in the novel, and draw what you imagine the garden to look like.
3. Several flowers are mentioned in the novel, for example, delphinium, columbine, snapdragons, crocuses, roses, irises, lilies, campanulas, and poppies. Find out their Latin names, descriptions, conditions for cultivation, and care. Present this information in a booklet or a multimedia presentation.
4. Colin demonstrates the power of optimism and laughter for good health. Locate an article in a magazine or newspaper that discusses this connection between laughter and health. Summarize the article.
5. Dickon can communicate with animals. Locate information in a magazine on a real person, such as a horse whisperer, who has this ability. Write a brief biography about this person, emphasizing his or her work with animals.
6. The Sowerbys speak the Yorkshire dialect. Find out what dialects exist in this country. Compile a dictionary of phrases that are unique to certain parts of this country.

Vocabulary

Each of the following quotations chosen from *The Secret Garden* includes one or more vocabulary words in **bold print**.

1. "... by the time she was six years old she was as **tyrannical** and selfish a little pig as ever lived."
2. "... but she only **stammered** that the Ayah could not come...."
3. "... as long as she stayed with them they called her 'Mistress Mary Quite **Contrary**....'"
4. "He lives in a great, big, **desolate** old house in the country...."
5. "Mary sat in her corner of the railway carriage and looked plain and **fretful**."
6. "They were **obsequious** and **servile** and did not presume to talk to their masters as if they were their equals."
7. "... evidently not in the least aware that she was **impudent** ..."
8. "Martha looked **indignant**."

9. "The next day the rain poured down in **torrents** again. . . ."
10. ". . . and one of the things that made the place look strangest and loveliest was that climbing roses had run all over them and swung down long **tendrils** which made light swaying curtains. . . ."
11. ". . . when the grass and weeds had been **smothering** them."
12. "Mary looked at the fire and **pondered** a little."
13. "Dickon laughed so that he was obliged to **stifle** the sound by putting his arm over his mouth."
14. "She just grew sour and **obstinate** and did not care what happened."
15. ". . . he tried to **modify** his dialect so that Mary could better understand."
16. "Dr. Craven dreaded and **detested** the difficulties of these visits."
17. ". . . the lamb began to suck it with **ravenous** ecstasy."
18. ". . . he threw out his arms **exultantly**."

About the Author

Frances Hodgson Burnett was born in Manchester, England, in 1849 and moved to the United States with her family in 1865. Her first published writings were stories written for women's magazines, serialized novels, and adult novels. She began to publish children's novels in 1879, and her first major success in this genre was *Little Lord Fauntleroy*, which she also adapted for the stage. Her career as a children's writer flourished, but Burnett's marriage was not a happy one, and her teenage son died of tuberculosis. Her final years were spent on her estate on Long Island, where she enjoyed gardening. She died on Long Island in 1924.

Secrets at Hidden Valley
Author: Willo Davis Roberts
Publication date: 1997

Award

Edgar Allan Poe Nominee

Characters

Steffi Thomas
Audri Thomas, mother
Victor Tomaschek, grandfather
Bo and Casey Chapman, father and son
Kurt Vail
Chester and Burt Taylor, father and son
Helen Risku
Other residents of the Hidden Valley RV Park

Setting

Present day—Hidden Valley RV park, Michigan

Plot

When Steffi Thomas's father, a Hollywood stuntman, dies as a result of an accident, her mother must return to work, and Steffi is forced to go to her grandfather, a man she has never seen. Arriving at Hidden Valley RV Park, Steffi learns that her grandfather is not anticipating her arrival nor is he happy to see her. Unwelcome and suffering from homesickness, Steffi starts to learn about the residents of the park. She meets Casey Chapman, who lives here with his father, and Mrs. Risku, who hides each time a new camper comes to the park. A new camper, Kurt Vail, arrives the same day as Steffi, and something in his manner makes Steffi uneasy. From Casey, Steffi learns of the other park tenants, Chester Taylor and his son, Burt, the Montoni's, Oliver Mandell, and Elwood Grisham.

As Steffi becomes part of the life in the RV park, she is accepted by the others but rejected by Victor, her grandfather, who refuses to even call her by name. She soon learns that her father and Victor had long ago fallen out because Larry Thomas had become a stuntman and never gotten what Victor considered a decent job. She also learns that the Taylors are not to be trusted. Kurt Vail, the new camper, seems less intent on vacationing and more interested in finding out about the campers, worrying both Steffi and Mrs. Risku. It seems as if everyone in the RV park had something to hide.

When Victor is injured falling from a ladder, Steffi learns from the doctor that Victor had doted on her father and that they had been a very loving family. Steffi takes over the running of the park as well as the care of her grandfather and has little time to enjoy the pool that she and Casey had cleaned. Casey and Steffi begin to suspect that Mrs. Risku is right in her assumption that Kurt Vail is a detective. They start to investigate on their own and discover Vail's FBI credentials. Mrs. Risku is assured that he is not searching for her so that her daughter can put her in a nursing home. Casey admits to Steffi that he and his father are hiding from his mother, who has sole custody of him. Vail is after bigger fish; Chester Taylor is wanted for bank robbery. When a trap has been set for the Taylors, Chester grabs Steffi as a hostage. Victor, who attacks Chester with his crutch to prevent him from kidnapping his granddaughter, saves her. Victor, though not calling her by name, has finally acknowledged their relationship.

Questions for Discussion

1. How does Victor react to Steffi's unexpected arrival at the RV park? How would you feel in Steffi's place? Do you think she is right in being annoyed at her mother? Why do you think Victor will not acknowledge their relationship?

2. When Kurt Vail arrives at the park, Helen Risku hides and Vail makes Steffi uneasy. Do you think this is a foreshadowing of his importance to the story? Have you any idea who he might be?

3. What does Steffi find out about the Taylors when she is avoiding Vail? Is Chester Taylor someone whom you would like to know? Why?

4. When Casey and Steffi are cleaning the pool, the park residents stop by to watch. Do any of them offer to help? What does this tell you about them? Have you ever had this same experience when you were trying to accomplish a task?

5. What does Victor answer when Steffi asks why he hated her father? What did he think of her father's line of work? What did he want for his son? Do you agree with his disappointment at his son's choice? Is it common for parents and children to have different expectations for the future? Have you any ideas how the father and the son might have reached a mutual acceptance of each other?

6. Why do you think Buddy is a consolation to Steffi in her sorrow? Do you think animals can be a source of comfort? Why?

7. How does Steffi feel when Victor removes the box of photos that she found? Why does she feel pain that she is allowed no contact with family members? How do you think you would feel if you had little or no contact with members of your family? How can a family be a source of comfort and strength? What others can also be a source of comfort?

8. What does Steffi observe when Burt Taylor goes in the pool? What does Casey tell her about the bruises? Does this story make her consider the re-

lationship between her father and Victor? Why do you think these thoughts disturb her?

9. How do the campers react when Helen announces that Kurt Vail is a detective? How does Steffi feel about their reactions? Do you think she has a right to be concerned?

10. Both Mrs. Evans and Mrs. Risku are eager for company. Is it common for elderly people to be lonely? Why is that? Do you know anyone like them? What are some things you could do for that person?

11. When Victor is injured, Dr. Daniels comes to treat him. What does he tell Steffi about Victor's feelings for his son and the relationship between father and son? What do you think either of them might have done to improve the relationship?

12. What is Dr. Daniels' advice to Steffi about her grandfather? How does she feel about this advice?

13. Though Steffi was scared of Chester Taylor, she confronts him when he attempts to steal the carton of cigarettes. What does this tell you about Steffi? Is it okay to be scared of persons or situations but still face up to them?

14. Not only does Steffi take care of her injured grandfather, but she also takes over the management of the RV park. Does Victor show any gratitude? Why do you think he acts this way?

15. What happens when Chester Taylor takes Steffi as a hostage? Does this show the hidden softer side of Victor? Why do you think he never showed it before? What does he say that warms Steffi's heart?

Projects

1. Steffi cooks foods that are common in California but almost unheard of in Michigan. Select a section of the United States or a country of the world, and create an illustrated cookbook of recipes from that area.

2. Select either the fraternal or maternal side of your family and create a family tree for it. You may do this by talking to relatives or by investigating vitals records, such as birth, death, and marriage certificates.

3. Using the Internet or by contacting your local FBI office, research the Federal Bureau of Investigation from its founding to its present status. Write a report of your findings.

4. Elwood Grisham tells Steffi that a visit to Boston is like a walk through history. Select a city steeped in history, and write to the Chamber of Commerce requesting information about historical sites. With this information, develop an illustrated and annotated brochure of the historical sites in your selected city.

5. Imagine that you are a film or television stuntman, and write a story of your most dangerous or amusing stunt.

Vocabulary

Each of the following quotations chosen from *Secrets at Hidden Valley* includes one or more vocabulary words in **bold print**.

1. "It didn't look as if any of the **alternatives** Steffi had thought of were going to work."
2. ". . . she wished she had **fortified** herself with a bag of peanuts or a candy bar from the vending machine at the bus station."
3. "She waited until the snake disappeared into the weeds on the other side of the drive, then moved **cautiously** ahead."
4. "He sounded **incredulous** that she had come here."
5. "It was impossible to keep her **consternation** under control."
6. "At least the dog wasn't **antagonistic**."
7. ". . .she'd set an **elegant** table to showcase whatever they fixed."
8. "She was only beginning to **comprehend** what a **catastrophe** her arrival might be for her grandfather. . . ."
9. "It was **mortifying**, when Steffi thought about it."
10. "Maybe Helen's **paranoia** was catching."
11. ". . . she took one of the paths that **meandered** all around the area."
12. "**Instinctively**, she glanced toward the parking spaces."
13. ". . . in what seemed a **gruff** and **grudging** manner."
14. "He sat by her feet when she ate, although under her grandfather's **scrutiny** she didn't dare sneak him tidbits."
15. "Steffi was **confounded** by the expression on Casey's face."
16. "A **wariness**, a trace of **apprehension**?"
17. ". . . Buddy had **surreptitiously** hoisted himself up to rest his head on her feet."
18. "A person would have to be **demented**."
19. ". . . besides sit around reading the **decrepit** old Westerns. . . ."
20. "Oliver Mandell and Elwood Grisham lived **frugally** on small pensions."

About the Author

Now living in Washington State, Willo Davis Roberts grew up in Michigan, the setting for many of her novels. Though originally a writer of adult novels, the suggestion of her publisher that she change *The View from the Cherry Tree* to a young adult novel led her to writing primarily for children and young adults. Her novels have received recognition and awards from many sources, including the Edgar Award for Juvenile Fiction several times. Much of her time is spent in workshops helping aspiring writers.

From the Author

"*Secrets at Hidden Valley* was written after we met an eleven-year-old girl named Stephanie at an RV park in Florida. Her mother was the manager, but we never saw her or any other adult. Stephanie signed us in, took our money/credit cards, sold us goods out of the store, and appeared to be efficiently running the place by herself. I sensed a story and asked if she'd come down to our coach after supper and talk to me. I learned that she liked working in the office better than cleaning the swimming pool and my writer's 'what if' component clicked into gear.

"As a child, I lived briefly in a run-down trailer park, and I never got well enough acquainted with any of the inhabitants to find out if they had any mysteries in their lives. So imagination provided that. I often use real events and situations that can be enlivened by imagination, and also my own detailed recollections of being in that age group, helpless to affect my own destiny while uncaring adults swept me along whether I wanted to go or not. I think a lot of kids can identify with that."

Shiloh
Author: Phyllis Reynolds Naylor
Publication date: 1991

Awards
Newbery Medal

Characters
Marty Preston
Mother and father
Sisters, Becky and Dara Lynn
Judd Travers
Doc Murphy
David Howard

Setting
Present day—Friendly, West Virginia

Plot
Eleven-year-old Marty Preston finds a young beagle that belongs to Judd Travers, a man who mistreats his dogs. Made to return the dog by his father, Marty is assailed with the ethical question of which is the greater wrong, returning the dog to be abused or keeping him from his rightful owner. In his mind, Marty decides that if the dog turns up again he will keep it in secrecy. When the beagle shows up, Marty builds a pen in the woods. Besides not telling his family, he must also feed the dog without depriving his already hard-strapped family. His life becomes a tangle of lies to his family and friends.

Shiloh, the name given to the beagle by Marty, is hurt badly when a German shepherd attacks him in his pen. Treated by the local doctor, he is returned to the Prestons to heal. Judd discovers the dog's whereabouts and demands his property back.

On the day of Shiloh,s return, Marty catches Judd in the woods with a deer he has shot out of season. They reach a bargain: for Marty's silence and twenty hours of work, Shiloh belongs to Marty. After he has completed more than half the work, Judd threatens that Marty is working for naught since there were no witnesses to the agreement. In spite of this fact, Marty continues to fulfill his part of the bargain.

Judd grows to respect Marty, and Marty realizes that Judd's childhood of abuse has caused his cruelty. Marty knows how fortunate he is to be surrounded by family love.

The dog becomes Marty's.

Questions for Discussion

1. Why does Shiloh follow Marty home? What are the reasons that Marty does not like Judd Travers?
2. Why do you think Marty is first attracted to the dog, Shiloh? Would these qualities influence you to dislike him as well?
3. Marty and his father talk about Judd's treatment of his dogs, with the father saying it is none of their business. Do you agree with this position? Why?
4. Marty deals with the dilemma of being one hundred percent honest and carrying the dog back to Judd "so that one of God's creatures can be kicked and starved all over again" or not returning the dog. How would you resolve this problem?
5. " 'Funny thing how one lie leads to another and before you know it your whole life is a lie.' " Do you feel this statement is true? How is the statement illustrated in the book?
6. The Preston family finances are tight because they must share the expenses for their elderly grandmother. Do you know of anyone in your family or community with this same problem? How do they cope with the situation?
7. Marty feels better when he tells David about Shiloh. Why do you think this is so? Do you sometimes share your problems with a friend? Does it make you feel better?
8. What does Marty catch Judd doing? What deal does he strike with Judd? Do you think this was the right thing to do? What would you have done in this situation?
9. There is good and evil in everyone. How does Judd show his goodness? How does Marty demonstrate less than admirable qualities? Was there a cause for Judd's cruelty?
10. What does Marty learn from saving Shiloh from Judd Travers?

Projects

1. Contact the local Society for the Prevention of Cruelty to Animals to find what is being done in your community to protect animals from cruelty. Prepare an oral presentation of the facilities and regulations in your community to prevent animal abuse.
2. Select a breed of dog; find out its place of origin, the purpose of the breed, its evolution, and its care and feeding. Prepare an informational booklet presenting these facts.
3. If you have a pet at home, for one full week take over its complete care, including feeding, exercising, and training. Keep a daily log of all the activities involved.
4. Compare the life of eleven-year-old Marty living with his family in Friendly, West Virginia, with yours. Write a summary of all the similarities and differences, then tell which lifestyle you prefer and why.
5. After reading *Shiloh*, rewrite the ending, fashioning a solution that does not involve dishonesty.

6. View the video, *Shiloh,* after reading the book. In a written report compare and contrast the two. Decide which version made a greater impact upon you.

Vocabulary

Each of the following quotations chosen from *Shiloh* includes one or more vocabulary words in **bold print**.

1. "Dog goes down on his stomach **groveling** about in the grass."
2. "Mr. Wallace, he is so **frustrated** he just digs in the money drawer and gives Judd change for a twenty."
3. "Shiloh leaping almost shoulder high to lick my cheek **nuzzling**, my hands, my thighs."
4. " 'You got a **bargain**.' "
5. " 'The thing we got to worry about is **infection**.' "
6. "Seems as if the whole sky is **swirling** around above me. . . ."
7. " 'But I got him sewn back up and full of **antibiotics**.' "
8. ". . . but he's already **suspicious** about me. . . ."
9. "He's wearing this army **camouflage** shirt, a brown cap, and the weirdest grin that could fit on a human face."
10. "I blush then, 'cause my dad would die of **embarrassment**. . . ."

About the Author

As a writer for children, Naylor enjoys writing books about realistic problems and is truly happiest when she sees one of her characters come alive on paper. A family person, her husband and two sons often appear in her books, but the chief inspiration for *Shiloh* is an abandoned dog she saw on a trip to West Virginia. *Shiloh* has become a trilogy with the publication of *Shiloh Season* and *Saving Shiloh.*

From the Author

"I didn't even know I was going to write *Shiloh* until I found such a dog in West Virginia. And I had no intention of writing a sequel, much less two. But I was disturbed by the rage that children expressed toward Judd Travers in their letters to me, and I did not want to leave them with all that anger without some understanding of what made Judd the way he was. The first book, *Shiloh,* explores the gray area between right and wrong; the second book, *Shiloh Season,* is about redemption, in the social/moral sense; and the third, *Saving Shiloh,* deals with restitution—what it would take a community to forgive a man like Judd."

Skellig
Author: David Almond
Publication date: 1998

Awards
   Booklist, Top Ten Fantasy Novels for Young Readers
   Michael L. Printz Honor Book
   Whitbread Children's Book of the Year

Characters
   Michael
   Mina
   Skellig
   Michael's parents

Setting
   Present day—England

Plot

The day after Michael and his family move to a new house, he discovers Skellig in the garage. Until Skellig opens his eyes and asks Michael what he wants, Michael thinks this being, white-faced, thin, and covered with dust and cobwebs, is dead. Half-believing this is a dream, Michael returns to the garage and warns Skellig that the garage is in danger of collapsing. Skellig merely continues to eat insects and asks Michael for aspirin and " '27 and 53,' " which Michael figures out later are Chinese menu items. On another visit, Michael feels something " 'springy and flexible' " beneath each of Skellig's shoulder blades.

Living in Michael's new neighborhood is Mina, an outspoken and precocious child who is educated at home by her mother. Mina takes Michael to her secret place, an abandoned house where tawny owls make their nest in the attic. Michael takes Mina to the garage, and Skellig agrees to let them take him to a safer place. They carry him to Mina's secret place. Mina takes off his jacket, and Skellig's wings are released.

Michael and Mina continue to visit Skellig. Once they find Skellig on the top floor of the building with owls feeding him. Michael, Mina, and Skellig join in a circle as if they are one. Michael sees wings on Mina's back and feels them on his own. " 'Remember this night,' " Skellig tells them.

At the same time this is happening, Michael's baby sister is very ill and needs a heart operation. When Skellig disappears, Michael feels his own heart stop and believes his sister is dead. She does survive, and Michael's mother tells him that during the night, in what she believes was a dream, she saw a man with " 'a great hunch on his back' " lift the baby. In the slow dance he did with her, Michael's mother saw wings on her daughter's back. Later when she sees a picture of Skellig drawn by Mina, she is stunned. Skellig returns and admits he's visited Michael's sister and says he is now going away. When Michael asks him what he is, Skellig responds, " 'Something like you, something like a beast, something like a bird, something like an angel.' "

Questions for Discussion
1. What does Michael think when he first sees Skellig? Why isn't he afraid?
2. Describe Skellig. Mina says he is beautiful. Can you understand her reaction?
3. What kind of girl is Mina? What special talents does she have? Does she have any qualities that you do not admire? Why does Michael trust her enough to introduce her to Skellig? Would you like her for a friend?
4. What impact is the illness of Michael's baby sister having on his family? Why does he ask Skellig to think about her? Why did Michael and his father fight the day of his sister's operation? Have you ever shared Michael's feelings?
5. When Michael rides the bus to school, he realizes how little he knows about people just from their appearance. Does this message apply to any other situations in this novel?
6. How does Michael feel when his friends come to play football? Have you ever experienced feelings similar to this?
7. After Michael and Mina fight, she says, " 'It's possible to hate your friend. You hated me today.' " Do you agree with Mina?
8. What is Skellig? How can you explain his human form and human requests for such things as aspirin and Chinese food? How do you explain his pain, his weakness, and his tears?
9. Why does Skellig struggle to the top floor of the house?
10. Michael, Mina, and Skellig join together in a slow dance. How is this scene important to the novel?
11. Why doesn't Michael tell his parents about Skellig?
12. Why did Skellig become part of Michael and Mina's lives? Do you think he chose them specifically?
13. Skellig tells Michael and Mina that they are angels. Do you agree?
14. When Michael asks him what he is, Skellig says he is, " 'Something like you, something like a beast, something like a bird, something like an angel.' " Do you agree with Skellig's description?
15. Michael and Mina find a heart scratched into the floor of the attic with the words " '*Thank you. S.*' " Inside the heart were three white feathers. Who left this message? What are they being thanked for? What do the feathers represent? Why do the owls bring them a dead mouse and bird?

Projects
1. Both Michael and Mina draw; for example, she has a book of bird pictures, and he draws his family and the world through his sister's eyes. Both draw Skellig. Duplicate their drawings of Skellig at various points in the novel;

for example, as he is when Michael finds him, as he is during their dance, and as Michael's mother sees him with the baby.

2. Mina introduces Michael to the work of the poet William Blake; she says, " 'He painted pictures and wrote poems. Much of the time he wore no clothes. He saw angels in his garden.' " Find out about the life of this poet. In an anthology of his poetry, locate two poems that appeal to you. Prepare an oral presentation about the life of Blake, and recite the two poems.

3. Miss Clarts tells Michael's class about Icarus, whose wings melted when he got too close to the sun, and about Ulysses, who was trapped with the one-eyed monster Polyphemus. Read either of these myths from Greek mythology, writing a summary of the myth.

4. Owls inhabit Mina's secret place and feed Skellig. Prepare a written report on the habits of owls as they are shown in this novel.

Vocabulary

Each of the following quotations chosen from *Skellig* includes one or more vocabulary words in **bold print**.

1. "It was more like a **demolition** site or a rubbish dump or like one of those ancient warehouses they keep pulling down at the wharf."
2. ". . . there were dozens of **massive** planks nailed across the entrance."
3. "I shoved the door and it **lurched** half shut on its single hinge."
4. "The dust was **clogging** my nostrils and throat."
5. "I put the skeleton picture on the table and looked at it but couldn't **concentrate** on it."
6. "She pointed to the back wall, a **gaping** hole where some plaster and bricks had fallen in."
7. "She saw the **blotch**es on my skin."
8. " 'We believe that schools **inhibit** the natural curiosity, creativity, and intelligence of children. The mind needs to be opened out into the world, not shuttered down inside a gloomy classroom.' "
9. "She **teetered** on the brink."
10. "She grinned and **beckoned** me over the wall when she saw me standing there."
11. " 'You think you're special but you're just as **ignorant** as anybody.' "
12. "The door was open behind us, letting a **wedge** of light out into the dark."
13. "What would I feel when they opened the baby's **fragile** chest, when they cut into her tiny heart?"
14. "And then we fought, my dad and I, while we crunched burnt toast and swigged **tepid** tea."
15. "The parents waited, **wary** of us. . . ."

About the Author

David Almond grew up in northeast England. He worked as a teacher, mailman, editor, and brush salesman, but always wanted to be a writer. He has written a great deal for adults. He says, "Writing can be difficult, but sometimes it really does feel like a kind of magic."

Somewhere in the Darkness
Author: Walter Dean Myers
Publication date: 1992

Awards
Newbery Honor Book
Boston Globe/Horn Book Award
Booklist Editors' Choice
ALA Best Books for Young Adults
Coretta Scott King Award

Characters
Jimmy Little
Mama Jean
Cephus "Crab" Little

Setting
Present day—United States

Plot
Unlike many books written for young adults, Walter Dean Myers writes of young boys growing up in the inner city. Jimmy Little is one such boy living in the care of a woman he calls Mama Jean. His real mother is deceased, and his father is in jail for allegedly murdering a guard during an armored truck holdup.

Returning home from school one day, he is met by a tall, thin man who tells Jimmy he is his father. When Mama Jean gets home from work, Crab, Jimmy's father, tells her he is taking Jimmy with him to Chicago, where he has a job, and that they must leave immediately. Before Jimmy leaves, Mama Jean secretly gives him fifty dollars to come home if the need arises. On the trip to Chicago, Jimmy learns that his father has not been paroled but has escaped from prison, has something wrong with his kidneys, and claims that he did not kill the guard. No matter what else he has done in his life, Crab wants Jimmy to know that he did not kill the guard. He tells Jimmy the story of the holdup and of the man Rydell Dupuis, who can prove his innocence. Crab knows that Rydell will not go to the police but he might tell Jimmy the truth. Rydell has returned home to Arkansas, and that is where he and Jimmy are headed.

On their way to Arkansas, they stop in Chicago, where Crab hopes to get a thousand dollars to finance their trip. While in Chicago, Crab becomes very ill, and Jimmy is afraid he might die. Though wanting to return to Mama Jean, Jimmy knows that he will go to Arkansas and begins to spend his emergency money. Since they did not get the thousand dollars, Crab uses a stolen credit card to rent a car.

As they travel, Crab tells Jimmy about his life, of his father who had no time for him, of his mother, of his playing the saxophone, and of the sights and sounds and people of his hometown, Marion, Arkansas. He tries hard to make a connection with his son but all Jimmy can see is the darkness of the man.

Instead of proclaiming Crab's innocence to Jimmy, Rydell turns him in to the police. Crab dies shackled to a hospital bed. On his way home to Mama Jean, Jimmy thinks of having his own child and how he will share everything with him all the time from the very beginning so there will not be darkness between them.

Questions for Discussion

1. How does Jimmy feel when he first meets his father? What is his father's reaction to Jimmy?
2. Why had Crab been in prison? What does Crab say about his crime? Does Jimmy believe him? How would you feel if you were Jimmy?
3. Why did Crab never send any letters? Have you ever tried to write a letter that just does not say what you mean?
4. What does Mama Jean tell Jimmy when he is about to leave? Do you think this helped, knowing he had a place to come back to?
5. What does Crab tell Jimmy about the other prisoners in the jail? What does he say about jail? Do you agree?
6. How had Jimmy imagined his father? Is Crab anything like his thoughts? What do you think Crab is doing at the closed filling station? Does Jimmy trust his father? How would you feel toward Crab?
7. What does Jimmy want to do when he learns that Crab has escaped from prison? How does he feel toward Crab? Would you be scared if you were Jimmy? Why?
8. Why does Crab feel that he could not wait for parole? What does he want Jimmy to know?
9. As they drive to Chicago, Jimmy's whole body is tense. Why? Can you understand his dilemma?
10. In Chicago, they visit Mavis Stokes and her son, Frank. Frank, a fledgling boxer, tries to intimidate Jimmy. What does Jimmy do in response? Do you think this is an effective way to stop a bully? Why?
11. When Jimmy wonders about whether Crab loves him or even likes him, he can't find the answer. What is it about Crab that confuses him? Do you know people who act differently with different people? Do you think this is a good trait?
12. What happens that makes Jimmy know that he is going to Arkansas even though he wants to return to Mama Jean?
13. What does Crab use to rent the car? How does Jimmy feel about this? Do you share Jimmy's feelings?
14. " 'I need to look in the mirror and see something I can respect.' " What does Crab mean when he says this? Is this an important value to live by?
15. Jimmy tries to find out about the relationship between Crab and his father. Why is this important to him?

16. Why is Crab pleased with himself when he corrects Jimmy's grammar? Why is he unhappy with Jimmy's response? How does Jimmy lighten the situation?
17. How does Crab describe segregation? Why was it so degrading to black people? What has been done to correct some of these evils? Do you think more needs to be done? What?
18. Crab goes to see High John, the conjure man. Do you know what a conjure man is? What does he mean when he tells Crab, " 'Sometimes a man grows a cloud over his eyes and can't see the work of his own hand, or the truth in his own heart' " ? Has the trip helped Crab to lift the cloud? How has it affected Jimmy?
19. Though both Crab and Jimmy try to build a true father-and-son relationship they both know that it cannot be done. Why?
20. As Jimmy returns to New York, he thinks of having his own son. What does he want with that child? How does he intend to get that connection?

Projects

1. Crab tells Jimmy of segregation and how blacks were not allowed to eat or drink at the lunch counter. Research where this form of segregation was first defied. Write a skit to dramatize the event.
2. Research the important events in the history of the Civil Rights movement and develop an illustrated time line to show them.
3. Write a report on the life of Martin Luther King, Jr.
4. Draw or paint a picture of how you envision the hallway and staircase in Jimmy's apartment building.
5. From New York City where Jimmy lives with Mama Jean, plot the route taken by Jimmy and Crab from there to Marion, Arkansas. Estimate the mileage covered and the amount of gasoline used.

Vocabulary

Each of the following quotations chosen from *Somewhere in the Darkness* includes one or more vocabulary words in **bold print**.

1. "When they got home Mama Jean had **lectured** him on how important reading and writing were."
2. "As a result he had to see a **psychologist** who came around once a month."
3. "Already the familiar smells of garlic and fried **plantains** was in the air."
4. "The boy looked at Jimmy **sullenly**, then backed off."
5. "It **splattered** against the window, making patterns against the dirt-frosted glass."
6. "Maurice made a **ceremonious** bow and left."
7. "Mama Jean opened a drawer, pulled out an **adjustable** wrench, and put it on the counter."
8. "The voice was flat, **hard-edged**."
9. "Jimmy watched him go toward the small **bodega** where Johnny Cruz's father worked."

10. "Crab's hand reached over his shoulder and pushed the **cradle** down, cutting him off."
11. "Jimmy **sniffled** and was sorry that he did."
12. "He took his right hand off the steering wheel and **flexed** his fingers."
13. " 'It's twenty–four **carat** and all but it don't mean nothing in the real world.' "
14. "Looking at Crab in the car, as the day **waned** and the neon lights flashed against the sharp angles of his face . . . "
15. "Crab got out quickly, then **winced** as the pain in his back got to him."

About the Author

Though born in the South, Myers spent most of his growing-up years in Harlem being raised by foster parents. Knowing he could not afford college, he quit high school to join the army. Many years later he received his bachelor's degree from the Empire State College. His writings are varied: picture books, fantasy, mystery, adventure, historical fiction, and nonfiction. In his statement, " 'Young people need ideals which identify them, and their lives, as central . . . guideposts which tell them what they can be, should be, and indeed are,' " Myers states the purpose of *Building Character through Literature*.

Stone Fox
Author: John Reynolds Gardiner
Publication date: 1980

Characters
> Little Willy
> Grandfather
> Searchlight
> Doc Smith
> Clifford Snyder
> Stone Fox

Setting
> Nineteenth century—Rural Wyoming

Plot

"One day Grandfather wouldn't get out of bed. He just lay there and stared at the ceiling and looked sad." Grandfather often plays jokes, so little Willy thinks he is having fun. When he doesn't get up and get dressed, Willy runs to Doc Smith for help. Her diagnosis is that Grandfather is physically fit but has just given up on life.

Little Willy is not daunted and decides he will find the reason and make it better. His big black and white dog, Searchlight, who is just his age, ten years old, supports him. Though a ten-year-old boy cannot run a farm, little Willy does not know that and is determined to grow potatoes just as Grandfather did.

After the harvest that is only a few weeks away, little Willy is sure everything will be all right. Doc Smith says Grandfather is getting worse, and other plans will have to be made for little Willy and Searchlight. Little Willy says they are a family and must not be split up. As he prepares for the harvest, little Willy finds there is no money to rent a horse. Searchlight solves the problem by insisting on being hitched to the plow. The harvest is a big one, but it is not the source of grandfather's worry.

The tax man comes, and little Willy finds they owe five hundred dollars in back taxes. Now little Willy is sure that Grandfather will be well when the taxes are paid. All attempts to raise the money fail, so little Willy enters the dog sled race against Stone Fox and his five Samoyeds. Little Willy wins the race with help from Stone Fox and restores Grandfather to health, but at a great cost. Searchlight has given her all for little Willy and Grandfather.

Questions for Discussion

1. Doc Smith diagnoses Grandfather as perfectly healthy but says he has given up on life. Do you think this really happens? What might cause a person to give up? How would Grandfather be treated today?
2. Little Willy is determined to find out what is wrong with Grandfather and make it better. Who is his supporter? How does Searchlight show his support?
3. Searchlight displays some human qualities; what is this called in literary terms? What human qualities do you see in Searchlight?
4. Little Willy is sure that harvesting the potato crop will cure Grandfather. Does Doc Smith agree? What is her solution to the problem? How does Searchlight react? Why? What is little Willy's answer? How would you have answered?
5. How does little Willy get ready for the harvest? What does he need that he does not have? What makes this impossible to achieve? How is the problem solved? Is the crop what Grandfather is worried about?
6. Who awaits Willie and Searchlight when they return from school? How does he threaten their home life?
7. What does Little Willy sacrifice to enter the dog sled race? Why does he not tell Grandfather of his decision?
8. Why is it important to Stone Fox that he win the race? What has he accomplished with his winnings?
9. Why do you that think Stone Fox helped little Willy win the race?
10. What do you think are some of the good qualities that little Willy and Stone Fox exhibited?

Projects

1. Investigate the history of the Shoshone Indians from their earliest times in North America to the settlement on the Indian reservation in Wyoming. Tell their story in your own words.
2. Make a diorama or a poster depicting life in a typical Shosone village. Illustrate the clothing, housing, modes of getting and preparing food, and forms of entertainment.
3. The pen and ink drawings in *Stone Fox* greatly add to the story. Select five scenes from the story, and illustrate them in a medium of your choosing.
4. The Iditerod in Alaska is a world-famous dog sled race. On a map of Alaska, plot its course. Calculate the time needed to run the course, determine the number of rest stops necessary, and list the supplies to be carried on the sled.
5. Doc Smith in *Stone Fox* is a woman physician, an uncommon occurrence in the nineteenth century. Find the names of some of the women pioneers in the medical field. Write a report about one of these women, telling her family life, her education, her career, her accomplishments, and the obstacles she faced in the pursuit of her education and her career.

6. Locate the Teton Mountains, investigate the plants and animals found there, and present this information orally to the class. The presentation must include visuals of the plants and animals discussed.

Vocabulary

Each of the following quotations chosen from *Stone Fox* includes one or more vocabulary words in **bold print**.

1. "He was a handsome **palomino**."
2. "She **forged** ahead with such speed that the sled seemed to lift off the ground and fly."
3. "They were so **exhausted** when they arrived at the house. . . ."
4. "He was holding a small **derringer** and pointing it at Searchlight."
5. "In fact, they were the most beautiful **Samoyeds** little Willy had ever seen."
6. "The dogs held their heads up proudly and **strutted** in unison."
7. "Stories and legends about the **awesome** mountain man followed shortly."
8. "Little Willy's sled flew by the schoolhouse on the **outskirts** of town, and then by the old **deserted** barn."
9. "They also pulled a large—but by no means lightly **constructed** man."
10. "The voice cut through the air like the twang of a **ricocheting** bullet. . . ."
11. ". . .with **moccasins** that came all the way up to his knees.

About the Author

A nonreader as a child, Gardiner had the imagination to tell a story but not the skill to spell or phrase the story properly. He did not read his first novel until age nineteen and did not write his first book until he was in his thirties. Living in California, he is a thermal analyst for aerospace engineering firms and an inventor as well as a writer.

From the Author

"We read nonfiction to *know*. We read fiction to *feel*. But the author must feel first, before the reader will feel. Was I sad when I wrote **Stone Fox**? You better believe it!"

Stranger with My Face
Author: Lois Duncan
Publication date: 1981

Awards
ALA Best Books for Young Adults
New York Times Best Books for Children
Ethical Culture School Book Award
Library of Congress' Best Books
English Teacher's Journal Best Books of the Year for Young Adults
University of Iowa Best Books of the Year for Young Adults
Best Novel Award, National League of American Pen Women

Characters
Laurie Stratton
Lia
Mr. and Mrs. Stratton
Neal, Laurie's brother
Meg, Laurie's sister
Helen Tuttle
Jeff Rankin

Setting
Present day—Brighton Island, in New England

Plot
Eighteen-year-old Laurie Stratton recounts the details of the previous year. The year began with Laurie finally part of the "in crowd" of Brighton Island teenagers. However, before long, strange things begin to happen. Laurie doesn't go to a party because she is ill, but her friends think they see her on the beach and are angry with her. She feels she is being followed and that someone has been in her room. Her father thinks he sees her in the house when, in reality, Laurie is at school. She looks in a mirror and realizes that the face looking back at her does not belong to her. In her sleep one night, her twin sister comes to her. On another visit, Laurie's twin introduces herself as Lia.

Laurie does not know how this is all happening until her friend, Helen, who had learned about it from her Navaho boyfriend when she lived in the Southwest, suggests that Laurie has been using astral projection. Through this phenomenon, the soul or mind or spiritual part of a person separates from the body and travels wherever it wants to go. However, it is Lia, not Laurie, who is using this technique to come to Brighton Island.

When Laurie confronts her parents about her twin, they admit that she was adopted as a baby. They had gone to the Southwest and met both Laurie and her twin, the children of a Navaho mother and white father. Finances did not allow them to adopt both children. They chose Laurie because they sensed a strange quality in Lia and didn't think they could love her as a daughter.

When Laurie tells Helen that she wants to know her sister, Helen cautions that Lia is evil. Soon after, Helen has a serious accident that renders her an invalid. Jeff, another friend, falls to the rocks below Laurie's house. Laurie realizes that Lia has caused both of these accidents. Laurie learns to use astral projection herself to visit Helen in the hospital and to learn about Lia, who has killed the child of her foster parents and is in a mental institution in the Southwest.

When Laurie attempts to return to her body, she cannot because Lia has taken it over. She behaves so differently from Laurie that many people, especially Laurie's younger sister, Meg, notice the difference. In the end, the eagle fetish, a defense against evil spirits given to Laurie by Helen, stuns Lia and allows Laurie to return to her own body.

Questions for Discussion

1. How does Laurie become part of the "in crowd" on Brighton Island? How important is this to her? Do you understand Laurie's desire to be part of the group?

2. What kind of girl is Helen? Why is it difficult for her to make close friends? How would you go about being a friend to Helen? How does the island group treat her when Laurie brings her to the lunch table? How does Laurie feel when Gordon objects to her friendship with Helen? How would you react to the actions of the group and Gordon if you were in Laurie's place?

3. Laurie appreciates Helen as a friend because Helen is "nonjudgmental" when Laurie is totally honest with her. How important is it to have a friend with whom you can be honest and be yourself?

4. Laurie eventually realizes that Darlene, Mary Beth, and Natalie are "surface friends." What does she mean by this comment? Have you been friends with anyone in this way? How important is this kind of friendship to you?

5. Laurie is initially angry that her parents have not told her she was adopted. Do you understand why she was not told of the adoption? Do you understand how Laurie feels? In a relatively short time, their family life is back to normal. What does this say about the relationship between Laurie and her parents?

6. Helen's parents are not happy about their daughter's friendship with Jeff and eventually blame him for her injury. Why do they feel this way? Are you critical of them, or do you understand their feelings at all?

7. How does Helen feel about Jeff? What does this tell you about the kind of person she is?

8. In what ways does Laurie come to understand her own parents better? What does she learn about them from the concern they show for Helen and Jeff?

9. How are Laurie and Lia different? Can you explain how identical twins came to have such different personalities and values? Can you understand at all how Lia turned out as she did? What happens to Lia at the end of the story?
10. What is Laurie's attitude as she finishes her story? How is she changed by her experience with her twin?

Projects

1. Helen gives Laurie a turquoise eagle that, according to Navaho tradition, will protect against evil from above. Find out what other symbols and traditions exist in Navaho culture, and present these in the form of a poster.
2. Laurie's mother is an artist. Laurie paints a picture in words of her home, Cliff House, as it juts out from the rocks. Draw a picture of your vision of Cliff House from Laurie's words.
3. Laurie's father comments that adoption is more openly talked about today. Read and summarize a magazine article on a current issue dealing with adoption.
4. Using the Internet or other current sources, find out how many children are waiting to be adopted, what ages of children are more or less likely to be adopted, and how many children are adopted from this country and from foreign countries. Summarize your findings into a brief report.
5. Lia and Laurie are very different, but they are still connected with a unique bond. Locate information on the special relationship that exists between twins. Present your information in a written report, a multimedia presentation, or a poster.

Vocabulary

Each of the following quotations chosen from *Stranger with My Face* includes one or more vocabulary words in **bold print**.

1. "Even the beauty of the ocean is no **solace**."
2. "I swung my legs over the side of the bed and **hoisted** myself gingerly to my feet."
3. "I was **bewildered** by the summons."
4. ". . . pretending it didn't matter that the 'in' group was bunched together on the bow, laughing and joking around, **oblivious** to my existence."
5. "I could feel the vibrations of **hostility** stretching to meet me."
6. " 'Gordon, you've got to be crazy!' I stared at him **incredulously**."
7. "He was furious. I had never seen Gordon so **livid**."
8. "Up ahead, perched **precariously** on its ledge, Cliff House was **silhouetted** against the glare of the afternoon sun."
9. "The spread was smooth and **taut**. There was no **indentation** to show that someone had rested there."
10. "I forgot my locker combination and had to attend my first two classes without books, which did little to **endear** me to my teachers."
11. ". . . my mind was in such **turmoil** that I missed every problem that was given me."

12. ". . . **clambering** onto the dock . . ."
13. "I reached over and **groped** for the bedside lamp. . . ."
14. ". . . when he is **confronted** with something that he does not know how to handle."
15. "I found his silent company more to my liking than the **incessant** chatter of the group below."
16. "Her sympathy gave me a **twinge** of guilt, for I did not deserve it."
17. ". . . her pillow would be **drenched** with sweat."
18. ". . . it was **contorted** with pain."
19. ". . . the water came **surging** up through the **crevices** in bursts of **froth**."
20. ". . . the sound of the tardy bell **reverberating** through the empty hall . . ."

About the Author

Lois Duncan was born in Philadelphia and educated at Duke University and the University of New Mexico. When she was a teenager, she began to write stories for magazines. One of her first attempts at a book was a love story for teenagers that won a publisher's contest. Her characters are frequently based on people she knows, and her plots combine reality and a surprise that is often supernatural. Lois Duncan lives in Albuquerque, New Mexico.

Summer of My German Soldier
Author: Bette Greene
Publication date: 1973

Awards

Golden Kite Award—Society of Children's Book Writers
ALA Notable Books for Children
New York Times Notable Books of the Year
National Book Award Finalist

Characters

Patty Bergen
Harry and Pearl Bergen, Patty's parents
Ruth
Frederick Anton Reiker
Freddy Doud
Maternal grandparents

Setting

The 1940s—Jenkinsville, Arkansas

Plot

It was the 1940s and the United States was at war with the Axis powers, Germany, Japan, and Italy. Hitler had long been waging his persecution of the European Jews. On the home front, loyal Americans were following the war news, feeling the pinch of rationing, and reveling in stalwart patriotism.

Patty is the twelve-year-old daughter of Harry and Pearl Bergen, owners of the local department store. In this primarily Christian community of Jenkinsville, Arkansas, they are the only Jews and therefore not completely accepted by the townspeople. Patty's home life is not a happy one, for her father, an arrogant and frustrated man, beats Patty for the slightest or imagined infraction of his rules. Her mother, an immature, vain woman, does not physically abuse Patty but undermines her self-esteem through constant putdowns. Patty is always attempting to gain their approval and love but is forever rejected. Her only support comes from Ruth, the black housekeeper, and her maternal grandparents.

When a POW camp is set up on the outskirts of town, Patty meets Anton, a twenty-two-year-old German prisoner. Upon his escape, Patty shelters and feeds him. As the two talk, Patty is moved by his gentle kindness and comes to love this stranger, who calls her a "person of value." When Anton moves on, Patty supplies him with civilian clothing, including a monogrammed blue shirt, a present she had given to her father. When Anton is shot resisting arrest in New York City, the shirt is traced to Patty. When her father asks why she, a Jewish girl, helped Anton, she answers, " 'He was kind to me.' "

For her part in Anton's escape, Patty is sent to a girl's reformatory for six months. Through the gifts and love bestowed on her by Anton and Ruth, Patty realizes that she is a survivor, and her father can beat her but not defeat her. She further comes to realize that she is not bad but a "person of value" as Anton had said.

Questions for Discussion

1. Patty daydreams that her parents are stranded in a blizzard, she saves them, and is rewarded by their love. Why does she feel that this would be a miracle?

2. Why did the residents of Jenkinsville drive the Chu Lees out of town? Does their reasoning make any sense to you?

3. Why does Mr. Bergen resent his in-laws? Do people dislike being indebted to someone? What could he have done to help this situation?

4. When the family is driving to Memphis, both Sharon and Patty make an attempt at humor. How do their parents respond to them? Why do you think the children are treated so differently? Do you think this is fair? Why does Patty think her mother rejects her?

5. What does Grandpa mean when he says that bending is better than breaking? How can you apply this to your life? Is this strategy always the right way to go? Can you see that there are times when it is not the answer?

6. Why does Patty lie to Sister Parker about what Anton said? Does Patty often make trouble for herself by talking too much? Why do you think she does this?

7. Patty dreams of having a black horse named Evol. What does this mean to her? Can you understand her need for love?

8. Why does Patty feel shame and anger when her mother sends her to Mrs. Reeves, the hairdresser? What happens when she tries to rebel?

9. Anton describes his mother to Patty. How does she compare to Patty's mother?

10. Why is Patty, a Jewish girl, helping Anton, an escaped German POW? Would you do the same if you were Patty? Do you think Patty would have reacted in the same manner if she were used to gentle kindness and attention?

11. How did Dr. Robinson describe Anton? How was he different from some of the other prisoners? Do you think it is possible that among our enemies as among friends there can be good and bad people?

12. Why does Patty feel an empathy with Freddy Doud? What does Mr. Bergen do when he finds him with Patty? What is Anton's reaction? How does Ruth describe his action? Do you agree with her?

13. Patty describes Freddy to Anton. What does she say about him? Do you agree with Anton that he sounds delightful? Why does Patty's father not like him? Do you know any people who feel as Patty's father does?

14. Patty, Anton, and Ruth talk about making better people. What are the three things that Patty brings up? Do you think they would be helpful? What does Anton believe is the answer? Can you explain his answer?

15. Patty is torn with making a decision to side with what her father would want or to continue helping Anton. What helps her make her decision?

16. Why does Anton give Patty his ring when he leaves? What does he give her that is even more valuable?

17. Patty brings trouble down on herself by showing Anton's ring and lying about how she got it. How does her father react? How does the sheriff react? What is it about each man that made him accept the story so differently?

18. When Patty is implicated in Anton's escape, how do her parents react? Do they do anything that would help her in her trouble? What has Patty learned about herself and her parents that makes this bearable?

19. After Patty's arrest, her parents are harassed by the townspeople. Why do you think the townspeople are doing this? Do you think the reaction would have been the same if the Bergens were not Jewish? Does prejudice often color people's actions? Why do you think this is so?

20. Ruth is Patty's only support while she is in the reformatory. As they talk Ruth makes an observation about Patty's parents. Do you agree with her? What does Patty realize about herself? Is it important to know that you are a good person with value? How would that knowledge affect your actions?

Projects

1. Yom Kippur and Chanukah are Jewish religious holidays mentioned in this book. Research the origins of each and the manner in which they are celebrated. Prepare an oral presentation for the class.

2. The capture of General Wainright and the Russian offensive on the Kalinin Front are two news items discussed by the family. Locate the facts about one of these, and write a television segment or a newspaper article on your findings.

3. Locate pictures of Franklin Roosevelt, Winston Churchill, Joseph Stalin, or Adolf Hitler, and create a pictorial biography of their war years.

4. Go to your school or community library, and compile a bibliography of its holdings dealing with child abuse. Copy and distribute this to your class.

5. Locate the services available to victims of abuse, and design a poster containing the hot-line phone numbers.

6. Locate someone in your community who is a Holocaust survivor or a descendant of a survivor. Interview him or her concerning the memories of this period. Videotape the interview.

7. Find recordings of the old radio programs cited in this book and play one for the class. Moderate a discussion of your classmates' impressions.

Vocabulary

Each of the following quotations chosen from *Summer of My German Soldier* includes one or more vocabulary words in **bold print**.

1. "Their **ravaged** faces would tell a story of defeat, disgrace, and downfall."
2. " 'A real **fastidious** wife.' "
3. ". . .he couldn't in good conscience consider it a **priority** item."
4. "And there were the lofty cheekbones that gave mother's face form, **symmetry**, and on occasion, great beauty."
5. "By the time they finish with her it's tight and unreal, like the hair on a department store **manikin**."
6. "She looked at me **reproachfully**, like Cinderella being disturbed while waltzing with the prince."
7. "As I walked down the only residential block in town it followed my footsteps, **evaporating** my energies."
8. "I **propelled** myself backward, falling into and finally through the tight little branches."
9. "I saw the hate that **gnarled** and snarled his face like a dog gone rabid."
10. "Hands that were in the **throes** of a fit worked to unfasten his belt buckle."
11. "A hundred frizzledy-fries ringlets **obstinately** refusing to flow into one another. . . ."
12. "Her face was a study in **martyred** innocence."
13. "Thin ones like **ego** and **ode**."
14. "Fat ones like **harmonic** and **palatable**."
15. "I tried to **calculate** how long it had been since Anton had eaten."
16. " ' I will not **jeopardize** this university' "
17. "My father chose **acquiescence** and life rather than resistance and death."
18. " ' I wouldn't wish to **implicate** him.' "
19. " '. . . and it is considered essential that he be quickly **apprehended**.' "
20. "Six o'clock came before my thoughts had **congealed** into plans."

About the Author

Bette Greene, born in 1934, spent her early years in Arkansas and Tennessee but later went on to study in Paris and New York. She had published short stories and articles for newspapers and magazines before writing this, her first novel for young adults, in 1973. Her novels deal with the serious themes of prejudice and religious hypocrisy and stir the reader to think and question. Greene hopes that her novels, which are frequently semiautobiographical, are a help to children.

Tangerine
Author: Edward Bloor
Publication date: 1997

Awards

ALA Top Ten Best Books for Young Adults
Horn Book Fanfare Book
American Bookseller Pick of the List
New York Public Library's One Hundred Titles for Reading and Sharing
The Bulletin of the Center for Children's Books Blue Ribbon Book

Characters

Paul Fisher
Erik Fisher
Mr. and Mrs. Fisher
Victor Guzman
Tino Cruz
Luis Cruz
Theresa Cruz
Joey Costello
Arthur Bauer

Setting

Present day—Tangerine County, Florida

Plot

Paul moves with his parents and brother Erik to an affluent neighborhood, Lake Windsor Downs in Tangerine County, Florida. Although he is legally blind, Paul can see well enough to be a very good soccer player. However, all of the family's attention, especially that of the father, is focused on Erik and his football exploits. Both boys will play for Lake Windsor teams.

Paul is devastated when he is removed from his soccer team because he is visually handicapped. Paul has fragmented memories of what happened to impair his sight, and many of these include his brother. Paul realizes that Erik can be cruel. When a member of his football team is struck by lightening and dies, Erik and his friend know they will no longer have to deal with competition from another talented player and laugh at the death. When a giant sinkhole swallows up several portable classrooms at his high school, Paul decides to go to Tangerine Middle School. With its old building, old books, and minority student population, Tangerine is very different from Lake Windsor. Knowing how much he wants to play soccer as well as how well he can play the game, his mother destroys Paul's individual educational plan, a requirement for handicapped students, and Paul is a back-up on the team. The War Eagles, made up of boys and girls, is a real team. When Paul shows how hard he can play, Victor, the team leader, welcomes him as part of the group.

When he works with Theresa and Tino Cruz on a science project, he meets their brother Luis, who runs a citrus nursery and cultivates new varieties of trees. Paul becomes fascinated with the work there and returns to help. During a sleepless and harrowing night, Paul helps fight the freeze that threatens to destroy the crop. When they work on the project at Paul's house, Erik and Tino fight. Later Luis confronts Erik, who then calls on Arthur Bauer to take care of Luis. Arthur strikes Luis with a blackjack, and Paul witnesses the entire scene from under the bleachers. Several days later Luis dies. Tino amd Victor crash the Senior Awards Night ceremony to avenge Luis's death. Paul enables Tino to escape as a melee ensues. Paul is expelled for assaulting a teacher.

Paul's mother discovers items stolen from neighborhhood homes in their storage locker. Erik and Arthur are responsible. Paul reveals what he saw from under the bleachers, and Arnold is arrested for Luis's death. Paul remembers that Erik sprayed paint into his eyes, causing him to lose his sight. Paul decides he will return to Tangerine Middle School the next year.

Questions for Discussion

1. Paul and Erik are brothers. What qualities do they share? How are they different? Which brother would you rather have for a friend? Why?

2. Why does Erik do the things he does? Does he present different sides of himself to different people? How does he treat his parents, his brother, his friends, and others?

3. In what ways is Paul distressed about the way people behave after Mike's death? Do you agree with him?

4. How would you characterize Mr. Fisher's involvement with Erik's football career? Do you think he is doing what any good parent would do? Do you admire his behavior?

5. Why does Paul's mother destroy his individual educational plan? Do you think it is right for her to do this?

6. How are Lake Windsor Middle School and Tangerine Middle School different? What are the good things and the bad things about each? Which school would you rather attend?

7. How does Paul feel about going to Tangerine? How is he accepted by the other students? How does Joey behave when he transfers to Tangerine? Whose behavior do you admire more, Paul's or Joey's?

8. Do you think Mr. Fisher sees the fight between Erik and Tino? If he does, why doesn't he intervene? Why do you think Paul sees sorrow and fear, rather that anger, in Erik's face?

9. Luis tells Paul he shouldn't be afraid of Erik. Do you agree with Luis? If Erik were your brother, would you be afraid of him?

10. How does Paul react to Luis's death? Why doesn't Theresa want Paul to come to her brother's funeral? Do you agree with her?

11. Why does Paul enable Tino to escape when Tino and Victor come to the Senior Awards Night to avenge Luis's death? Theresa is mad that Paul messed up his own life; do you agree with her? Do you think Paul did the right thing?
12. Why does Paul have a hard time remembering the accident that nearly blinded him? What finally helped him to recall the accident?
13. Why did Mr. and Mrs. Fisher do nothing when they know how Paul's eyes had been injured? Is their inaction understandable or excusable?
14. How do Mr. and Mrs. Fisher deal with the fact that Erik has robbed several homes in their area? Do they propose a fair settlement to the victims? Is this the best for Erik?
15. Does Paul do the right thing by telling the truth about Luis's death? Do you respect what he does?
16. Paul's grandmother says that Mr. and Mrs. Fisher are paying the price for things they didn't do years before. What does she mean by this? Do you think the Fishers are good parents?
17. Lake Windsor is a community that is not what it seems to be at first glance. How is the community a metaphor for the people in the community?
18. Are you surprised that Paul wants to return to Tangerine the next year?
19. What do you think are the themes of this novel?
20. How is Tangerine, as a place that is beautiful on the outside but not strong, a metaphor for the characters in this novel?

Projects

1. Paul keeps a journal on his computer. Continue Paul's journal after the novel is finished. What happens to his brother, his parents, his friends from Tangerine, and Joey?
2. The osprey is native to Florida. Locate information on this bird, including classification, habitat, eating habits, and description. Include this information on a poster along with a picture of the bird.
3. Tangerine County is notable for the frequency of lightening strikes it experiences. Locate information on lightening, including its causes, effects, and the precautions people should take to be safe from its effects. Organize this information into a brief report.
4. Paul becomes interested in the citrus grove run by the Cruz family. Locate information on the ways in which new species of fruit are propagated. Organize your information into a multimedia presentation.
5. A big frost is frightening for citrus growers. Reread the section of the novel on the fight to save the Cruz family grove. Write a newspaper article that chronicles the events of that night.

Vocabulary

Each of the following quotations chosen from *Tangerine* includes one or more vocabulary words in **bold print**.
1. ". . . all neatly **wedged** into the back of Mom's Volvo wagon."
2. "I heard a loud roar like an animal's, like a **predator snarling**."

3. "Thousands upon thousands of trees in the red glow of sundown, perfectly shaped and perfectly **aligned** . . ."
4. ". . . same smoke **billowing** out."
5. ". . . but their goggles would be **intact**. Nothing can break these goggles."
6. "Over there they were **hurling** their bodies at a blocking sled. . . ."
7. "Soccer practice was a **colossal** drag."
8. ". . . the crowd buzzed **ominously**."
9. "**Menacing**-looking gangs, just standing around . . ."
10. "One big guy took his forearm and **swatted** me out of the way, like I was some kind of gnat."
11. "They turned to us and started **jeering** as we began our lap around the field."
12. ". . . in a **frenzy** that drove away all the fear and **intimidation** that I felt from our opening lap."
13. "Joey was **sulking** pretty heavily in the back."
14. "We ran into the building and **congregated** around the double doors in the back."
15. "I watched that hand, **mesmerized**."
16. "I stood outside the car door, **unflinching**. . . ."
17. ". . . **belching** foul-smelling smoke and shooting a dangerous wild flame out the top . . ."
18. ". . . as if nothing in their **pathetic** lives had changed."
19. "Dad tried to **regain** control."
20. "He looked out of place among humans, like an **ogre** in a storybook."

About the Author

Edward Bloor was raised in Trenton, New Jersey, and received a bachelor of arts from Fordham University. After teaching at the middle and high school levels in Florida, he began to work in educational publishing. In this job, he read many young adult novels, and this inspired him to write the type of novel he had enjoyed reading in his own youth. The book he wrote was *Tangerine*. He is living in Florida with his wife and two children and working on his second novel.

From the Author

"Paul Fisher triumphs over evil in this book, not by being a violent macho man, but by being himself and by sticking to his principles. Sometimes, it seems like it isn't worth it to have principles in life. But if you hang in there long enough, you will see that it is. You may even see that principles are worth more than anything else in life."

The Trouble with Lemons
Author: Daniel Hayes
Publication date: 1991

Awards
ALA Best Books for Young Adults
International Reading Association Young Adults Choice

Characters
Tyler McAllister
Linda LaMar, Tyler's mother
Chris, Tyler's brother
Lymie
Chuckie Deegan
Mrs. Saunders
Mary Grace
Mr. Blumberg
Mark Blumberg
Jack

Setting
Present day—Wakefield, in upstate New York

Plot
His mother and brother are famous movie stars, but Tyler McAllister thinks of himself as a lemon, like the car that needs constant attention because it is always broken down. He suffers from serious allergies and asthma attacks, sleepwalks, and has nightmares. In prep school, he was lonely and fought repeatedly, sometimes in defense of his bullied roommate, and he was asked not to return. He gets into a fight with the bully in his new school and is rescued by Chuckie, their groundskeeper, who has black belts in judo and karate. He feels responsible for his parents' divorce. If all of this is not enough to make Tyler feel jinxed, what happens when he and Lymie sneak out at night to swim in Wakefield Quarry convinces him. The boys see two people get into a car and drive away and find a dead body in the quarry.

The body is later identified as BooBoo Anderson, a retarded man in his early twenties who had workedaround the school. According to medical reports, he died of a broken neck. The report also states that chlorinated water in his lungs indicates that he had been in a swimming pool and was put in the quarry after his death.

In the school detention room, Tyler overhears two boys admit that they threw BooBoo in the quarry. One of the boys is Mark Blumberg, the son of the high school principal. He and his friend, Jack, gloat about inventing a story about two hitchhikers who become the primary suspects in the death of BooBoo. They realize Tyler has overheard them, and Tyler is petrified. Chuckie figures out that Booboo probably died in the chlorinated school pool. He also cautions Tyler against acting too rashly and reminds him of Edgar Allan Poe's "Tell-Tale Heart," a short story in which the character's own guilty conscience forces him to confess. Taking Chuckie's advice, Mary Grace devises a plan that they think will force Jack to confess. Mary Grace, Tyler, and Lymie post signs for a pool party with directions to contact Jack. Jack does get overwhelmed with guilt and tells Tyler that he, Mark, and BooBoo were drinking and went into the school with Mark's father's keys. BooBoo hit his head on the diving board; and when they couldn't revive him, they decided to take him to the quarry. Jack goes to the police to confess.

Besides helping Tyler to deal with bullies and to solve the crime, Chuckie shares his own humiliation with Tyler. This helps Tyler to understand himself better. He tells Tyler that his parents did not divorce because of him and that he should not expect to be perfect and shouldn't take on the guilt for everything.

Questions for Discussion

1. Tyler's brother started calling him Lemon because his hair is yellow, but Tyler compares himself to one of his mother's cars that she called a lemon because it always needed repairs. Why does Tyler think of himself this way? Do you think he's a lemon? Does he ever come to understand himself better?

2. How would you characterize the relationship between Tyler and his mother? Between Tyler and his brother? How would you characterize the relationship between Tyler and his father? What kind of memories does Tyler have of his father? How do these memories affect his attitude about himself.

3. Tyler's mother and brother are famous. Knowing this, would you, like Chuckie, have a preconceived idea of the kind of person Tyler is? Would your feelings about him change after you met him? What do you think are Tyler's best qualities? Is there anything about him you do not like? Would you like him for a friend?

4. After his father died, Tyler cried like he has never cried before. Why hadn't he cried before this time? How did it make him feel when he finally allowed himself to cry? Have you every shared Tyler's feelings? Did crying make you feel better or worse?

5. Why was Tyler so unhappy at prep school? Describe Tyler's roommate and their relationship. How did Tyler feel about the way his roommate was treated by other students? What does this tell you about him?

6. Tyler's mother taught him that having money didn't entitle a person to be disrespectful of others. At the prep school he attended, Tyler saw the students treat the workers with disrespect. How does Tyler treat Mrs. Saunders? Do you think his mother approves of the way Mrs. Saunders is treated by Mr. Blumberg?

7. Describe the friendship between Tyler and Lymie. What draws them together as friends? Do you think they treat each other in a typical way? Do you have a friendship similar to the one shared by Tyler and Lymie?

8. Mr. Blumberg is very critical of Tyler's mother. Does he have any reason to be this way? Is there anything in his own life that explains his attitude? Why does Tyler feel sorry for Mr. Blumberg? What does this tell you about Tyler?

9. What does Mrs. Saunders tell Tyler about his brother that surprises him? Do you think this affects the way Tyler views himself? Mrs. Saunders tells Tyler that both he and his brother are normal in their own ways, and both are uniquely special. What do you think of her opinion? Do you agree that there are many kinds of normal, and all are special? Think about what makes you both normal and special.

10. What does Tyler think of Chuckie before he knows him? How does Chuckie become a very important person in Tyler's life? How does he help Tyler understand himself better?

11. Why does Tyler feel compelled to wait outside the police station when Jack is confessing? Is this consistent with his character? Do you think that Tyler is correct in saying it is foolish to view people as either good or bad?

12. What can you learn from this book about human nature? What themes about individuals and human relationships are presented in *The Trouble with Lemons*?

Projects

1. Chuckie tells Tyler about Poe's "Tell-Tale Heart" and how a person's guilt drives him to confess. Read the story, and write a brief essay that traces how the main character's guilt forces him to confess.

2. Beaver and Mark are bullies. Create a poster that illustrates ways to deal with bullies.

3. With its isolation, pool of water, rock walls, and wildlife, the Wakefield Quarry is a place of fascination. Construct a diorama or draw a picture of the quarry as it appears to Tyler and Lymie on the night they discover Boo-Boo's body.

4. One of the lessons of this book is that people are often different from our preconceived ideas. Think of someone about whom your preconceived ideas were incorrect. Write a journal entry on how your ideas about the person changed and what you learned about yourself.

5. Tyler says, "Because sometimes a person will do something for you, some little kindness or whatever, and it's one of those things you know you'll never forget for the rest of your life, no matter what." Have you ever been the recipient of a kindness that you clearly remember and think you will remember forever? If so, write the person a thank-you letter for the kindness that you were given. Be sure to mention why this was so important to you.

Vocabulary

Each of the following quotations chosen from *The Trouble with Lemons* includes one or more vocabulary words in **bold print**.

1. ". . . everyone in the class giggling and **gawking** at me."
2. "And Lymie said to forget about the village police because the quarry was out of their **jurisdiction**, and they wouldn't care."
3. "Suddenly a new face appeared, an evil face, pale, bloated, and **leering**."
4. "As I **flailed** at the water, the face smiled."
5. "I **lunged** past him, knocking him to the floor."
6. "I raised and lowered and turned my head again and again, fascinated by the fish-eye lens **distortions** of my features."
7. "It had grown quieter, more **attentive**."
8. "I was so **groggy** I felt like I'd been drugged."
9. "My legs felt rubbery, but I tried to look **nonchalant**, like a normal kid walking home after a normal day at school."
10. "Chuckie **hoisted** me over the nearest sprinkler."
11. " 'That my son had the misfortune to happen upon a senseless fight is hardly **pertinent**.' "
12. "The other kids kicked him as he **writhed** like a fat worm. . . ."
13. "It seemed sometimes that my whole life, and especially the last few years, had been so **jinxed** that hardly anything went right for me."
14. "When I realized how self-centered I'd been, **dominating** the whole conversation with my problems . . ."

About the Author

Daniel Hayes was born In Troy, New York, and received degrees from State University of New York at Plattsburgh and State University of New York at Albany. He decided to become a writer when he was in college and worked for years to develop his own style. He begins his writing by learning about his characters, who they are and what they care about. Hayes is an English teacher in Troy, New York.

From the Author

"Almost twenty years passed from the time I decided to become a writer until I actually completed my first book, *The Trouble with Lemons*. During this time, I would always toss ideas around in my head about who I wanted my first narrator to be and what kind of story I wanted to tell. Consequently, when I started writing the book, I found that a lot of the work was already done, and I was able to complete the first draft in less than two months. The initial rejections I received turned out, actually, to be good for the book as they gave me time to rewrite scenes, sharpen dialogue, and make all those little changes that we hope make an edited book better than the original."

The True Confessions of Charlotte Doyle
Author: Avi
Publication date: 1990

Awards
Newbery Honor Book
Horn Book/Boston Globe Award
Judith Lopez Memorial Award

Characters
Charlotte Doyle
Zachariah
Captain Jaggery
Mr. Keetch
Mr. Hollybrass
Mr. Barlow
Fisk
Ewing
Cranick

Setting
1832—Aboard the brig *Seahawk,* crossing the Atlantic

Plot
It's 1832, and Charlotte Doyle, the daughter of an officer in a shipping firm, sets sail on the *Seahawk,* a brig crossing the Atlantic Ocean from Liverpool, England, to Providence, Rhode Island. She is the sole passenger, for her family has preceded her home, and the other families scheduled to sail have canceled at the last minute. The very prim and proper thirteen-year-old of the times is sure she should not sail without a chaperone but is thrust aboard by her father's agent, Mr. Grummage.

A sense of foreboding occurs even before Charlotte boards the *Seahawk,* when the porters carrying baggage will not approach a ship mastered by Captain Jaggery. Aboard Mr. Barlow warns her that she would be better off far from the *Seahawk.* Zachariah, the elderly black cook, offers friendship and a knife, both of which Charlotte rejects, but Zachariah succeeds in giving her the knife. Seeing Captain Jaggery with his fine clothes and dignified way, Charlotte immediately decides that he is a gentleman. "A man to be trusted. In short, a man to whom I could talk and upon whom I can rely."

Having tea with the captain in his cabin each day, Charlotte tells of all her encounters with the seamen who have befriended her and of the dirk given her by Zachariah. Finally, she tells him of the pistol in Ewing's chest, the round-robin, and her belief that the ship harbors a stowaway. The captain calls all hands, crushes the proposed mutiny, kills Cranick, and orders fifty lashes for Zachariah. Charlotte, in attempting to stop the whipping, inadvertently flicks the whip toward Captain Jaggery, cutting his cheek and making an enemy of him.

Cast aside by the captain, Charlotte joins the crew, earning her place by climbing to the top of the royal yard. Clad in seaman's clothes previously given to her by Zachariah, Charlotte battles through a terrible storm, is accused of killing Mr. Hollybrass, the first mate, is condemned to be hanged by Captain Jaggery, and eventually becomes the captain of the *Seahawk*.

Returning home, Charlotte finds that she does not belong, for she is no longer the prim and proper young lady expected by her family. At her first opportunity, she returns to the sea with her friends aboard the *Seahawk.*

Questions for Discussion

1. Why does Charlotte board the *Seahawk* even though she will be without a chaperone? Are there differences in her training and of a child today? What do you think they are? What are the good and bad points of each?
2. When Mr. Barlow advises Charlotte that she should not be on the ship, she scorns his advice. Why? What does this tell you about Charlotte and her family? Have you ever had similar feelings?
3. Charlotte accepts Captain Jaggery as a gentleman and someone to trust. What about him leads her to these perceptions? Are these accurate measures of a person's character? What are better indicators of character?
4. " 'Justice is poorly served when you speak ill of your betters,' " is Charlotte's answer to Zachariah when he tells her the savage tale of the *Seahawk*'s previous voyage. Who has instilled this philosophy in her? What is Charlotte's opinion of this tale? What about Zachariah leads Charlotte to the conclusion?
5. What is Charlotte's reaction to the captain's killing Cranick and having Zachariah lashed? Why does the captain single out Zachariah for fifty lashes? Why does the crew react as it does?
6. Why does Charlotte decide to become a member of the crew? What does Charlotte do to earn acceptance by the crew? What character traits does Charlotte exhibit in her work as a member of the crew?
7. Captain Jaggery and Mr. Doyle display similar qualities in their expectations of Charlotte's behavior and in their treatment of those in their charge. What are the similarities? Are these qualities you admire? What was the word they both used in describing Charlotte's behavior? Do you think this word is an accurate descriptor?
8. How do you think Charlotte changed during her voyage on the Seahawk? What do you think caused these changes?
9. Who is the better man—Mr. Doyle, Captain Jaggery, or Zachariah? Why?
10. Why do you think Charlotte returned to the sea? Do you think she made the right decision? Why or why not?

Projects

1. Build a model of the *Seahawk* from the drawings in the appendix.
2. Create an alphabetic dictionary of the nautical terms in this novel. Each entry must have the correct pronunciation and one definition. You may include illustrations for some of the entries if you wish.
3. Discover the articles of clothing considered mandatory for a thirteen-year-old girl of Charlotte's station in the 1830s. Design a poster illustrating each item, or clothe a doll in the proper attire.
4. Create an imaginary two-week adventure, and keep a journal chronicling each day's happenings.
5. Research the shipping history for New England in the 1800s. Write a report showing your findings.

Vocabulary

Each of the following quotations chosen from *The True Confessions of Charlotte Doyle* includes one or more vocabulary words in **bold print**.

1. "And a stench of rot **permeated** the air."
2. ". . . that I burst into tears of **vexation**, crying with fear, rage, and humiliation."
3. "I followed with **trepidation**, stopping at the threshold to look about."
4. "I tried to grasp what I heard but I gave it up as **incomprehensible**."
5. "Captain Jaggery smiled brilliantly, then laughed—a **beguiling**, manly laugh."
6. "As **loathsome** as the food appeared, hunger dictated."
7. ". . . he received not one word of **censure**."
8. "Never had I met such **impertinence**!"
9. " 'I am a **punctilious** man, Miss Doyle.' "
10. "**Chaos** on shipboard is sailing without a rudder."
11. "Barlow was **dexterous** as a monkey."
12. "So **engrossed** was I in the explorations of my trunk. . . ."
13. "A **grotesque** carving, I told myself."
14. "The ship, festering in her own **malodorous** breath, moaned and groaned."
15. "He grunted an **affirmation**."
16. "The flesh upon my hands broke first into oozing, running sores, then **metamorphosed** into a rough new hide. . . ."
17. ". . . the captain was the principal subject of endless **scuttlebutt** in the forecastle. . . ."
18. ". . . with perfect **equanimity**—upon the final judgement."
19. "Small points perhaps, but not for a man of his **fastidiousness**."
20. "He gazed at me in **perplexity**."

About the Author

A former librarian, Avi feels that his first step to writing professionally was reading extensively. Avi now writes exciting and readable books for children and young adults. Writing in many genres including mystery, adventure, historical, supernatural, and teen life, he often offers thought-provoking themes and realistic questions about the American culture, both past and present. In whatever genre, his writing is always fast-paced and gripping, even to the reluctant reader.

Weasel
Author: Cynthia DeFelice
Publication date: 1990

Awards
Notable Children's Trade Book in the Field of Social Studies
International Reading Association and Children's Book Council Young
    Adult Award
Hodge Podger Society Award for Fiction
School Library Journal Best Books of the Year

Characters
Nathan Fowler
Molly Fowler
Pa Fowler
Ezra Ketcham
"Weasel"

Setting
1839—Ohio

Plot
    Nathan and Molly have been home alone for six days when a speechless stranger appears at the door holding their mother's locket. Since their mother's death, their father has worn the locket around his neck. Fear strikes them; they know that their pa would never part with the locket unless there was something seriously wrong. Though he does not speak, the stranger indicates that they should follow him.

    After traveling through the woods all night, the children become tired and pause to rest. At this time, Nathan catches his first glimpse of Weasel, called that by the Indians because of the shock of white in the midst of his brown hair. Weasel had been an Indian fighter hired by the government to drive the Indians off the land. With the removal of the Indians, he has turned to killing the white settlers. When they ask the stranger if the stories they heard are true, he shows them his mouth with his missing tongue cut out by Weasel and prints his name, Ezra, in the dirt.

    Reaching Ezra's we-gi-wa, Nathan and Molly find their pa near death with a leg wound. They learn that he was caught in one of Weasel's traps. When Weasel discovered him, he stole Pa's gun and left him to die. With the herbs Molly has brought with her and the healing skills taught by her mother, Molly, with Ezra's help, begins to nurse her father. Slowly he responds to the care.

Nathan suddenly realizes that they have left the animals untended, and he must return to care for them. At the cabin, he finds the pigs and chickens slaughtered and the horse and mule gone. After burying the slaughtered animals, Nathan sets out for Ezra's we-gi-wa but is stalked and captured by Weasel. During the capture Nathan causes Weasel to shoot himself in the leg. As he nurses himself with whiskey, Weasel tells Nathan how he and Ezra had been Indian fighters together. Ezra, sickened by the killing, married a Shawnee woman. Weasel killed her and the child she was expecting and mutilated Ezra. Escaping his bonds, Nathan grabs the gun from the intoxicated Weasel and escapes on the horse, Job.

Returning to the we-gi-wa, Nathan is ashamed that he did not kill Weasel when he had the chance. He is filled with hatred, and feels a bond with Ezra, who is also consumed with hate. Though Pa, Molly, and Nathan return to their home and their usual lives, Nathan cannot rest. With the arrival of spring, he returns to Weasel's cabin to discover him dead of natural causes. He and Ezra bury him; this act of civilized men begins the healing process for them. Urged by Molly, Ezra heads for Kansas to join his wife's people, and Nathan lets go of the hatred.

Questions for Discussion

1. Why did the Indians call Weasel by that name? Do you think it is appropriate?
2. What did Weasel do to Ezra and to his family? How would you feel if you were treated in this manner?
3. When Molly opens Mama's medicine bag, the aroma brings back memories of her. Has a smell, a sound, or a sight ever triggered memories for you? What were some of these?
4. Pa says, "A man who mistreats a poor, dumb beast is no better than a beast himself." What does he mean by this? Do you agree with him?
5. When Nathan returns to the farm, he feels that the woods are cold and uncaring rather than friendly and familiar. Why does he feel this way? What literary device is this an example of?
6. What does Nathan find when he reaches the cabin? What is his reaction? Have you ever wanted to go back to a safer time or place? Is this a common reaction to fear?
7. Why does Pa say that the white men called the Indians savages? Do people still do this? Can you think of some examples?
8. How does Nathan try to overcome his fear of the darkness and Weasel? Is this a good strategy? Is it one that you could use?
9. How do you feel about Weasel's remarks about what he did to Ezra? Why does he find them funny? Does this tell something about the man?
10. Why does Nathan feel ashamed that he did not kill Weasel? Would you feel the same way? Why?
11. Why do thoughts of Weasel haunt Nathan? What does his dream about the river mean? Why can't he and Ezra get to the other side? What do they need to cross?

12. What does Pa tell Nathan about killing Weasel? Why doesn't Pa dwell on Weasel's evil? Is this a good way to live?
13. Why does Nathan want to kill Weasel? What does Pa tell Nathan about revenge?
14. Why do Nathan and Ezra bury Weasel? How does this act separate them from Weasel?
15. List all the qualities that made you like Pa. List all the qualities that made you dislike Weasel. Which qualities do you see in yourself? Are you pleased with what you see?

Projects
1. Research how the Shawnee Indians built and furnished their we-gi-was. Build a three-dimensional model of one.
2. Molly brings Mama's leather medicine pouch to Ezra's we-gi-wa. Prepare a medicine pouch with the herbs that the settlers used for healing. Label each herb with its name and medicinal purpose.
3. When Nathan hears the night animals, he realizes he does not "really belong in their nighttime world." Name five creatures of the night and make a chart or a multimedia presentation, identifying their niches, feeding habits, physical description, and an interesting fact about each.
4. With a partner, research the history of the Removal Act. Present the positions of the proponents and opponents of the act to the class in the form of a formal debate.
5. Discover the many feats of Daniel Boone, and write a report presenting the facts. See what information you can find about his time in Ohio.

Vocabulary
Each of the following quotations chosen from *Weasel* includes one or more vocabulary words in **bold print**.
1. "We fed the animals, we **fetched** the water, we did everything we knew to keep things right."
2. "The twisted paths weren't familiar to me, and it took all my **concentration** just to stay on my feet and keep up."
3. "His eyes got all **squinty**, looking right past us like we weren't even there in front of him."
4. "They said he **preyed** on settlers like us."
5. "He's **cunning**."
6. "When the bag opened, Mama came back in a rush of **exotic** smells."
7. ". . . what she called **infusions**, or **poultices**, or soothing **ointments**."
8. " It did seem that Pa's face was a more normal color, and the **hectic** red spots on his cheeks were gone."
9. "In the quiet of the little room, my **outburst** seemed very loud."
10. "I looked carefully as Ezra **emphasized** by pointing, shaking, or nodding his head. . . ."
11. "I'd fill up the pig's **trough** with plenty of feed, and scatter lots of corn for the chickens."

12. "I could forget the hunger **gnawing** at my stomach and the urge to look over my shoulder."
13. "He held the knife in midair and continued speaking, his voice filled with **loathing**."
14. " 'To the **privy**,' I explained."
15. "Weasel slashed through the ropes that held my hands and watched **scornfully** as I forced my cramped arms and legs to move."
16. ". . . digging my heels into his **flanks**, and off we flew, heading west, as the sun rose in the east."
17. "For a moment I felt surprised that the river was still flowing along, unaware of my **predicament** and uncaring."
18. "I sat as silent as Ezra, **brooding** about Weasel."
19. "Pa **faltered** and didn't seem to know what to say next."
20. "I felt my lips **twitching** into a smile, thinking about what Pa said."

About the Author

Born in Philadelphia DeFelice received her bachelor of arts from William Smith College and her master of library science from Syracuse University. As a school librarian, she noticed how good books entranced children and decided that she would like to write books that cause children to want to know what happened next.

From the Author

"Before I began writing, I was a school 'media specialist' or librarian, a job I loved. As a child I was an avid reader so it was an education for me to meet reluctant readers, many of whom seemed to be boys. When I was writing *Weasel*, I was thinking about those reluctant readers. I wanted to write a book that teachers and librarians could give to them and say, 'You think reading is boring? Try this!'

"When I read the Removal Act, passed by Congress in 1830, which said to Native Americans that they had to willingly surrender and go out to the Indian Territories or be killed by the army, I was stunned, I didn't remember learning about this in my childhood studies of the westward movement. I knew I wanted to write about that experience, and about the clash of settlers and native peoples. I wanted to write about a young person's confrontation with evil, and about coping with feelings of hatred and revenge. Most of all, I wanted to write a rip-roaring adventure story!"

The Westing Game
Author: Ellen Raskin
Publication date: 1978

Awards
Newbery Medal

Characters
The Tenants
    The Wexlers —Grace, Jake, Tabitha Ruth "Turtle," Angela
    The Theodorakises—George, Theo, Chris
    The Hoos—James Shin, Sun Lin, Doug
    Judge J. J. Ford
    Sydelle Pulaski
    Flora Baumbach
Sandy McSouthers, the doorman
Otis Amber, the delivery boy
Berthe Crow, the cleaning woman
Dr. D. Denton Deere, Angela's fiancé
Barney Northrup, the real estate agent
Samuel Westing
Ed Plum, lawyer
Dr. Sikes

Setting
Present day—Wisconsin

Plot
By the first of September, the tenants of the new Sunset Towers, the Wexlers (Jake, Grace, and their daughters, Turtle and Angela), the Theodorakises (George, his wife, and sons, Theo and Chris), the Hoos (James Hin, Sun Lin, and son, Doug), Flora Baumbach, J. J. Ford, and Sydelle Pulaski, have all occupied the apartments rented by Barney Northrup. Also occupying the building are the cleaning lady, Berthe Crow, Dr. Wexler's office, the Theodorakises' Coffee Shop, and the Shin Hoo Restaurant. On Halloween, Turtle Wexler enters the haunted Wexler house and discovers the dead body of Samuel Westing. The next day sixteen people receive letters requesting their attendance for the reading of Mr. Westing's will. In addition to the occupants of the Sunset Towers, Sandy McSouthers, the doorman; Otis Amber, the sixty-two-year-old delivery

boy; Berthe Crow, the cleaning woman; and Dr. Deere, Angela's fiancé, have also received invitations to the reading of the will.

The will states that each of the invitees are the nieces and nephews of Mr. Westing and that one is his murderer. The will sets up eight teams, each of which receives ten thousand dollars and a set of clues. Mr. Wexler and Madame Hoo forfeit their clues and money since they do not appear for the reading of the will. The will hints that what you do not have is important and that some of the heirs are not who they say they are and some are not who they seem to be. As each team searches for the answer, each member develops an understanding of his or her partner and learns that each has talents.

When called to meet again, each team has some part of the solution, but it is only Turtle who fully solves the mystery of Mr. Westing's death and becomes his true heir.

Questions for Discussion

1. Describe your first impression of Turtle Wexler. Describe your first impression of Angela Wexler. How do the sisters differ? Why do you think their mother treats them differently? How does Angela's offer to hem Turtle's costume affect your first impression of her? Can you see why Angela may have been the easier daughter for her mother to like and understand?

2. What is Doug Hoo's ambition? What does his father want for him? Is it common for teenagers and their parents to disagree on what is important? Does this ever happen to you? How do you handle the situation?

3. What does Sydelle Pulaski want from the occupants of Sunset Towers? How would you feel if no one ever took notice of you? What could you do to rectify the problem?

4. What is Mrs. Wexler's attitude at the reading of the will? Does she consider herself better than the other heirs? Does she have a realistic picture of herself?

5. What do Angela and Sydelle hear when the others examine their clues? Do you think this is a good strategy? What two things do they accomplish?

6. Why does Sydelle, who was usually ignored, become the center of attention? How does she capitalize on her notoriety?

7. What four things does the Westing will imply? Why does Judge Ford think the players will stay in the game? Do you agree with her? Is greed a common failing of many people?

8. How does Turtle feel when her mother brushes and braids her hair? What is her motive in doing this? How does she react when Turtle refuses to give her any clues?

9. Why does James Hoo resent Mr. Westing? Do you think he has a good reason? How would you feel in his place?

10. Do you agree with Turtle that people hide their true selves behind a crutch or a prop? Why do you think this is done? Have you ever tried to hide your true self? Why and how did you do this?

11. What is wrong with the phrase, "English-speaking ears"? How would you correct it?
12. Why does Turtle grow so fond of her partner, Flora Baumbach? Why is she jealous of Flora's daughter? Does she wish her mother felt about her the way Flora feels for her daughter?
13. What makes Theo ashamed of his spying? How does he feel about Sam Westing and the game? What does this tell you about Theo? Does it make you like him better?
14. Why does Turtle set a bomb and confess to the other bombings? What does this tell you about her feelings for her sister? How has Angela showed her love for Turtle? How does her mother react to Turtle's actions? Are you surprised by Jake's response to her? What is the result of their talk?
15. What statement in the will leads Turtle to the solution of the mystery? Were you able to solve the puzzle along with her?

Projects

1. Be a bird watcher like Chris Theodorakis, and create a field guide for ten birds indigenous to your area. For each bird include a picture, either drawn or copied, the common and scientific name, a physical description, and the mating, nesting, feeding, and migratory habits.
2. Develop an interest in the stock market like Turtle. Select five stocks and follow the fluctuation of their prices for two weeks. Create a poster that charts these figures on a graph.
3. Design a wedding dress for Angela. Describe the material chosen, the yardage needed, and the probable cost of the dress and veil.
4. Create a menu for the Shin Hoo Restaurant that describes each dish and lists the price of each entrée.
5. Each of the heirs receives more than monetary gifts from playing the game. Make a list of each of the heirs and tell how their lives were improved and how they helped others.

Vocabulary

Each of the following quotations chosen from *The Westing Game* includes one or more vocabulary words in **bold print**.

1. "It was indeed, an **exclusive** neighborhood; too exclusive for Mr. Hoo."
2. "She was close to a **tantrum**."
3. ". . . Sandy reported as he **hoisted** a full briefcase from the trunk of the car."
4. " 'And high above the **putrid** corpse a crystal chandelier is tinkling.' "
5. "She had moved to the Sunset Towers hoping to meet **elegant** people. . . . "
6. "Under the long black cape the pockets of her jeans bulged with the necessities for the night's dangerous **vigil**."
7. "The spectacular **pyrotechnic** display could be viewed thirty miles away."
8. ". . . Turtle said, **relinquishing** her chair and stomping to the far end of the table."

9. "Some stared at the **afflicted** child with **morbid fascination**, but most turned away."
10. "Several months before he had argued before her court, **bumbling** to the point of incompetence."
11. "I have verified the **signatures**. . . ."
12. "Although the will you are about to hear may seem **eccentric**, I pledge my good name and reputation on its legality."
13. " 'I am just as appalled by our **purported** relationship.' "
14. " 'Your wife is quite lovely, you know, so doll-like and **inscrutable**.' "
15. "Grace Windkloppel Wexler, heir pretender, **pretentious** heir."
16. ". . . awarding a medal to the murderer might be **incriminating**."
17. "Which heir was the target of Westing's **vindictiveness**?"
18. "In spite of the **impeccable** logic, Angela looked over her shoulder several times on the way to 3c."
19. "Smiling without good reason was **demeaning**."
20. ". . . if only he was less **obsequious**—and less of a gossip."

About the Author

Ellen Raskin was in every sense of the word a Renaissance person, talented in the fine arts of music, art, and literature as well being an accomplished stock market analyst. After graduating from the University of Wisconsin, her home state, she proceeded to New York, where she became a freelance illustrator. After completing one thousand book-jacket designs, she embarked on her own writing career and devoted herself entirely to writing and illustrating children's books. In *Blake's Songs of Innocence*, she was able to combine all her talents by setting the poems to music and illustrating them. The American Institute of Graphic Arts selected this book as one of the Fifty Books of the Year 1996. In 1984, Ellen Raskin, at the age of fifty-six, died of complications from connective tissue disease.

What Jamie Saw
Author: Carolyn Coman
Publication date: 1995

Awards
Newbery Honor Book
ALA Notable Book for Children
Booklist Editors' Choice
National Book Award Finalist

Characters
Jamie
Patty, Jamie's mother
Nin, Jamie's sister
Van
Earl
Mrs. Desrochers

Setting
Present day—New Hampshire

Plot
Nine-year-old Jamie lives with his mother, his infant half-sister, Nin, and his mother's boyfriend, Van. One night he is awakened to the sound of Nin's cries and the sight of Van throwing the baby across the room. Fortunately, Jamie's mother, Patty, catches the baby, and, that very night, she takes the children to the apartment of her best friend, Earl. Soon they move to Earl's tiny trailer, at the base of a mountain near a pond. Earl is reluctant to relocate them at his remote place because he fears they will be "sitting ducks." Patty assures Jamie that he doesn't have to worry about where they will live, but Jamie is afraid of Van finding them and even thinks of punching holes in the bottom of the drawer Nin sleeps in so that he can quickly shut the drawer if Van surprises them. Both Jamie and Patty are terrified when they think they see Van at a holiday fair in the local high school.

After this episode, Jamie stays home from school and his mother from work for a week until Jamie's teacher, Mrs. Desrochers, visits them. She overcomes Patty's antagonism by reassuring Jamie's mother and offering to keep Jamie on Tuesdays so that Patty can attend a women's support group. When Patty leaves to return the bag his teacher has left behind, Jamie is terrified that she isn't coming back.

Some comfort and fun do come to Jamie during this time through the magic tricks that he enjoys performing. Van had given him a magic book, and he prac-

ticed many tricks, with Nin as an audience. Also, Earl gives Jamie an early
Christmas present of ice skates and teaches him to skate on the pond near the
trailer.

When Van finally does come to the trailer, Jamie is alone with Nin. His first
reaction is to hide with her, but he comes out from hiding to confront Van and
protect his sister. After Van goes outside to wait for Patty, Jamie invites him
back inside so that when Patty comes home and sees his truck she can go for
help if she wants. When Patty returns, Jamie refuses to leave. Patty tells Van to
go, and he does. After Van leaves, Jamie is consumed with tears, and Patty reas-
sures him that they are all right.

Questions for Discussion

1. What kind of man is Van? How does he react after he throws the baby?
   When Patty tells him to leave?
2. How does Jamie feel about Van? When Van stands by the crib? When he
   comes to the trailer? How do you feel about Van?
3. Why does Patty take her children away? Does she make a good decision to
   take them to the trailer? In what ways do you admire her as a mother?
4. What kind of man is Earl? What admirable qualities does he have? Is Patty
   right in considering him her best friend?
5. How does fear affect Jamie and his mother? Do you think they handle their
   fear in the right way? Have you ever been really afraid? How did you react?
6. At one point Jamie kicks the drawer in which his sister is sleeping; another
   time he kicks his mother. How can you explain the temper that Jamie
   shows?
7. How does Mrs. Desrochers reassure Jamie and Patty? What admirable
   qualities does she have?
8. How does Jamie act to protect his sister and mother when Van comes? Do
   you think he makes the right decisions? Do you admire what he does? Why
   does he refuse to leave when his mother asks him to?
9. After Van leaves, Jamie cries and cries. Is this understandable? Have you
   ever reacted like this after a crisis is over?
10. Do you think the events of this story will make Jamie's family stronger?
    Why?

Projects

1. Think about Jamie, his mother, and his sister one year later. What has happened to them? Write an afterword to this novel that details what their lives
   have become one year later.
2. Jamie loves to do magic tricks. Locate a book on magic, and learn to do a
   trick that you perform for your class.
3. Throughout the book, Patty smokes. Locate information on the dangers of
   smoking; prepare a poster or a multimedia presentation that details the dangers of smoking for the smoker and anyone in the same place with a
   smoker.

4. Jamie's family members are the victims of abuse. Find out what services are available in your community, through social service agencies, churches, or community groups, to help the victims of abuse. Make a list of these services including what they offer and how they can be contacted.

Vocabulary

Each of the following quotations chosen from *What Jamie Saw* includes one or more vocabulary words in **bold print**.

1. ". . . her words were slow and **deliberate** and powerful."
2. "**Frigid** winter air **encased** them."
3. "His mother had shifted the car into reverse with a **decisive**, deep-bellied thunk. . . ."
4. "How quickly her one word stopped the **ferocious** pounding in his heart."
5. "It was the gravel of Earl's U-turn driveway crunching under the tires that **jostled** Jamie awake again. . . ."
6. ". . . that didn't seem to **clinch** anything either. . . ."
7. ". . . but it **embarrassed** him to feel sorry for a grownup. . . ."
8. ". . . **hoisting** the bag stuffed with diapers and wipes and bottles."
9. "Maybe he asked her for one more time, one more round, but she wasn't **budging**. . . ."
10. ". . . the car felt dark and **cavernous** to Jamie. . . ."
11. ". . . her body released and **slumped** in on itself."
12. ". . . sunlight that was pouring through the window, **drenching** them."
13. "It struck two days before Christmas and covered every **exposed** thing with a **delicate** but strong layer of ice."
14. ". . . her **enraged** and terrified face . . ."
15. ". . . kicked her legs in **anticipation** of being lifted up."

About the Author

Born in Evanston, Illinois, Carolyn Coman received a degree in writing from Hampshire College in Amherst, Massachusetts. After apprenticing with a master bookbinder, she operated her own bindery. She has worked as an editor for an educational publisher and taught writing at Harvard Extension and Harvard Summer School. She is currently on the faculty of Vermont College in the Masters in Fine Arts Writing for Children Program. She has said, "I am drawn to characters who make me feel deeply—make me mad, confuse me, make me wonder, break my heart, stagger me with what they are up against . . . I listen carefully to the sounds of their voices, and to what they are trying to say."

When Zachary Beaver Came to Town
Author: Kimberly Willis Holt
Publication date: 1999

Awards
National Book Award for Young People's Literature

Characters
Toby Wilson
Zachary Beaver
Cal McKnight
Otto Wilson, Toby's father
Paulie Rankin
Miss Myrtie Mae
The Judge
Sheriff Levi Fetterman

Setting
1971—Texas

Plot
Thirteen-year-old Toby and his friend, Cal, pay money along with many other people in town to walk through Zachary Beaver's trailer and see fifteen-year-old, six hundred and forty-three-pound Zachary, the world's fattest boy. When Paulie Rankin, Zachary's guardian, who had pulled Zachary's trailer into town, leaves, Toby and Cal start to leave food for Zachary on the trailer steps. They also throw rocks at kids who are taunting Zachary and accidentally break a window in Zachary's trailer. When the sheriff asks the boys to accompany him to the trailer to check on Zachary and find out when Paulie will return, they find Zachary rude and obnoxious. However, he does not tell the sheriff that Toby and Cal broke the window in his trailer. They rationalize that Zachary doesn't squeal because he has secrets of his own, namely about where Paulie has gone and why his baptism was not recorded in his Bible although he claimed to have been baptized.

The boys decide that they will try to get Zachary out to the drive-in theater. They build stairs so that Zachary can climb into the back of their truck and coerce Cal's sister into driving their pickup truck. When Toby sees the finger pointing and hears the fat-boy taunts, he realizes that Zachary hides in his trailer to escape and has invented the stories about all the exotic places he's been and about his baptism. In the meantime Toby's mother goes to Nashville for a singing contest and decides to stay. Toby lies about why she has not returned and realizes that his lies are not very different from Zachary's. Toby refuses to deal with his mother's absence and does not even open the letters she has sent him. At the same time, Cal's family is struggling with the absence of Cal's brother, Wayne, who is fighting in Vietnam. When Cal stalls about writing Wayne, Toby writes to the soldier and signs Cal's name. The family receives word that Wayne is killed, but Toby cannot bring himself to go to the wake or the funeral even to support his friend.

Cal confesses that he wishes he had written to his brother instead of Toby, who apologizes for not being able to go to the funeral. Toby's father explains that he shouldn't have expected his wife to change and give up her dreams, and Toby reconnects with his mother. Cal and Toby arrange for Zachary to be baptized. When Paulie returns, he pulls Zachary's trailer out of town, and Toby knows that he and Cal will never hear from Zachary again. However, they have accepted Zachary for who he was, and have both learned to accept their changing lives.

Questions for Discussion

1. How do others treat Zachary? How does he react to this treatment? Why has he allowed Paulie to put him on display?
2. How do Toby and Cal defend Zachary when he is picked on by other kids? Would you do the same thing in a similar situation?
3. Why is Zachary sometimes sarcastic and rude? How do Toby and Cal deal with his behavior? Do they try to understand why he behaves the way he does? Do you admire the way they treat him?
4. Why does Toby feel the need to write to Wayne? Why does he sign Cal's name? Why does Cal procrastinate about writing to his brother? Does this procrastination make him feel worse about his brother's death?
5. Why does Toby lie about his mother staying in Nashville? What are the similarities between Toby's lying and Zachary's lying?
6. Why can't Toby go to the wake and the funeral for Wayne? Do you think he lets his friend, Cal, down? Do you respect him for the way he acts? What does Toby's father think about Toby's actions? How does Cal react to Toby's not coming to the services? Have you ever made yourself do something that you did not want to do?
7. Do you think Toby and Cal understand each other at the end of the novel? What does this tell you about their friendship?
8. Miss Myrtie Mae's brother, the Judge, is old and forgetful. How does Toby treat him? Why is it important to be kind and considerate to the elderly?
9. Why does Toby's mother leave home? Do you admire her for doing this? How does Toby deal with her actions?
10. What kind of relationship does Toby have with his father? Do you think he comes to understand him better as the novel progresses?
11. Why is it important to Toby and Cal to baptize Zachary?
12. What are the themes of this novel? What are the important life lessons presented in this novel?

Projects

1. Cal and Toby go to the library to see if Zachary is included in the *Guinness Book of World Records*. Look at a recent copy of this book for world records that you find especially unique and interesting. Also find out how a record is determined to be one that can be included in this book. Organize all of this information into a multimedia presentation on the *Guinness Book*.
2. Wayne McKnight is serving in the Vietnam War. Locate historical information on this conflict, including the dates, causes, participants, and involvement of the Unites States. Organize your information into a report.
3. Toby believes that they will never hear from Zachary again; however, they experience several memorable things together. Begin a correspondence between Zachary and Toby one year after the novel ends. Include their feelings about what they did together and what happened to them afterward.
4. Toby's father raises worms, and Toby is able to explain some of the uses beyond fishing bait. Make a poster that outlines the beneficial uses of worms.
5. Each year, Cal's family releases sacks of ladybugs in their cotton fields to combat bollworms. The scene of the ladybugs being released, the "Ladybug Waltz," is particularly descriptive. Draw a picture of this scene.

Vocabulary

Each of the following quotations chosen from *When Zachary Beaver Came to Town* includes one or more vocabulary words in **bold print**.

1. ". . . with two dollars **clutched** in hand . . ."
2. ". . . it's not as flat and **sparse** as most of the Panhandle."
3. ". . . while people come by to **gawk** at him."
4. "Cal and I **straddle** our bikes. . . ."
5. ". . . except for his usual eye **twitch**, his face looks blank."
6. "I'm not a **snitch** like Malcolm."
7. "Sheriff Levi **grimaces**, and his voice becomes firm."
8. "Her voice **quivers**. . . ."
9. ". . . **fumbling** with his pocket watch."
10. "The sight of the Judge breathing down my face doesn't **fluster** her at all."
11. ". . . she's so **engrossed** in it, she doesn't see me."
12. "I **traipse** over to the kitchen drawer. . . ."
13. "Zachary **snarls** as I **devour** my slice. . . ."
14. "Dad studies me and I **squirm**, wishing I could **vanish**."

About the Author

Kimberly Willis Holt has lived all around the world and now resides in Texas with her family. Her first novel, *My Louisiana Sky*, received many awards and was named an ALA Notable Book. Her idea for this book came from seeing the fattest boy in the world at the Louisiana State Fair when she was thirteen years old.

From the Author

"Like most of my stories, the voice of the main character came first. And like most of my books, the first words came easily, then left me wondering where do I go from here. The rough draft of *When Zachary Beaver Came to Town* was awful. I felt like a huge failure. After I finally figured out how Toby and Cal would help Zachary the story fell into place."

Wringer
Author: Jerry Spinelli
Publication date: 1997

Awards
Newbery Honor Book

Characters
Palmer LaRue, nickname "Snots"
Mother and father
Dorothy Gruzik, "Fishface"
Arthur Dodds, "Beans"
Billy Natola, "Mutto"
Henry

Setting
Present day—Waymer, a rural community in the United States

Plot
Birthdays for young people are something to be eagerly anticipated, but for eight-year-old Palmer LaRue each birthday brings him closer to the tenth, when he can or must become a wringer. In Palmer's hometown of Waymer, Pigeon Day is the climax of the annual summer Family Fest. To raise money for the community park, sharpshooters from the area pay a fee to shoot at ten or twenty birds released from crates. A few of the pigeons escape, many are killed outright, and some are only wounded. It is the privilege of ten-year-olds to retrieve the downed birds, wringing the necks of the wounded and placing all in boxes to become fertilizer.

Palmer's ninth birthday party initiates him into the gang, joining "Beans," "Mutto," and Henry. As he strives to be "Snots," a true gang member, he turns his back on his innate sense of right and wrong. Becoming a true member of the gang involves tormenting his neighbor and friend, Dorothy, and pretending a happy anticipation of becoming a wringer when he reaches ten. But then a visitor taps on his window and enters his room and his life. The visitor, a pigeon that Palmer names Nipper, becomes his well-loved pet and a secret that he shares only with Dorothy. Palmer knows that he cannot participate in Pigeon Day, but how can he get the courage to disappoint his father, a former wringer and sharpshooter, and to go against the gang? For Palmer, love becomes stronger than fear; he defies the gang and the whole town to save Nipper's life.

Questions for Discussion

1. "It was simply a whisper of featherwings, reminding him of the moment he dreaded above all others." What does the phrase "a whisper of feather-wings" mean to you? Have you ever experienced a similar feeling? What words would you use to describe it?

2. Palmer describes his happiness following his birthday party, "New birthday. New Friends. New feelings of excitement and pride and belonging." Why then does he burst into tears?

3. After viewing his first Pigeon Day, Palmer learns that the role of the wringer is to put the wounded pigeons out of their misery. What questions does this knowledge present to him? What questions does this statement arouse in you?

4. How does Palmer acquire a pigeon for a pet? What does Palmer do to keep his pet a secret from his family? How does he distract the gang from coming to his house? Why is Palmer afraid to have people find out about Nipper?

5. The gang has been tormenting Dorothy for days, and Palmer has been expecting consequences. What does the gang do to torment Dorothy? How does she react? What does Beans want her to do? When she finally responds, what does she do? How does this affect Palmer?

6. When the gang sees Nipper land on Palmer's head, what do they think? How does Palmer react to their accusations? What would you do?

7. When the gang invades Palmer's room, what do they discover? How do Palmer's thoughts about the gang and Henry make him realize something about himself? How does Palmer first rebel against the gang?

8. What does Palmer learn about his parents in the story? Do you think this is true of many parents?

Projects

1. Jerry Spinelli is the prize-winning author of many books for children. Using your school or community library or the Internet, investigate the life and works of this author. Report your findings in a book format including a title page, a table of contents, titled chapters, and a list of sources where your information was found.

2. Search your library or the Internet for information about pigeons. If using the Internet, two helpful websites are:

   http://www.weast-world.com/pigeons/sjhpc-2.htm
   http://www.interbug.com/pigeons

   Make a poster illustrating the facts located. The poster may be manually or electronically produced.

3. Pigeons were used as a source of communication before the invention of the telegraph or the telephone. Locate historical instances where pigeons were used. Create a short story or a play about one of these instances.

4. Many people raise pigeons as a hobby. Locate someone in your community with this hobby. Interview him or her about the care and training of such

pets. Record this conversation on either video or audiotape for class presentation.

Vocabulary

Each of the following quotations chosen from *Wringer* includes one or more vocabulary words in **bold print**.

1. "The red fingers and lips of a man cheering, **spewing** specks of barbecued chicken."
2. "Palmer even saw one crossing a street with a crowd of people on a green light, just another **pedestrian**."
3. "The pigeon was on his pillow, sounding like someone **gargling** water."
4. "At times the Ferris Wheel seemed to be **winching** minutes."
5. "Jogging through the dark and sleepy alleyways, **skirting** pools of streetlight. . . "
6. "They picked up sticks and **racketed** along the slats."
7. "Palmer fired without **restraint**."
8. "He bopped Mutto again with the muskrat **carcass**, chased him twice around the table and out the kitchen."
9. "Brown hair **funneled** into a ponytail by a plain rubber band."
10. "Several times in the noise and **jostle**, he thought he heard Bean's voice."
11. "Words were **etched** into a shiny panel below the statue."
12. "He tumbled lifelessly through July, feeling as dry and empty as the **cicada** husks on the trees."

About the Author

Jerry Spinelli lives in Pennsylvania with his wife, who is also an author, and their six children. A Newbery winner for his *Maniac Magee*, he is noted for his accurate and humorous descriptions of adolescent life. His sure ear for adolescent dialogue is greatly assisted by hearing it at home, for his children are often the inspiration for his characters and themes.

From the Author

"Every year my morning newspaper carried an article about a small-town pigeon shoot. I knew this was story material, but how to get into it? Then it occurred to me: tell it through one of the boys. Better yet: make him not want the job he inherits on his birthday. Start it: he did not want to be a wringer. I was on my way."

A Wrinkle in Time
Author: Madeleine L'Engle
Publication date: 1962

Award

Newbery Medal

Characters

Meg Murry
Charles Hamilton Murry
Sandy and Dennys Murry
Mrs. Murry
Calvin O'Keefe
Mrs. Whatsit
Mrs. Who
Mrs. Which
Mr. Murry
Aunt Beast
It

Setting

The Universe

Plot

Mr. Murry, a scientist for the government, disappeared two years ago while on a secret mission. Two of his four children, Meg, an awkward adolescent, and Charles Hamilton, a brilliant four-year-old with special abilities, join with Calvin O'Keefe to search for him. They are aided in their venture by Mrs. Whatsit, Mrs. Who, and Mrs. Which, who for lack of a better term, will be called witches. The three witches are accomplished at tessering, the project on which Mr. and Mrs. Murry have been working. A tesseract, as explained by Charles Hamilton, is the fifth dimension or a way of traveling through space without actually covering the miles. Another way of explaining a tesseract is a wrinkle in time or space.

The six tesser to Uriel, where the witches begin to explain about themselves and about Mr. Murry's mission. When Mrs. Whatsit turns into her true form, a beautiful winged centaur, she brings the children up into the atmosphere and shows them the Black Thing, evil, and explains that this is what Mr. Murry is fighting. The Black Thing is trying to take over the earth. Meg, Charles Hamilton, and Calvin, after several learning adventures, finally arrive on Camazotz where Mr. Murry is imprisoned. Mrs. Whatsit, Mrs. Who, and Mrs. Which tell the children that they must battle the Black Thing without their help but leave them with a talisman and helpful advice. Mrs. Who gives Meg her glasses, and Mrs. Which commands them to enter the town and admonishes that they should never separate. Mrs. Whatsit warns Charles Hamilton that his pride and arrogance are his greatest liabilities, to Meg she gives her faults, and for Calvin she strengthens his ability to communicate.

The first thing the threesome notices is that every house and yard are exactly alike and the children and their mothers do all motions in unison. They proceed to the CENTRAL Central Intelligence Building, where they encounter the man with the red eyes who can communicate directly to their brains. After several failed attempts to control Charles Hamilton's brain, Charles Hamilton, thinking that he can keep part of himself back, becomes controlled by It. Charles Hamilton leads Meg and Calvin to a transparent column in which Mr. Murry is imprisoned. With the aid of Mrs. Who's glasses, Mr. Murry, Meg, and Calvin escape, leaving Charles Hamilton behind.

Only one person can save Charles Hamilton and that is Meg, who must return to Camazotz alone. Though fearful, she realizes that the only thing she has that It does not have is love, and this she gives to Charles Hamilton, breaking It's hold over him.

Questions for Discussion

1. Why does Meg feel that she is a monster or an oddball? How does she feel about being different? Are her insecurities common for girls her age? Do you ever feel that you are different from the others around you? Does that feeling make you happy or sad?

2. What do Calvin and Charles Hamilton have in common? Calvin says to Charles Hamilton, " 'I must remember I'm precoditioned in my concept of your mentality.' " What does he mean by that statement? Why does Meg have it tough in Charles Hamilton's estimation?

3. Why did Meg lose her fear when they entered the haunted house? Does it help with your fears and worries to know that someone is concerned?

4. Calvin feels he is going home for the first time when he is invited to the Murry house. Why? Why does he not feel this way about his own house and family?

5. Though Calvin comes from a terrible home life, he has something that Meg lacks. Do you know what it is? How does he help Meg to feel better about herself?

6. How does Mrs. Who explain "tessering"? Do you think it is possible to do? Have any space explorations used this technique? Do you think it might ever be possible?

7. What are Mrs. Whatsit's talents? How does Mrs. Whatsit feel about her own talents? Do you know any talents that you may have? How have you used them?

8. When Meg sees Calvin's mother in the Happy Medium's globe, what does she do? Why does she want to help and protect Calvin?

9. What gifts does Mrs. Whatsit give the three children? What did Mrs. Who and Mrs. Which give them? How do you think they may be of help?

10. What is the first thing the children notice about Camazotz? Do you ever feel that you are expected to be like everyone else? Do you want to be like everyone else, or do you enjoy your individuality? How do the differences in people contribute to the welfare and improvement of the world?

11. For what reason does Charles Hamilton choose to go into It? What does the red-eyed man say will be the result of this decision? How does Charles Hamilton's pride and arrogance contribute to his being taken in by It?

12. What does Charles Hamilton tell Meg and Calvin about the planet, Camazotz? What happens to those who are ill or deformed? Has this evil ever occurred on our own planet? What happened because of this evil?

13. On Camazotz, everyone is alike. What do Meg and Calvin feel about this for themselves? Why does Meg feel that you must be unhappy sometimes? Do you agree with her?

14. How does Meg release Mr. Murry from the transparent column? Why is Meg disappointed with her father's response to the situation? Do children often think that their parents can accomplish anything? Why do you think this is so?

15. Why does Calvin tell Mr. Murry to tesser? What is Meg's reaction when Calvin and Mr. Murry try to explain their reason for leaving Charles Hamilton behind? Do people often lash out in hatred or meanness when they are greatly hurt or disappointed?

16. When Meg thinks, "It was she who was limited by her senses, not the blind beasts, for they must have sense of which she could not even dream," what does she mean?

17. What does she mean when Aunt Beast says, " 'For the things which are seen are temporal. But the things which are not seen are eternal.' "?

18. How does Meg defeat It? Is love a strong force against evil? Why? Is this a wise lesson for you to learn?

19. Review the children's time on Camazotz. Analyze the ways in which the witches' gifts helped them.

Projects

1. Make a list of the famous sixteen people suggested by the three children as fighters against the darkness. Research the accomplishments of each, and make a chart of your findings.

2. Make a poster of earth's galaxy. Be sure that the distances and sizes of the planets are in proportion.

3. Research one of the elements mentioned by Meg, and write a report. Things to be included should be its symbol, atomic weight, atomic mass, history, physical properties, chemical properties, uses, and methods of obtaining it from nature. A drawing of its Bohr model should also be included.

4. Read about what a sonnet is and what form it must have; then write a sonnet of your own.
5. Select a poet who is famous for writing sonnets; then explain what one of the sonnets means to you.

Vocabulary

Each of the following quotations chosen from *A Wrinkle in Time* includes one or more vocabulary words in **bold print**.

1. ". . . the trees tossing in **frenzied** lashing of the wind."
2. " '**Prodigious**,' Mrs. Murry said. "
3. "Mrs. Whatsit untied a blue and green **paisley** scarf. . . ."
4. ". . . Mrs. Whatsit said, still **supine**."
5. "Meg **flounced** out."
6. "Try to be a little less **antagonistic**."
7. " 'I'm third from the top of eleven kids. I'm a **sport**.' "
8. "Charles and Fortinbras **gamboled** on ahead."
9. "She was watching a pale blue fluid move slowly through a tube from a beaker to a **retort**."
10. ". . . he announced **judiciously**."
11. ". . . but her happiness had fled and she was back in a **morass** of anger and resentment."
12. "The **corporeal** Meg simply was not."
13. "A deaf person can feel **vibrations**."
14. ". . . Mrs. Which, despite her looks and **ephemeral** broomstick. . ."
15. ". . . across a plateau of granite-like rock shaped into enormous **monoliths**."
16. ". . . when they reached the **corona** of clouds."
17. "His voice took on the dry, **pedantic** tones of Mr. Jenkins."
18. ". . . and scorn and disapproval seemed to **emanate** from him."
19. "The red **miasma** swan before her eyes. . . ."
20. ". . . **catapulted** his sleek black body right through the screened door of the kitchen."

About the Author

Madeleine L'Engle, born in 1918 and named for her mother and grand-mother, is one of the most widely read writers for children and young adults. Since the 1960s she has written more than forty science fiction, coming-of-age, mystery, and suspense novels, which have enraptured her readers. In addition to these, she has also written plays, poetry, and adult fiction. One of the truly cap-tivating features of her writing is the continuity of her characters, for as the reader grows up and matures, so do Meg, Charles Hamilton, and Calvin in many of her succeeding works.

Titles Arranged by Genre and Theme

Frequently when working with middle readers, the selection of a book may depend upon the needs of the reader. One purpose may be to enlighten the reader concerning the different literary genres; another may be the need to stress a theme. In order to help the teacher, librarian, or parent, we have chosen several genres and themes and placed our selected novels in the appropriate categories. Be aware that most novels will appear in more than one category.

Genre

Adventure
Around the World in Eighty Days
Deathwatch
Harry Potter and the Sorcerer's Stone
Holes
The Indian in the Cupboard
The Maze
Save Queen of Sheba
Stone Fox
The True Confessions of Charlotte Doyle
Weasel

Animals
Animal Farm
Bambi
Shiloh
Stone Fox

Classics
Animal Farm
Around the World in Eighty Days
Bambi
Pudd'nhead Wilson
The Secret Garden

Fantasy/Science Fiction
Animal Farm
Ella Enchanted
The Giver
The Indian in the Cupboard
Skellig

Fantasy/Science Fiction (continued)
Stranger with My Face
A Wrinkle in Time

Historical Fiction
Bud, Not Buddy
Holes
The Indian in the Cupboard
Jacob Have I Loved
Lily's Crossing
A Long Way from Chicago
The Midwife's Apprentice
Nightjohn
Out of the Dust
Save Queen of Sheba
The True Confessions of Charlotte Doyle
Weasel

Mystery
The Face on the Milk Carton
Holes
Pudd'nhead Wilson
The Séance
Secrets at Hidden Valley
Stranger with My Face
The Westing Game

Theme

Coming-of-Age
Belle Prater's Boy
Crazy Lady!
Dancing on the Edge
Dear Mr. Henshaw
Dicey's Song
Ella Enchanted
The Giver
Jacob Have I Loved
The Maze
The Midwife's Apprentice
The Moves Make the Man
Out of the Dust
The Pigman
The Secret Garden
Secrets at Hidden Valley

Coming-of-Age (continued)

Shiloh
Somewhere in the Darkness
Stone Fox
Summer of My German Soldier
Tangerine
The Trouble with Lemons
The True Confessions of Charlotte Doyle
Weasel
The Westing Game
What Jamie Saw
Wringer
A Wrinkle in Time

Discrimination

Animal Farm
Crazy Lady!
Jacob Have I Loved
A Long Way from Chicago
The Moves Make the Man
Nightjohn
Petey
Pudd'nhead Wilson
Somewhere in the Darkness
Summer of My German Soldier
Tangerine
Weasel
When Zachary Beaver Came to Town

Family

After the Rain
Amber Brown Goes Fourth
Belle Prater's Boy
Bud, Not Buddy
Dancing on the Edge
Dear Mr. Henshaw
Dicey's Song
The Face on the Milk Carton
The Giver
Harry Potter and the Sorcerer's Stone
Jacob Have I Loved
Lily's Crossing
A Long Way from Chicago
Missing May
On My Honor
Out of the Dust

Family (continued)

Pudd'nhead Wilson
Save Queen of Sheba
The Secret Garden
Secrets at Hidden Valley
Shiloh
Skellig
Somewhere in the Darkness
Stone Fox
Summer of My German Soldier
Tangerine
The Trouble with Lemons
The True Confessions of Charlotte Doyle
Weasel
When Zachary Beaver Came to Town
Wringer
A Wrinkle in Time

Friendship

Amber Brown Goes Fourth
Belle Prater's Boy
Harry Potter and the Sorcerer's Stone
Holes
The Indian in the Cupboard
Lily's Crossing
The Maze
The Moves Make the Man
On My Honor
Petey
The Pigman
The Secret Garden
Skellig
Summer of My German Soldier
What Jamie Saw
When Zachary Beaver Came to Town

Intergenerational

After the Rain
Bud, Not Buddy
Dicey's Song
The Giver
Jacob Have I loved
A Long Way from Chicago
Missing May
Petey

Intergenerational (continued)
The Pigman
Stone Fox

Sports
Harry Potter and the Sorcerer's Stone
The Moves Make the Man
Stone Fox
Tangerine

Survival
Deathwatch
Dicey's Song
Ella Enchanted
Holes
The Maze
The Midwife's Apprentice
The Moves Make the Man
Nightjohn
Out of the Dust
Save Queen of Sheba
Somewhere in the Darkness
Stranger with My Face
Summer of My German Soldier
The True Confessions of Charlotte Doyle
Weasel
Wringer

Character Traits in the Novels

Teachers, librarians, and parents with children and young adults may at times recognize a special need in a youngster for a heightened awareness of a particular character trait. They may wish to suggest specific titles in the hopes that reading about it in a fictional work will positively influence the reader. We have selected twenty-three admirable character traits and listed titles in which the protagonist or subordinate person either positively or negatively illustrated them.

Citizenship

Deathwatch
Lily's Crossing
A Long Way from Chicago
The Maze
The Moves Make the Man

Nightjohn
Shiloh
Somewhere in the Darkness
Summer of My German Soldier
Weasel

Compassion

After the Rain
Belle Prater's Boy
Dancing on the Edge
The Indian in the Cupboard
Jacob Have I Loved
A Long Way from Chicago
The Midwife's Apprentice
Missing May
The Moves Make the Man

Nightjohn
The Pigman
Skellig
Stranger with my Face
Summer of My German Soldier
True Confessions of Charlotte Doyle
When Zachary Beaver Came to Town
Wringer
A Wrinkle in Time

Cooperation

Animal Farm
Around the World in Eighty Days
Harry Potter and the Sorcerer's Stone
Holes
Jacob Have I Loved
The Maze

Save Queen of Sheba
Stone Fox
Summer of My German Soldier
Tangerine
The Westing Game
A Wrinkle in Time

Courage

Around the World in Eighty Days
Bambi
Belle Prater's Boy
Bud, Not Buddy
Dancing on the Edge
Deathwatch
Ella Enchanted
The Giver
Harry Potter and the Sorcerer's Stone
Holes
A Long way from Chicago
The Maze
The Midwife's Apprentice
The Moves Make the Man
Nightjohn
Petey
Save Queen of Sheba
Shiloh
Somewhere in the Darkness
Stone Fox
Stranger with my Face
Tangerine
True Confessions of Charlotte Doyle
Weasel
Wringer
A Wrinkle in Time

Dependability

After the Rain
Around the World in Eighty Days
Belle Prater's Boy
Crazy Lady!
Dicey's Song
The Giver
The Indian in the Cupboard
The Maze
The Midwife's Apprentice
Petey
Save Queen of Sheba
Secrets at Hidden Valley
Stone Fox
The Westing Game
A Wrinkle in Time

Fairness

Amber Brown Goes Fourth
Animal Farm
The Giver
A Long Way from Chicago
The Moves Make the Man
Summer of My German Soldier
Tangerine

Generosity

Around the World in Eighty Days
Belle Prater's Boy
Dear Mr. Henshaw
Ella Enchanted
Jacob Have I Loved
A Long Way from Chicago
The Pigman
What Jamie Saw
When Zachary Beaver Came to Town

Helpfulness

After the Rain
Around the World in Eighty Days
Crazy Lady!
Dicey's Song
Ella Enchanted
Holes
A Long Way from Chicago
The Midwife's Apprentice

Petey
The Secret Garden
Secrets at Hidden Valley
Skellig
Tangerine
The Trouble with Lemons
What Jamie Saw
When Zachary Beaver Came to Town

Integrity

Animal Farm
Around the World in Eighty Days
Bambi
Belle Prater's Boy
Deathwatch
Dicey' Song
Ella Enchanted
The Face on the Milk Carton
Holes
The Indian in the Cupboard
Lily's Crossing
A Long Way from Chicago
The Maze
The Midwife's Apprentice
Missing May

Nightjohn
On My Honor
The Pigman
Pudd'nhead Wilson
The Séance
Shiloh
Stranger with My Face
Summer of My German Soldier
Tangerine
The Trouble with Lemons
True Confessions of Charlotte Doyle
Weasel
When Zachary Beaver Came to Town
A Wrinkle in Time

Kindness

After the Rain
Around the World in Eighty Days
Belle Prater's Boy
Crazy Lady!
Dancing on the Edge
Harry Potter and the Sorcerer's Stone
Jacob Have I Loved
A Long Way from Chicago
The Maze
Missing May
Nightjohn
Petey
The Pigman

Pudd'nhead Wilson
The Secret Garden
Secrets at Hidden Valley
Stone Fox
Stranger with My Face
Summer of My German Soldier
Tangerine
True Confessions of Charlotte Doyle
The Westing Game
What Jamie Saw
When Zachary Beaver Came to Town
A Wrinkle in Time

Loyalty

Amber Brown Goes Fourth
Animal Farm
Belle Prater's Boy
The Face on the Milk Carton
Harry Potter and the Sorcerer's Stone
Holes
On My Honor
The Secret Garden

Stone Fox
Tangerine
The Trouble with Lemons
True Confessions of Charlotte Doyle
The Westing Game
What Jamie Saw
Wringer

Optimism

Around the World in Eighty Days
Ella Enchanted
Missing May
Nightjohn
Petey

The Secret Garden
Secrets at Hidden Valley
Skellig
Stone Fox
Stranger with My Face

Patience

After the Rain
Belle Prater's Boy
Deathwatch
Dicey's Song
Holes

Nightjohn
Out of the Past
Petey
The Secret Garden
The Westing Game

Perseverance

After the Rain
Animal Farm
Around the World in Eighty Days
Bud, Not Buddy
Crazy Lady!
Dancing on the Edge
Deathwatch
Dicey's Song
The Face on the Milk Carton
The Giver
Holes

Nightjohn
On My Honor
Out of the Dust
Petey
Save Queen of Sheba
The Secret Garden
Stone Fox
Tangerine
True Confessions of Charlotte Doyle
When Zachary Beaver Came to Town
A Wrinkle in Time

Resilience

Around the World in Eighty Days
Belle Prater's Boy
Bud, Not Buddy
Dancing on the Edge
Deathwatch
Dicey's Song
Ella Enchanted
The Maze
The Midwife's Apprentice
On My Honor
Out of the Dust
Nightjohn

Petey
Pudd'nhead Wilson
Save Queen of Sheba
Somewhere in the Darkness
Summer of My German Soldier
Tangerine
The Trouble with Lemons
True Confessions of Charlotte Doyle
What Jamie Saw
When Zachary Beaver Came to Town
A Wrinkle in Time

Resourcefulness

Amber Brown Goes Fourth
Animal Farm
Bud, Not Buddy
Crazy Lady!
Dear Mr. Henshaw
Deathwatch
Dicey's Song
Ella Enchanted
The Face on the Milk Carton
The Giver
Harry Potter and the Sorcerer's Stone
Holes
Lily's Crossing
A Long Way from Chicago
The Maze

The Midwife's Apprentice
Petey
Save Queen of Sheba
The Secret Garden
Secrets at Hidden Valley
Stone Fox
Stranger with My Face
Tangerine
True Confessions of Charlotte Doyle
Weasel
The Westing Game
What Jamie Saw
When Zachary Beaver Came to Town
A Wrinkle in Time

Respect

After the Rain
Around the World in Eighty Days
Bambi
Belle Prater's Boy
The Giver
Harry Potter and the Sorcerer's Stone
The Indian in the Cupboard
A Long Way from Chicago

The Maze
The Moves Make the Man
Petey
The Pigman
Pudd'nhead Wilson
Shiloh
True Confessions of Charlotte Doyle
A Wrinkle in Time

Respect for the Environment

Bambi
Deathwatch
Jacob Have I Loved
The Maze

The Secret Garden
Weasel
Wringer

Responsibility

After the Rain
Crazy Lady!
Deathwatch
Dicey's Song
The Giver
The Indian in the Cupboard
The Moves Make the Man
On My Honor
Petey
Save Queen of Sheba

The Séance
Secrets at Hidden Valley
Shiloh
Somewhere in the Darkness
Tangerine
True Confessions of Charlotte Doyle
Weasel
What Jamie Saw
A Wrinkle in Time

Self Control

Around the World in Eighty Days
Dancing on the Edge
The Giver

A Long Way from Chicago
The Maze
A Wrinkle in Time

Self Respect

Belle Prater's Boy
Crazy Lady!
Dancing on the Edge
Dicey's Song
Harry Potter and the Sorcerer's Stone
Jacob Have I Loved
The Midwife's Apprentice
The Secret Garden

Somewhere in the Darkness
Summer of My German Soldier
The Trouble with Lemons
True Confessions of Charlotte Doyle
Weasel
Wringer
A Wrinkle in Time

Tolerance

Animal Farm
Around the World in Eighty Days
Belle Prater's Boy
Crazy Lady!
Harry Potter and the Sorcerer's Stone
The Indian in the Cupboard
 A Long Way from Chicago
The Moves Make the Man

Nightjohn
Pudd'nhead Wilson
Somewhere in the Darkness
Summer of My German Soldier
Tangerine
True Confessions of Charlotte Doyle
Weasel
A Wrinkle in Time

Trustworthiness

Around the World in Eighty Days
The Face on the Milk Carton
The Giver
Holes
The Indian in the Cupboard
Lily's Crossing

On My Honor
Pudd'nhead Wilson
The Séance
Secrets at Hidden Valley
Stranger with My Face
Tangerine

Interesting and Useful Websites

In doing the research for this book, numerous websites, which might be of great use to those working with the novels, were discovered. Several of the authors cited in this book have created their own home pages, offering a personal contact with the authors and their works. Though the websites differ, biographical information about the author, insights into the writing of the novels, ideas for teaching the novel in the classroom, and future projects of the author are usually included.

In addition to these home pages, some publishers of children's novels offer websites that allow you to find data about the authors and their novels as well as ideas for teaching; they also comment on the novels or other sections of the website. Universities and other sources have also provided thought-provoking websites. The following is a list of those we found to be the most interesting and useful; the list does not purport to be all-inclusive.

Authors' Home Pages
Avi: Books, Bios: Bulletin Boards
    http://www.avi-writer.com
Ben Mikaelsen's Web Site
    http://www.BenMikaelsen.com
Cynthia Rylant
    http://www.rylant.com
Home Page of Daniel Hayes
    http://www.danielhayes.com
Lois Duncan
    http://www.iag.net/~barq/lois.html
The Official Katherine Paterson
    http://www.terabithia.com
Official Website of Award-Winning Children's Book Author, Will Hobbs
    http://www.willhobbsauthor.com
Paula Danziger
    http://www.maquoketa.k12.ia.us/paula_danziger.html
The Tesseract: A Madeleine L'Engle Bibliography in 5 Dimensions
    http://hometown.aol.com/kfbofpql/LEngl.html
A Warm Welcome from Lynne Reid Banks
    http://www.lynnereidbanks.com

Publishers' Websites
Harper Children's
    http://www.harperchildrens.com

Houghton Mifflin Education Place
   http://www.eduplace.com
Puffin Books
   http://www.puffin.co.uk
Random House
   http://www.randomhouse.com/features/garypaulsen/
   http://randomhouse.com/teachersbdd/
Scholastic
   http://www.scholastic.com
Simon Says Kids
   http://simonandschuster.com/kids
Young Readers Penguin Putnam, Inc.
   http://www.penguinputnam.com/yreaders/index.htm

Miscellaneous Websites
ALA Website Site Map
   http://www.ala.org/sitemap.html
Carol Hurst's Children's Literature Site
   http://www.carolhurst.com/index.html
Children's Book Council Online
   http://www.cbcbooks.org/index.htm
Children's Literature Web Guide
   http://www.acs.ucalgary.ca/~dkbrown/authors.html
ERIC Clearinghouse on Reading, English, & Communication
   http://www.indiana.edu/~eric_ rec/
The Internet Public Library Youth Division
   http://www.ipl.org/youth/HomePage.html
Kay Vandergrift's Authors and Illustrators
   http:www.scils.rutgers/special/kay/authors.html
Meet Harry Potter
   http://www/scholastic.com/harrypotter/index/htm
The Not Especially Fascinating Life So Far of J. K. Rowling
   http://www.okubooks.com/harry/rowling.htm
The Reading Corner
   http://www.car.lib.md.us/read/index.htm
Reading Plans from the Teacher's Desk
   http://www.knownet.net/users/Ackley/reading_plans.html
Yahoo Author Series
   http://www.promotions.yahoo.com.promotions/authors
Yahooligans
   http://www.yahooligans.com

Bibliography

Novels

Almond, David. *Skellig*. New York: Delacorte, 1998.

Avi. *The True Confessions of Charlotte Doyle*. New York: Orchard Books, 1990.

Banks, Lynne Reid. *The Indian in the Cupboard*. Santa Barbara: ABC-Clio, 1980.

Bauer, Marion Dane. *On My Honor*. New York: Clarion Books, 1986.

Bloor, Edward. *Tangerine*. San Diego: Harcourt Brace, 1997.

Brooks, Bruce. *The Moves Make the Man*. New York: Harper Row, 1984.

Burnett, Frances Hodgson. *The Secret Garden*. New York: Henry Holt, 1987.

Cleary, Beverly. *Dear Mr. Henshaw*. New York: William Morrow, 1983.

Coman, Carolyn. *What Jamie Saw*. New York: Puffin Books, 1995.

Conly, Jane Leslie. *Crazy Lady!* New York: HarperCollins Children's Books, 1993.

Cooney, Caroline B. *The Face on the Milk Carton*. New York: Bantam, 1990.

Curtis, Christopher Paul. *Bud, Not Buddy*. New York: Delacorte, 1999.

Cushman, Karen. *The Midwife's Apprentice*. New York: Clarion Books, 1995.

Danziger, Paula. *Amber Brown Goes Fourth*. New York: Putnam, 1995.

DeFelice, Cynthia. *Weasel*. New York: Macmillan, 1990.

Duncan, Lois. *Stranger with My Face*. New York: Little, Brown, 1981.

Gardiner, John Reynolds. *Stone Fox*. New York: HarperCollins, 1980.

Giff, Patricia Reilly. *Lily's Crossing*. New York: Troll, 1997.

Greene, Bette. *Summer of My German Soldier*. New York: Dial Books, 1973.

Hayes, Daniel. *The Trouble with Lemons*. Boston: David R. Godine, 1991.

Hesse, Karen. *Out of the Dust*. New York: Scholastic Press, 1997.

Hobbs, Will. *The Maze*. New York: Morrow Junior Books, 1998.

Holt, Kimberly Willis. *When Zachary Beaver Came to Town*. New York: Henry Holt, 1999.

L'Engle, Madeleine. *A Wrinkle in Time*. New York: Farrar, Strauss, Giroux, 1962.

Levine, Gail Clark. *Ella Enchanted*. New York: HarperCollins, 1997.

Lowry, Lois. *The Giver*. Boston: Houghton Mifflin, 1993.

Mazer, Norma Fox. *After the Rain*. New York: William Morrow, 1987.

Mikaelsen, Ben. *Petey*. New York: Hyperion Books for Children, 1998.

Moeri, Louise. *Save Queen of Sheba*. New York: E. P. Dutton, 1981.

Myers, Walter Dean. *Somewhere in the Darkness*. New York: Scholastic Press, 1992.

Naylor, Phyllis Reynolds. *Shiloh*. New York: Atheneum, 1991.

Nixon, Joan Lowery. *The Séance*. New York: Harcourt Brace Jovanovich, 1980.

Nolan, Han. *Dancing on the Edge*. New York: Harcourt Brace, 1997.

Orwell, George. *Animal Farm.* New York: Harcourt Brace, 1956.

Paterson, Katherine. *Jacob Have I Loved.* New York: Thomas Y. Crowell, 1980.

Paulsen, Gary. *Nightjohn.* New York: Delacorte, 1993.

Peck, Richard. *A Long Way from Chicago: A Novel in Stories.* New York: Dial Books for Young Readers, 1998.

Raskin, Ellen. *The Westing Game.* New York: E. P. Dutton, 1978.

Roberts, Willo Davis. *Secrets at Hidden Valley.* New York: Atheneum, 1997.

Rowling, J. K. *Harry Potter and the Sorcerer's Stone.* New York: Arthur A. Levine Books, 1998.

Rylant, Cynthia. *Missing May.* New York: Orchard Books, 1992.

Sachar, Louis. *Holes.* New York: Farrar, Strauss, Giroux, 1998.

Salten, Felix. *Bambi.* New York: Simon and Schuster, 1928.

Spinelli, Jerry. *Wringer.* New York: HarperCollins, 1998.

Twain, Mark. *Pudd'nhead Wilson.* Cutchogue: Buccaneer Books, 1997.

Verne, Jules. *Around the World in Eighty Days.* New York: William Morrow, 1988.

Voigt, Cynthia. *Dicey's Song.* New York: Atheneum, 1982.

White, Ruth. *Belle Prater's Boy.* Farrar, Strauss, Giroux: New York, 1996.

White, Robb. *Deathwatch.* New York: Doubleday, 1972.

Zindel, Paul. *The Pigman.* New York: Harper Row, 1968.

Sources

Authors & Artists for Young Adults. Detroit: Gale Research, Inc. Multiple volumes.

Felix Salten (1869-1945). Feuchtwanger Memorial Library, USC, May 1997. <http://www.usc.edu/isd/locations/ssh/special/fml/Salten.html>, [accessed 7 July 2000].

Gallo, Donald R. ed. *Speaking for Ourselves.* Urbana: National Council of Teachers of English, 1990.

Gallo, Donald R. ed. *Speaking for Ourselves Too.* Urbana: National Council of Teachers of English, 1990.

Junior Book of Authors series. New York: H. W. Wilson. Multiple volumes.

Major Authors and Illustrators for Children and Young Adults. Detroit: Gale Research, Inc. Multiple volumes.

The McGraw-Hill Encyclopedia of World Biography. New York: McGraw-Hill Book Company, 1987

Something about the Author series. New York: Gale Group. Multiple volumes.

Vandergrift, Kay. *Learning about the Author and Illustrator.* <http://scils.rutgers.edu/special/kay/author.html>, [accessed 16 June 2000].

Index

Fictional characters are found in italic.